MW00594029

CiTY·SMaRT™
GUIDEBOOK

Austin

Second Edition

Eleanor S. Morris, Paris Permenter, and John Bigley

John Muir Publications
Santa Fe, New Mexico

Acknowledgments

Many thanks to Gwen Spain, Director of Public Relations/Advertising, and the entire staff of the Austin Convention and Visitors Bureau for their assistance.

John Muir Publications, P.O. Box 613, Santa Fe, New Mexico 87504

Copyright © 1999, 1997 by John Muir Publications
Cover and maps copyright © 1999 by John Muir Publications
All rights reserved.

Printed in the United States of America.
Second edition. First printing August 1999.

ISBN: 1-56261-503-3
ISSN: 1093-3220

Editors: Marybeth Griffin, Elaine Robbins
Graphics Editor: Bunny Wong
Production: Rebecca Cook
Design: Janine Lehmann
Cover Design: Suzanne Rush
Typesetter: Kathy Sparkes–White Hart Design
Map Illustration: Julie Felton
Printer: Publishers Press
Front Cover: © Laurence Parent/Texas State Capitol
Back Cover: © Laurence Parent/University of Texas tower

Distributed to the book trade by
Publishers Group West
Berkeley, California

While every effort has been made to provide accurate, up-to-date information, the author and publisher accept no responsibility for loss, injury, or inconvenience sustained by any person using this book.

CONTENTS

MAP CONTENTS

See Austin the CiTY·SMaRT™ Way

The Guide for Austin Natives, New Residents, and Visitors

In *City•Smart Guidebook: Austin*, local authors Eleanor S. Morris, Paris Permenter, and John Bigley tell it like it is. Residents will learn things they never knew about their city, new residents will get an insider's view of their new hometown, and visitors will be guided to the very best Austin has to offer—whether they're on a weekend getaway or staying a week or more.

Opinionated Recommendations Save You Time and Money

From shopping to nightlife to museums, the authors are opinionated about what they like and dislike. You'll learn the great and the not-so-great things about Austin's sights, restaurants, and accommodations. So you can decide what's worth your time and what's not; which hotel is worth the splurge and which is the best choice for budget travelers.

Easy-to-Use Format Makes Planning Your Trip a Cinch

City•Smart Guidebook: Austin is user-friendly—you'll quickly find exactly what you're looking for. Chapters are organized by travelers' interests or needs, from Where to Stay and Where to Eat, to Sights and Attractions, Kids' Stuff, Sports and Recreation, and even Day Trips from Austin.

Includes Maps and Quick Location-Finding Features

Every listing in this book is accompanied by a geographic zone designation (see the following page for zone details) that helps you immediately find each location. Staying in Downtown Austin and wondering about nearby sights and restaurants? Look for the Downtown Austin label in the listings, and you'll know that museum or café is not far away. Or maybe you're looking for the University of Texas. Along with its address, you'll see a North Austin label, so you'll know just where to find it.

All That and Fun to Read, Too!

Every City•Smart chapter includes fun-to-read (and fun-to-use) tips and trivia to help you get more out of Austin, (Did you know that Texas was once a separate country, complete with its own ambassadors?), and illuminating sidebars (The Hill Country Flyer introduces you to Texas' Hill Country, see page 87 for more details). And well-known Austin residents provide their personal "Top Ten" lists, guiding readers to the city's best sights, restaurants, activities, and more.

AUSTIN ZONES

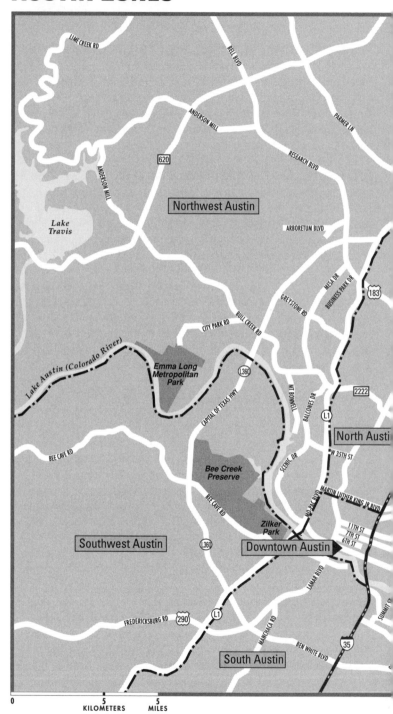

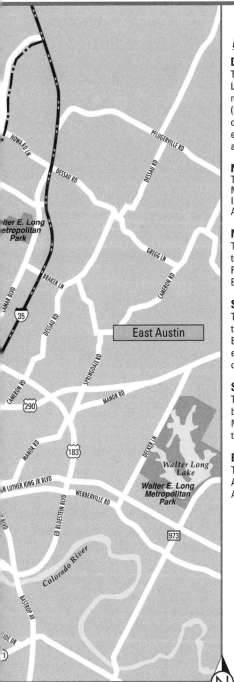

AUSTIN ZONES

Downtown Austin (DA)
The area bounded by Martin Luther King Jr. Boulevard on the north, Mo-Pac Expressway (Loop 1) on the west, Town Lake on the south, and I-35 on the east. Includes the state capitol area.

North Austin (NA)
The area north of downtown, Mo-Pac Expressway (Loop 1). Includes the University of Austin-Texas campus.

Northwest Austin (NWA)
The area northwest of downtown, bounded by the Colorado River on the south and Mo-Pac Expressway (Loop 1) on the east.

Southwest Austin (SWA)
The area southwest of downtown, bounded by Mo-Pac Expressway (Loop 1) on the east and the Colorado River on the north.

South Austin (SA)
The area south of Town Lake, bounded by I-35 on the east and Mo-Pac Expressway (Loop 1) on the west.

East Austin (EA)
The area east of I-35, including Austin-Bergstrom International Airport.

© Permenter and Bigley

1

WELCOME TO AUSTIN

Austin is a multilayered, multifaceted city, and its residents enjoy a high quality of life that combines progress and an appreciation for relaxed living. These are the values admired by Austin's visitors and so fiercely protected by the folks who live here. An open-minded, down-home kind of place that not only tolerates, but likes, respects, and welcomes people who are different, Austin is a city where folks consider greeting strangers in passing as just plain good manners.

Maybe it's because the city's residents are highly educated that they promote and respect cultural diversity. Whatever the reason, Austin is a magnet for creative souls and a community everyone loves to love. The capital of Texas and the seat of Travis County, Austin has an estimated population of 608,921 inhabitants within the city and just over a million in the metropolitan area. The population has grown substantially within the last decade.

Getting to Know Austin

Austin is a beautiful lake city with broad streets and period architecture, but it's also a bustling metropolis and high-tech haven. The city is known both nationally and internationally for its top-notch research and development in the rapidly expanding microelectronics industry. High-tech whiz kids barely out of college come to Austin to begin Fortune 500 computer and software companies.

Austin is also a city with a rich intellectual climate. In the midst of town there is a major research university, the University of Texas, as well

TRIVIA

Texas' own statue of liberty, the Goddess of Liberty—1½ tons of zinc and iron—stood atop the Capitol dome from 1888 to 1985. She was eventually removed because of damage from exposure to the elements, and in 1986 she was replaced by an aluminum replica.

as three other universities. One of them, Huston-Tillotson College, is the oldest African American university in the nation. Per capita, Austin has one of the most highly educated populations in the country.

Sixth-highest in the nation for its large number of artists and musicians, Austin is a place where hopefuls follow legends like Willie Nelson, who put Austin on the map as a major music venue when he moved here in 1970. Musicians might get a start in one of the 100 live music clubs featuring local, national, and international talent every night. This artistically inclined city also offers symphony, opera, theater, museums, galleries, and exotic street markets.

A Brief History of Austin

Austin is the capital of Texas, but it didn't begin as such, and it didn't capture the title without a struggle. Originally it was a small village called Waterloo, settled by Jacob Harrell in 1835 along the mouths of Waller, Shoal, and Barton Creeks, which drained into the Colorado River. Several other

Statue of Stephen Austin at the Elisabet Ney Museum

© Permenter and Bigley

settlers joined Harrell, building log cabins and erecting a stockade for protection against Indians. After winning the Texas War of Independence (1835–1836) the Republic of Texas declared its independence from Mexico in 1836. When Mirabeau B. Lamar, vice president of the Republic, came to Waterloo on a buffalo hunt, he was so impressed with the beauty of the area that he decided to make it the Republic's capital. Without delay, he renamed the city Austin, after Texas colonizer Stephen F. Austin. After hastily renaming the city, Lamar had to battle for several years with Sam Houston, president of the Republic, who insisted that the capital be either Houston (the city named for himself) or the original site of Washington-on-the-Brazos to the east. Houston got his way until 1844, when new president Anson Jones changed the capital's name back to Austin. When Texas joined the United States a year later, Austin managed to remain as the capital. The issue was permanently settled when it passed two statewide voter referendums, one in 1850 and another in 1852.

During the years of the Republic, various diplomats lived in the city, and today the old French Legation is still maintained as a historic site. The governor's mansion, built in 1853, is adjacent to the Capitol's large grounds and is a showplace of southern colonial architecture.

Austin flourished from the beginning, growing from 856 citizens in 1840 (when the first capitol was a one-story frame building that had to be protected from Indians by an eight-foot stockade) to 3,494 citizens in 1860. Large-scale growth began with the arrival of the railroad in 1871. A new capitol, built in 1853, was gutted by fire, and the present building was erected in 1888.

In 1938 the Lower Colorado River Authority began constructing a series of dams along the Texas length of the Colorado River, forming the beautiful chain of Highland Lakes and giving Austin two refreshing bodies of water, Town Lake and Lake Austin. Town Lake flows west to east through

Austin's Convention Center

The Austin Convention Center has gained national attention since its completion in 1992. "The convention center has been recognized as one of the most technologically advanced in the nation," explains Gwen Spain, Director of Public Relations/Advertising for the Austin Convention & Visitors Bureau. "It's already 'plugged in' if your group needs any Internet capabilities. It's prewired for any high-tech needs, which saves the time and money of bringing someone in to get that done." The facility offers the latest in technological aids for any type of meeting: ISDN, fiber optics, in-house simulcast services, satellite links, plug and play access to the Internet, and more. The 400,000-square-foot facility includes 126,000 square feet of column-free exhibit space, a 24,000-square-foot ballroom, and 29 meeting rooms for groups of 10 to 500 delegates. Currently work is underway to expand the center.

TRIVIA

The high-tech industry has been responsible for focusing a great deal of national attention on Austin. In 1995 Austin ranked seventh in *Fortune* magazine's "Best Cities for Business" list. It was the smallest city on the list.

the city, dividing it into north and south sections. A leafy hike and bike trail lines both banks of the river within walking distance of downtown's tall office buildings. Along with Lake Austin, on the west side of town, Town Lake provides a cool green oasis for outdoor recreational pleasures.

The business district, lying on both sides of the river, is bisected by Congress Avenue, which runs from south of the river to the north, ending at the spacious lawns of the Capitol complex. The pink granite structure, constructed of fossilized native stone from Hill Country quarries, boasts a dome seven feet higher than that of the United States Capitol in Washington, D.C. Beyond the Capitol rises the 27-story bell tower of the University of Texas, founded in 1881. The university is the home of the Lyndon B. Johnson Library, the largest presidential library in the country. The enormous main campus is located just north of downtown, making Austin a noted educational center.

People of Austin

Austin's population is as diverse as its history. Having flown under six different flags, the Lone Star State boasts residents with ethnic backgrounds ranging from Mexican to German to Alsatian. In fact, the Institute of Texan Cultures in San Antonio documents more than 30 ethnic groups, many of which are represented in the city of Austin.

The influence of Texas' southern neighbor is strongly felt in Austin, where many citizens trace their ancestry to Hispanic roots. It's not uncommon to hear Spanish spoken anywhere in the city. The city celebrates Mexican holidays such as Cinco de Mayo, the May fifth victory over French troops by the small Mexican army, with as much exuberance as it bestows upon other festive days.

It's also not uncommon to see members of Austin's diverse population side by side throughout the city. For example, you might see a lobbyist in a three-piece suit next to a person who's obviously a frequent visitor to one of the city's many tattoo and body-piercing parlors. All of Austin's population comes together at the many coffeehouses, Tex-Mex restaurants, and local bars to partake of the food, music, and fun.

A sense of good-naturedness permeates Austin, from its nightlife to its festivals and outdoor recreation. Maybe it's the college population, which tops 50,000 students, that gives the city its casual feel. Maybe it's the live music industry, which has made this city a haven for fans and performers alike. Or maybe it's just the geography: Austin is situated on a downtown lake and perched at the edge of a rambling Hill Country lake that offers everything from windsurfing to nude sunbathing.

Sure, the city is home to both high-tech industry and countless state officials, but residents will use any excuse to toss off the ties and formal attire. They don hippie costumes for an annual party in Pease Park to celebrate, believe it or not, the birthday of Eeyore, pal of Winnie the Pooh. And those costumes are just a dress rehearsal for the Halloween party that takes place on Sixth Street, which attracts as many as 70,000 merrymakers.

At night, the clubs are the place to be. But during the daylight hours Austin shows off her beauty at places like the shores of Town Lake, the clear waters of Barton Springs swimming hole, and the manicured lawn of the Capitol. Regardless of political interest, many Austinites who work downtown like to sneak off to the Capitol grounds for a picnic lunch. Sitting out on the rolling lawn under tall oaks, feeding squirrels, and watching the flurry of legislative comings and goings provides one of the best shows in town.

In the late afternoon hours, locals grab their sneakers and head to Zilker Park or Town Lake's shores for a jog or just a leisurely walk. When the sun sets on summer days, attention turns to Congress Avenue Bridge, location of the country's largest urban colony of Mexican free-tailed bats. The bats make their nightly exodus after sunset to feed on insects in the Hill Country and the Austin area.

O. Henry

The humorist and short-story writer O. Henry (William Sydney Porter) was one of Austin's earliest famous citizens. According to O. Henry, the unlikely group of Stephen F. Austin, Daniel Boone, Davy Crockett, and Ponce de Leon, while navigating the Colorado River by canal boat, stopped at the foot of what is now Congress Avenue, and here's what happened:

"Suddenly an idea struck Stephen F. Austin. He was too generous a man to conceal it:

"'Boys, let's start a town site here and call it Austin.'

"'Just as you say,' they replied, and they laid out Austin. It has been laid out ever since."

AUSTIN TIME LINE

1835	Jacob Harrell settles along Waller, Shoal, and Barton Creeks and calls the settlement Waterloo.
1838	Mirabeau B. Lamar, vice president of the Republic of Texas, comes to Waterloo to hunt buffalo.
1839	France recognizes the Republic and sends Alphonse DuBois de Saligny to Austin as *chargé d'affaires*.
1839–44	Lamar struggles with President Sam Houston to establish Austin as the capital of the Republic.
1841	French Legation is built.
1844	New president Anson Jones declares Austin the capital of the Republic.
1845	The Republic of Texas joins the United States of America; Austin remains as capital of the new state of Texas.
1850	A voter referendum ensures Austin's status as state capital.
1851	Texas State Cemetery is founded.
1852	A second referendum ensures Austin's status as state capital.
1857	General Land Office is built (Austin's oldest surviving office building).
1860	Population has grown from 856 to 3,494 citizens.
1861	City residents vote against secession from the Union.
1869	First Congress Avenue Bridge, a pontoon bridge, is built.
1871	The railroads arrive.
1873	First library is founded.
1875	Second Congress Avenue Bridge is completed.
1876	Huston-Tillotson College, a black institution, is founded.
1880	Austin citizens vote to establish a public school system.
1881	The University of Texas is founded.
1883	Construction is begun on present Capitol building.
1885	St. Edward's University is founded.
1886	The Driskill Hotel is built.
1888	The Capitol opens for business.
1889	St. Edward's University is built.

Elisabet Ney, Texas' first eminent sculptor, builds her Hyde Park studio.	**1892**
Colorado River is dammed to generate electricity for street cars and Moonlight Towers.	**1893**
O. Henry (William Sydney Porter) publishes humorous weekly *The Rolling Stone*.	**1894**
City streets are paved with brick—Congress Avenue is the first.	**1905**
Present Congress Avenue Bridge is completed.	**1910**
The Paramount Theater is constructed.	**1915**
Austin's first airport is constructed on the south side of the city.	**1918**
City charter is written.	**1924**
Construction of seven dams along the Colorado River creates, among others, Town Lake.	**1930**
Year of the Great Flood.	**1935**
Tom Miller Dam is completed.	**1940**
Emma Long is the first woman elected to the City Council.	**1948**
Austin's first television station, Lyndon and Lady Bird Johnson's KTBC-TV, takes to the air. High-tech and real estate boom begins.	**1952**
Charles Whitman opens fire from the University of Texas' bell tower, killing 14 people and wounding 31.	**1966**
Tracor Electronics Company arrives in Austin.	**1967**
Willie Nelson moves from Nashville to Austin to initiate the Austin music scene.	**1970**
Willie Nelson's first Fourth of July picnic, now an Austin tradition, attracts more than 40,000 people.	**1973**
Treaty Oak is poisoned.	**1989**
The Austin Convention Center, a $69.4 million building, is dedicated.	**1992**
Capitol is rededicated after a six-year, $187 million restoration and expansion.	**1995**
Austin-Bergstrom International Airport opens its doors.	**1999**

Weather

Austin's location on the Colorado River where it crosses the Balcones Escarpment gives it a mild climate, with an average annual temperature of 70 degrees Fahrenheit. City elevations vary from 400 to 1,000 feet above sea level, and the climate is humid subtropical, with hot summers. Although the daytime temperatures are hot, summer nights are usually more pleasant, with average minimums in the lower 70s. The city enjoys an average of 300 days of sunshine each year.

Winters are mild, with below-freezing temperatures rarely occurring more than 25 days each year. Although rather strong winds and sharp drops in temperature (which Austinites call "a cold norther") sometimes occur during cold fronts, these are of short duration, rarely lasting more than a day or two.

The average annual rainfall is 27.86 inches, with the heaviest occurring in spring, though this is usually in the form of steady but light rain. Rainy days from April through September usually result from thundershowers, with large amounts falling in short periods of time. Snow is rare and is insignificant as a source of moisture; if it does fall, it generally melts rapidly when it touches the ground.

Prevailing winds are southerly throughout the year. When northerly

Austin Weather

	Avg. Temps (°F)	Humidity (percent)	Avg. Days of Rain
January	50	59	8
February	53	65	8
March	60	53	7
April	75	55	7
May	75	59	9
June	82	54	6
July	85	47	5
August	85	49	5
September	79	57	7
October	70	53	6
November	59	58	7
December	52	60	7

Source: City of Austin/National Weather Service

TRIVIA

Austin (Austin's Congress Avenue Bridge, to be exact) is home to the largest urban colony of Mexican free-tailed bats in the United States.

winds, accompanying colder air masses in winter, move over the Gulf of Mexico, they soon shift to southerly. Damaging hailstorms and destructive winds are infrequent; dissipating tropical storms affecting the city with strong winds and heavy rains are rare.

Dressing in the City

What to wear? Fashionwise, Austin is exceedingly informal. Just about anything goes so long as you won't be cited for indecent exposure. Visitors can hardly go wrong! The city is a mix of junior students, college students, ex-hippies who hate to dress up, style-conscious yuppies who love a casual-chic look, and traditionalists who won't go out without a coat and tie. At any event or eating establishment all of the above will be represented; there are few places in Austin where you'd feel uncomfortably dressed.

Jeans, shorts, T-shirts, camp shirts, sandals, and sneakers are legion depending upon the weather, not the time of year. Most restaurants really expect you to leave your dress-up clothes at home. (The few exceptions are noted in the restaurant section.) You wear what suits you—that's part of what being in a laid-back town means. Just don't get so laid back that

Town Lake Trail and the Austin skyline

© Permenter and Bigley

TRIVIA

Austin's first lots were sold at auction on August 1, 1839. Bidding began at $120. Congress Avenue, at 120 feet wide, was claimed to be the widest street in the country. But as it quickly became lined with log cabins and plank houses, it could hardly be considered an elegant thoroughfare.

you ignore the health code—shirts and shoes must be worn at all times in eating establishments.

Weatherwise, in spring, summer, and fall, cottons, shorts, short sleeves, and cool dresses are suitable. Wintertime might necessitate a sweater or a light jacket; there are only a few days during the coldest months when a heavy coat might be a good idea. An umbrella is useful for the few rainy days.

CALENDAR OF EVENTS

JANUARY
Red-Eye Regatta, Town Lake

FEBRUARY
Carnival Brasileiro, City Coliseum

MARCH
Austin/Travis County Livestock Show & Rodeo, Heritage Exposition
    Center
Capitol 10,000, a run through Austin streets
Jerry Jeff Walker's Birthday Celebration, Paramount Theater
Kite Festival, Zilker Park
SXSW Music and Media Conference, 25 city venues

APRIL
Austin Nature Center Safari, Austin Nature Center
Eeyore's Birthday Party, Pease Park
Highland Lakes Bluebonnet Trail, Highland Lakes
Texas Hill Country Wine and Food Festival, Four Seasons Hotel
Wildflower Days Festival, National Wildflower Research Center

MAY
Cinco de Mayo, Fiesta Gardens
Fiesta Laguna Gloria, Shores of Lake Austin
Flora Rama, Zilker Botanical Gardens
O. Henry Pun-Off, O. Henry Museum
Lone Star State Festival, East Sixth Street

JUNE
Ballet in the Park, Zilker Hillside Theater
Clarksville–West End Jazz and Arts Festival, West End
Hyde Park Historic Homes Tour, Hyde Park
Juneteenth Freedom Festival, Fiesta Garden

JULY
Annual Summer Musicals, Zilker Hillside Theater
Austin Symphony Fourth of July Concert, Town Lake
Bastille Day Celebration, French Legation
Freedom Festival and Fireworks, Zilker Park
Governor's Cup Sailing Regatta, Lake Travis

AUGUST
World's Largest Hot Sauce Festival, Farmer's Market

SEPTEMBER
Diez y Seis de Septiembre, Fiesta Gardens
Lone Star State Festival, East Sixth Street
Zilker Park Fall Jazz Festival, Zilker Park

OCTOBER
Fall Regatta on Town Lake
Great Tastes of Austin, Auditorium Shores
Halloween on Sixth Street
Pioneer Farm Fall Festival, Pioneer Farm

Elisabet Ney Museum

© J. Griffis Smith/Austin CVB

NOVEMBER

Los Días de los Muertos, Congress Avenue

Victorian Christmas, East Sixth Street

DECEMBER

Christmas at the French Legation, French Legation

Pioneer Farm Christmas Candle-light Tour, Pioneer Farm

West End Christmas Walk, West End

Wild Ideas: A Holiday Shopping Event, National Wildflower Research Center

Zilker Park Tree Lighting and Trail of Lights, Zilker Park

© Permenter and Bigley

Texas State Capitol building

Business and Economy

Austin's diverse economy revolves around state government, research, development, and high technology. Over 300 of its 800 manufacturers are considered high tech, thanks in a large part to a booming microchip industry. Sixty-five percent of the manufacturing workforce is employed by the high-tech industry, with a large number of workers employed by service-based high-tech businesses such as those engaged in computer programming and software design. Currently 1,750 firms are engaged in the high-tech business.

Many high-tech companies have relocated to Austin from Silicon Valley in search of a lower cost of living. South Korea's Samsung Electronics recently moved to Austin; it is the manufacturer's first installation outside of South Korea. The high-tech sector in Austin also includes Motorola, with over 10,000 employees; IBM, with over 6,500 employees; and Dell Computer, a leader in the field of personal computers, employing over 12,000 workers. So many high-tech companies have relocated to Austin that the city is often called "Silicon Hills."

Outside the high-tech field, the Texas Employment Commission reports that 26.5 percent of the workforce works for the state government (the

TRIVIA

Sixty percent of Austin's population uses computers, making it the most computer-literate city in the nation.

For more business information, check out the Business Information Center (BIC) at the Central Library at 800 Guadalupe Street. The collection includes business newspapers and journals, business directories, city guides, economic trends and forecasting, online database searching, and statistics.

leading employer) and 26 percent are employed in service industries. Other top employers include financial institutions and insurance companies, construction businesses, and transportation services.

The ACCRA Cost of Living Index measures the differences between regions by the cost of consumer goods and services and then compares the city to an "average" ranking of 100. Austin ranked 100.9 overall in most recent statistics. Groceries ranked 87.1, housing 100.2, utilities 117.6, transportation 105.1, and health care 106.7. On the same scale, Atlanta ranked 99.7 overall; Boston, 139.2; Dallas, 100.4; Los Angeles, 117.9; Phoenix, 100.8; Salt Lake City, 95.6; and San Francisco, 174.2. And, the most recent estimated household income for Travis County residents is $37,000.

Typical costs of everyday items and services include:

five-mile taxi ride	$9
hotel, double room	$80
average dinner	$10–$15
movie admission	$7
daily paper	$.50
gallon of gasoline	$.89–$.99
monthly bus pass	$10
club cover charge	$3–$5

Taxes

Texas has no corporate or personal income tax on either a state or local level. Sales tax in Austin is 8.25 percent, divided at 6¼ percent for state sales tax, 1 percent to the City of Austin, and 1 percent for the local transit authority.

Ad valorem property tax per $100 valuation is:

City of Austin	$ .60
Travis County	.5401
Austin ISD	1.4010
Austin Community College	.0500
TOTAL	$2.5911

Homes

Austin's booming economy has re-sulted in a tight real estate market. Higher home prices, higher rent prices, and a shortage of low-cost housing have taken some of the gleam off Austin's real estate appeal, although relocators, especially from the West Coast, find that prices are still favorable.

In 1998, the average price of a home was $113,900. Rental prices vary by neighborhood, but the aver-age price of a one-bedroom, one-bath apartment is $574 per month. Apartments can be tough to find with 1999 occupancy rates averag-ing 91 percent.

© Permenter and Bigley

Littlefield Fountain on the University of Texas campus

Schools

Austin is often touted as the most highly educated community in the United States among cities with populations of more than 250,000. More than 35 percent of adults boast 16 or more years of education; nearly half com-pleted high school and/or some college. One in nine adults is currently en-rolled in an Austin-area college or university.

Much of that education stems from the University of Texas at Austin, which enrolls nearly 50,000 students a year, making it the nation's biggest university. The University of Texas at Austin, or U.T. as it's more commonly known, includes top programs in liberal arts, engineering, business, and natural sciences. The campus includes the sixth-largest academic library in the country.

Other higher education campuses include Austin Community College, St. Edward's University, Huston-Tillotson College, and Concordia Lutheran College.

There are more than 15 school districts in the Austin area, although most of the city is covered by the Austin Independent School District, with nearly 100 campuses and over 77,000 students. District offices are located at the Carruth Administration Center, 1111 West Sixth Street, Austin, Texas 78703-5399, 512/414-1700. On the western edge of the city, Eanes Indepen-dent School District in Westlake Hills operates six elementary schools, two middle schools, and one high school. For information, write S. Don Rogers Administration Building, 601 Camp Craft Road, Austin, Texas 78746-6511, or call 512/329-3600. Enrollment at Eanes is 7,300 students.

© Permenter and Bigley

2

GETTING AROUND AUSTIN

City Layout

It doesn't take long to orient yourself with the many sections of Austin. You can usually tell east from west because land to the east is flat and land to the west is somewhat hilly. The beautiful Hill Country begins to rise on the west side of town, and there are scenic drives with curves and panoramic views well within the city. The river (Town Lake) divides the city into north and south sides quite neatly: Anything north of the river is North Austin; anything south of the river is South Austin.

Austin is located at the heart of the Lone Star State. Houston is a three-hour drive east; the Dallas/Fort Worth Metroplex is a little more than a three-hour drive north; and historic San Antonio is a little more than one hour south. Both the Dallas/Fort Worth Metroplex and San Antonio are reached via I-35, which goes right through Austin from the Texas/Mexico border all the way up to Canada. Houston can be reached by either U.S. 290 East or Highway 71 East to I-10.

Major Highways

The city is laid out at a slightly northeast/southwest slant, with three main north and south arteries. I-35, the first, has elevated express lanes above the downtown area. Mo-Pac Expressway (Loop 1), the second, takes its name from the Missouri-Pacific railroad tracks bisecting the expressway; trains still run on tracks between the northbound and southbound lanes. The third main north/south highway, U.S. 183, is known north of the city as Research Boulevard and to the south as Ed Bluestein Boulevard. U.S. 183 makes a northwest/southeast circle around Austin, crossing both I-35 and

Mo-Pac to intersect with RR 620 in far northwest Austin and U.S. 90/Highway 71 in southeast Austin.

On the north side of town, FM 2222 runs east and west, winding west into the hills from I-35 and meeting with RR 620 in far northwest Austin. East of the interstate it blends into U.S. 290. Coming from the east, U.S. 290 meets I-35 and follows it south until it connects with Highway 71. Then together they both head west and out of the city, diverging at the "Y" in Oak Hill. Ben White Boulevard on the south side runs east and west, as do both William Cannon Boulevard and Slaughter Lane. Other principal thoroughfares are Lamar Boulevard and Congress Avenue, both running north and south.

Loop 360 (Capital of Texas Highway) circles around the western half of the city from Mo-Pac north to merge with U.S. 90 and Highway 71 (Ben White Boulevard) on the south. Ongoing improvements include elevated lanes and flyways for access onto Mo-Pac and I-35.

Congress Avenue is the dividing line for addresses east and west. The river (Town Lake) is the dividing line for addresses north and south. Travis County includes all of Austin and the small communities of Jollyville to the north, Rollingwood and Westlake Hills to the southwest, and Sunset Valley to the south.

Walking the Historic Districts

If you're an ambitious stroller, pick up a brochure on historic Austin at the Convention and Visitors Bureau; they have divided the city into five historic areas for easy touring. The Historic Capitol touring area includes the Capitol, downtown, Sixth Street, and a 10-block walk through the Congress Avenue National Register District. The Historic University touring area includes both the University of Texas campus and the Hyde Park neighborhood, which is just north of the UT campus. Other tours are the Clarksville neighborhood (and Tom Miller Dam, but you'd need to drive to the dam) and the Historic Barton Springs touring area, which provides a hearty walk around Zilker Park and the springs (there's a train ride around the park if you don't want to walk). East of I-35 both the French Legation and the state cemetery make for interesting visits.

'DILLO EXPRESS

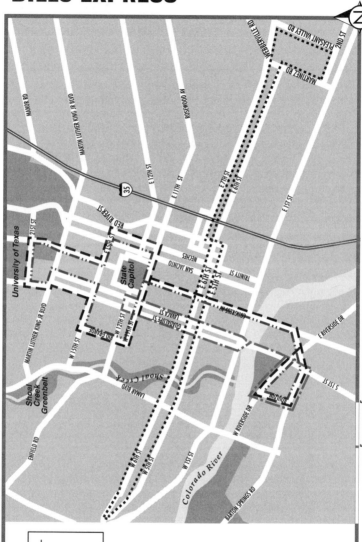

'DILLO LINES

Lavaca 'Dillo
Old Pecan St. 'Dillo
West Congress 'Dillo
East Congress 'Dillo

University of Texas

State Capitol

Shoal Creek Greenbelt

Colorado River

MANOR RD
MARTIN LUTHER KING JR BLVD
E 12TH ST
E 11TH ST
ROSEWOOD AV
E 7TH ST
E 8TH ST
E 1ST ST
WEBBERVILLE RD
PLEASANT VALLEY RD
2ND ST
MARTINEZ RD
21ST ST
RED RIVER ST
E 5TH ST
SAN JACINTO
NECHES
TRINITY ST
E 6TH ST
E 5TH ST
E RIVERSIDE DR
S 1ST ST
W 15TH ST
MARTIN LUTHER KING JR BLVD
ENFIELD RD
W 12TH ST
W 11TH ST
SAN ANTONIO
GUADALUPE ST
LAVACA ST
W CONGRESS AV
CONGRESS AV
LAMAR BLVD
W 6TH ST
W 5TH ST
W 1ST ST
W RIVERSIDE DR
BARTON SPRINGS RD

KILOMETERS   MILES
.5   .5

PUBLIC TRANSPORTATION

Bus Service
Capital Metro
512/474-1200
512/385 5872 TDD
512/478-9647 services for mobility impaired
Austin's clean-air Capital Metro city buses (they burn natural gas) serve passengers on 48 routes downtown and around town. The transit system is not only easy to use; it's a bargain at 50 cents per trip. Special services are offered for the mobility impaired, and the fare is 60 cents.

    Capital Metro's downtown information center is at 106 East Eighth Street (just east of Congress Avenue) on the ground floor of the Bremond Building. There you can purchase tickets and passes, have photos taken for identification cards, find or return lost items, and pick up service information. The center operates for walk-in customers Monday through Friday from 7:30 a.m. to 5:30 p.m.

'Dillo Express
512/474-1200
To get around only the downtown area, take the green 'Dillo Express—it's "free for the taking." The 'Dillo provides free circular service to downtown and the restaurants and clubs on Sixth Street, to ACC (Austin Community College) campus, UT (University of Texas) campus, and State Office Buildings Mon–Thu 6:30–midnight, Fri 6:30 a.m.–1:58 a.m., Sat 7:25 a.m.–1:53 a.m., Sun 7:25 a.m.–10:08 p.m. Buses run every 15 to 20 minutes.

Capital Metro Bus

© Permenter and Bigley

T I P

If you're driving in the downtown area you can park free at two Park & Ride lots, one at the City Coliseum (Barton Springs and Bouldin Roads) and the other at Austin High School (Mo-Pac Expressway and West First Street). From there, catch the 'Dillo to downtown.

The University of Texas Shuttle
512/474-1200
The university shuttle is available to everyone. It runs between the campus and many parts of the city. The cost is 50 cents per trip. Hours for each route vary, with 6:45 a.m. being the earliest and 11 p.m. the latest.

Taxi Service
The city has five licensed, metered taxicab companies and more than a dozen limousine services. All Austin taxicab companies work 24 hours a day, seven days a week, offering both smoking and nonsmoking cabs. Some take credit cards. Metered service is set by city ordinance and is based on $1.50

Transportation for Seniors

Seniors 60 years and older can enjoy special transportation thanks to the Austin Parks and Recreation Department's Senior Support Service. Reserve-a-Ride provides transportation from your home to meal sites and senior centers weekdays between 9 a.m. and 2:30 p.m. Contributions of 50 cents each way are encouraged.

For a contribution of $1 each way, Reserve-a-Ride will also arrange transportation to doctors and dentists (nonemergency), lawyers, banks, pharmacies, hair salons, to visit a friend in the hospital, to your volunteer work site, and to most other social engagements. The rides require 24 hours' notice.

Groups of 5 or larger (10 or more for out-of-town journeys) can schedule pleasure trips. Fees range from 50 cents to $10 a person. Previous trips have included the San Antonio River Walk, state parks, Hill Country communities, movies, plays, and concerts.

For reservations or more information, call 512/480-3012.

AMPCO Parking operates a 24-hour parking hotline, 512/499-7275, with up-to-the-minute information on airport parking availability and lot closures—a lifesaver if you need to catch a flight in a hurry. Radio station 1610 AM also provides parking and airport information.

the first one-sixth of a mile and $1.50 per mile thereafter. Average fare from the airport to downtown is about $12. Rates vary for travel to surrounding areas. Major taxi companies in Austin include: Ace Taxi, 512/244-1133; American Cab Company, 512/452-9999; American Yellow Checker Cab, 512/472-1111; Austin Cab Company, 512/478-2222; and Roy's Taxis, 512/482-0000.

Driving in Austin

Not too long ago, Austinites subscribed to the motto "Drive Friendly." Sadly this is no longer true. Perhaps it is because the city is growing so rapidly that traffic is becoming a problem. Rush-hour traffic, especially on I-35 and Mo-Pac, is fast catching up with the kind of five o'clock traffic you find in other large cities. Drivers in Austin are becoming much more aggressive. Motorists rushing through yellow lights, and even running red lights, are becoming all too common, so your best bet is to drive defensively.

Observe left turn lights closely; some are protected with an arrow, while others are not—usually there is a sign above the light. Speed limits are radar-enforced all over the city, in residential districts as well as major thoroughfares. Right turns on red lights are permitted after a stop; left turns are permitted onto one-way streets after a stop as well.

Parking
State law prohibits parking a vehicle within 20 feet of a crosswalk at an intersection, in front of driveways, or within 30 feet of a traffic signal or stop sign. Sidewalk ramps for persons with disabilities are usually located at crosswalks; keep these areas clear of vehicles. The Austin City Code prohibits parking in the sidewalk area or any place designated as "No Parking."

Parking meters, which take nickels, dimes, and quarters, come in several time limits, from 15 minutes to 2 hours. Be sure to check.

Biking in Austin

The Texas National Resource Conservation Commission (TNRCC), 512/239-1000, and Bicycle Users Group (BUG) work with the Austin Metropolitan

Austin-Bergstrom International Airport

PRESIDENTIAL BLVD

LONG TERM PARKING

LONG TERM PARKING

LONG TERM PARKING

EMPLOYEE PARKING

LONG TERM PARKING

LONG TERM PARKING

EXPRESS PARKING

EXPRESS PARKING

SHORT TERM PARKING GARAGE

TERMINAL BUILDING

Trails Council, the City of Austin Bicycle Advisory Council, and the Texas Bicycle Coalition to offer advice on the logistics of bicycle commuting and on the safest routes to ride to work. They also offer advice on the best bike shops, safe riding techniques, a cyclist's rights and responsibilities on the road, and the benefits of cycling. They support such major events each year as the Austin Bike-to-Work Day, the MS 150 Ride, the Clean Air Ride, and Pedal for the Planet.

Another great place to get all kinds of helpful information is the City of Austin Bicycle and Pedestrian Program, 512/499-7240.

Congress Avenue Bridge, p. 25

© Permenter and Bigley

Air Travel

Austin-Bergstrom International Airport
3600 Manor Rd.
512/369-6661 or 512/495-7515
The city's new Austin-Bergstrom International Airport, at the site of the former Bergstrom Air Force Base, intends to meet Austin's air traffic needs far into the twenty-first

Art in the Airport

To achieve the feel of Austin, the airport commissioned many Texas artists to translate that atmosphere into paintings, sculpture, and many finishing touches. Artwork found throughout the new Austin-Bergstrom International Airport includes:

- *Nine oil paintings on canvas by Thomas Evans that give a bird's eye view of Enchanted Rock*
- *Nine acrylic paintings on canvas by Fidencio Duran called* The Visit, *a representation of a family gathering*
- *A bronze bust of Barbara Jordan by David Deming*
- *A terrazzo map of the original Waller grid of Austin from 1839, executed by artist Jerry Ludwig*
- Texas Rivers *by Rudy Siliva: a terrazzo map of Texas portraying the rivers after which many Austin streets were named*
- The Creation of Texas *by David Santos and James Perez: a carved limestone and forged metal artwork found in the East Plaza Garden, set to be installed later*
- Texas Mythology/Texas Reality *by Jill Bedgood: etched mirrors in the baggage claim restrooms and cast metal medallions above the drinking fountains on the concourse level*
- *Six reverse paintings on glass shaped by luggage, created by Judy Jensen and seen on the walls of the escalators in baggage claim*
- Green Austin Series *by Jimmy Jalapeeno: seven acrylic paintings on canvas portraying Austin's greenbelts*
- *Forged steel handrails by Lars Stanley*
- *Carved granite glyphs by Philippe Klinefelter portraying each of the 12 trees that streets were named after in the original Waller Platte*

century. The airport opened with the potential for international passenger air service, which Austin did not have previously. The split-level 450,000-square-foot terminal building is the result of years of work by airport planners to meet the growing demand for expanded airport facilities.

The airport opened in the spring of 1999 and cost approximately $675 million. The new facility includes the $115 million Barbara Jordan Passenger Terminal, named for the first African American woman elected to the Texas Senate and a three-time Congresswoman. Known as the single

Airport Facts and Figures

- *Six million passengers (and 15 million people counting those coming to meet travelers) are expected to move through the terminal in its first year.*
- *The airport opened with 25 gates.*
- *The airport can expand to 55 gates if needed.*
- *The cost of the project is $675 million; the city's share was $585 million.*
- *Two parallel runways serve the facility.*
- *The airport includes parking for 8,000 cars in lots and 2,200 spaces in a parking garage.*

largest construction project in Austin history, the terminal will echo the atmosphere of Austin and central Texas through artwork and native materials such as pink granite from Marble Falls.

The terminal is a four-level facility. Many passengers spend time in The Market Place, and, in true Austin fashion, even a stage for live musicians on occasion.

Eateries at the airport include several Austin favorites: Schlotzky's Deli, Matt's Famous El Rancho, Amy's Ice Cream, The Salt Lick, Auntie Anne's Pretzels, and more.

Shops at the airport include Travelfest, www.new.austin and Bookpeople, Harlon's BBQ and News, Blue Bonnets Gifts and Collectibles, and more.

Train Services

Amtrak Station
250 N. Lamar Blvd. and W. Cesar Chavez St.

Major Airlines Serving Austin

America West, 800/235-9292

American, 800/433-7300

Continental, 800/525-0280

Delta, 800/221-1212

Northwest, 800/225-2525

Southwest, 800/435-9792

TWA, 512/454-8900 (domestic),

800/892-4141 (international)

United, 800/241-6522

USAirways, 800/428-4322

(a block north of Town Lake)
800/872-7245 (tickets, reservations, and information)
The Amtrak Eagle, a two-level passenger train, provides train service out of Austin. It provides daily direct service to major U.S. hubs. Trains leave for San Antonio, New Orleans, and Los Angeles on Monday, Wednesday, and Saturday; for Chicago on Sunday, Tuesday, and Thursday. Reservations are required for all trips.

Bus Services

Greyhound Bus Lines
Kerrville Bus Company
916 Koenig Ln. (across from Highland Mall Shopping Center)
512/389-1063 or 800/231-2222 (information and schedules)
Kerrville Bus Company offers daily direct service to Kerrville, Houston,

The Austin Rangers

Downtown, the Austin Downtown Rangers are at your service. Dressed in distinctive uniforms, they are Austin's goodwill ambassadors. On foot and on bicycles, they're on the alert for lost or displaced tourists. They don't carry weapons or make arrests; instead, they report criminal activity to the Austin Police Department. Armed only with maps of the city and two-way communication equipment, they provide assistance to visitors, answering questions and reporting problems to city agencies. They patrol the streets from Riverside Drive to Martin Luther King Boulevard (19th Street) north, and from the I-35 access road on the east and San Antonio Street on the west.

The Rangers are chosen from hundreds of qualified applicants after extensive background checks and personal interviews. They train extensively for downtown duty before they hit the streets. For some, being a Ranger is the first step toward a career with the Austin Police Department. "The Rangers express the friendly nature of Austin. Their presence contributes greatly to the downtown area," says former Mayor Bruce Todd.

The Congress Avenue Bridge

People who lived north or south of Town Lake had a transportation problem until the first bridge was built across the river in 1869. Unfortunately, it was a pontoon bridge and didn't last long; it washed away in a flood 11 months later. In 1875 the Congress Avenue Bridge was built. In 1910 it was replaced with the Congress Avenue Bridge.

Today the Congress Avenue Bridge is a tourist attraction, thanks to the millions of Mexican free-tailed bats that migrate and roost under the bridge every year. When they are in residence (late March through November), they fly out at dusk for dinner, consuming hundreds of thousands of mosquitoes each night. They're a boon to Austin!

Killeen, and Bryan-College Station, with service to numerous Texas cities and towns in between. In Austin, tickets must be purchased at the Greyhound station. Reservations are not accepted.

© Eleanor S. Morris

3

WHERE TO STAY

Although for one reason or another Austin never got around to building a group of historic hotels such as you might find in other large cities, in the early days there were two: the Stephen F. Austin—recently reopened—and the Driskill, Austin's pride. Today, as in any major city, Austin has no dearth of high-rise luxury hotels, but the Driskill still holds a special place.

Regardless of the type of accommodations you're seeking—luxury hotel, upscale chain, convenient motel, or homey bed-and-breakfast—you'll find what you're looking for in Austin. Luxury hotels are primarily located in the downtown region, near the State Capitol and Town Lake. Most chain properties are located north and south along I-35.

Bed-and-breakfasts are scattered throughout the city, with some of the most charming located in historic neighborhoods. More and more travelers and visitors are finding enjoyment in a change from the anonymity of a hotel. In a bed-and-breakfast, your hosts are not only pleasant, they are interested in you; and so, usually, are the other guests. People stay at bed-and-breakfasts because they enjoy this friendly exchange with other travelers and with gracious hosts. Wheelchair accessibility is indicated by the ఉ symbol.

Price rating symbols:
$ $50 and under
$$ $51 to $75
$$$ $76 to $125
$$$$ $126 and up

DOWNTOWN AUSTIN

Hotels

AUSTIN MARRIOTT AT THE CAPITOL
701 E. 11th St.
Austin
512/478-1111 or 800/228-9290
$$$$

Conveniently located downtown, this hotel includes everything needed to pamper the business or leisure traveler. An American grill serves a casual breakfast, lunch, and dinner; a sports bar and grill provides after-hours fun; and a lobby piano bar provides a soothing end to the day. Work out the travel kinks in the heated indoor/outdoor pool designed for swimming laps, or at the health club, complete with whirlpool and wet/dry sauna. ⚒ (Downtown Austin)

DOUBLETREE GUEST SUITES
303 W. 15th St.
Austin
512/478-7000 or 800/222-8733
$$$$

This all-suites hotel has 189 rooms with fully equipped kitchens, including 16 two-bedroom suites (four of which are penthouses). Facilities include an outdoor pool and Jacuzzi, a courtesy shuttle for trips within a two-mile radius, business and secretarial services, and a restaurant with indoor/outdoor dining. ⚒ (Downtown Austin)

DRISKILL HOTEL
604 Brazos St.
Austin
512/474-5911 or 800/527-2008
$$$$

Austin's most historic hotel is full of Texas history, architectural beauty, elegant furnishings, and artwork. Totally renovated and restored with all of it's original grandeur intact, this hotel has been host to dignitaries, heads of state, legislators, and lobbyists. The hotel has 177 luxuriously appointed rooms and seven suites, a full-service restaurant, lobby piano lounge, 24-hour room service, gift shop, concierge desk, and valet parking. It is located downtown, right on the corner of Brazos and Sixth Streets. The Driskill pampers guests with a complimentary coffee and newspaper each morning and a complimentary happy hour each evening. Restaurants, shops, the Capitol, and the Governor's Mansion are all within walking distance. ⚒ (Downtown Austin)

FOUR SEASONS HOTEL
98 San Jacinto Blvd.
Austin
512/478-4500 or 800/332-3442
$$$$

The Four Seasons prides itself on pampering guests in the same manner as fine European hotels, but the

Four Seasons Hotel

© Permenter and Bigley

DOWNTOWN AUSTIN

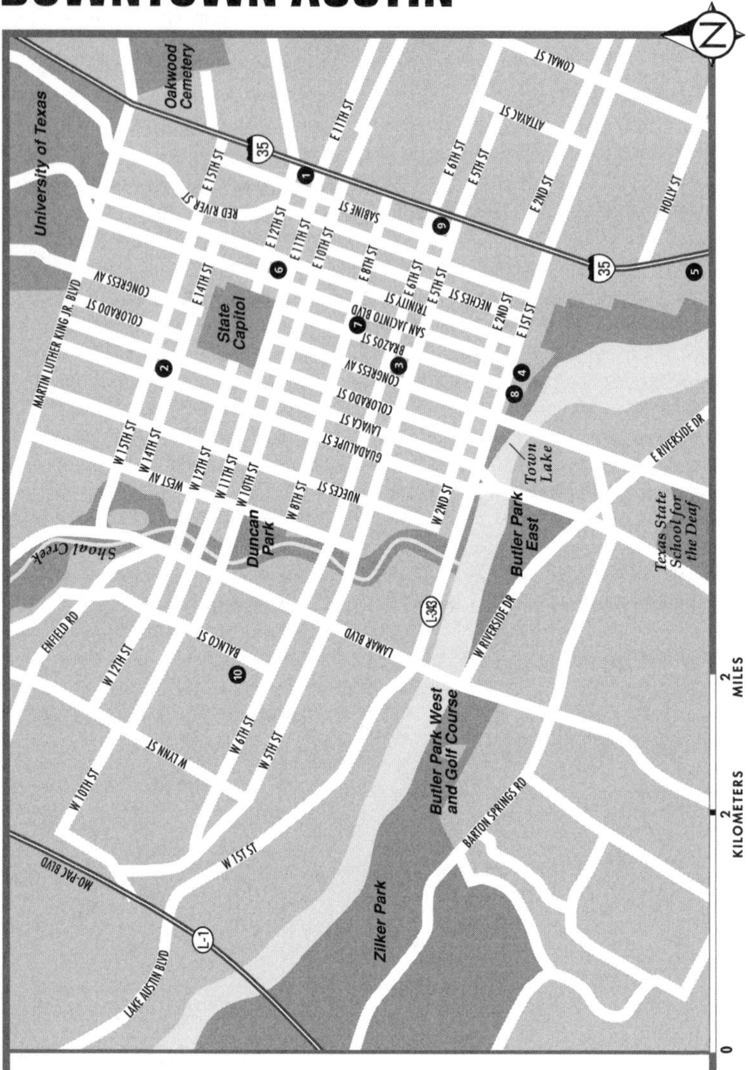

Where to Stay in Downtown Austin

1 Austin Marriott at the Capitol
2 Doubletree Guest Suites
3 Driskill Hotel
4 Four Seasons Hotel
5 Holiday Inn Town Lake
6 La Quinta at the Capitol
7 Omni Austin Hotel
8 Radisson Hotel and Suites on Town Lake
9 Sheraton Austin Hotel
10 Southard House

University of Texas

Oakwood Cemetery

State Capitol

Shoal Creek

Duncan Park

Town Lake

Butler Park East

Butler Park West and Golf Course

Texas State School for the Deaf

Zilker Park

MILES
KILOMETERS

Southwestern decor sets this place clearly in Texas. Lobby sofas are upholstered in brown-and-white steerhide. There are tables made of genuine Mission doors with ox yoke legs, and an elk head is mounted over the fireplace. Half of the 292 guest rooms offer views of Town Lake, and there's an outdoor pool overlooking the lake. The hotel is within walking distance of the Convention Center and Sixth Street. & (Downtown Austin)

HOLIDAY INN TOWN LAKE
I-35 and Town Lake Rd.
Austin
512/472-8211 or 800/HOLIDAY
$$$–$$$$
Overlooking both Town Lake and I-35, this 320-room hotel is only a mile from central downtown, Sixth Street, the Austin Convention Center, the Capitol, and the University of Texas. Amenities include work desks and computer hookups in rooms, a restaurant and lounge, a gift shop, valet service, bell service, and complimentary airport shuttle. & (Downtown Austin)

OMNI AUSTIN HOTEL
700 San Jacinto Blvd.
Austin
512/476-3700 or 800/THE OMNI
$$$$
With its high-rise atrium, the sophisticated, 304-room Omni offers all the amenities business and leisure travelers expect. The Club Floor on the 13th and 14th floors offers restricted access and upgraded amenities, including continental breakfast, afternoon hors d'oeuvres, beer and wine, and freshly baked cookies nightly. All guests have use of a fitness center. & (Downtown Austin)

RADISSON HOTEL AND SUITES ON TOWN LAKE
111 Cesar Chavez St.
Austin
512/478-9611 or 800/333-3333
www.radisson.com/austintx
$$–$$$$
Perched at the intersection of Congress Avenue and Town Lake Road, this hotel includes a health club, an outdoor pool, and a TGI Friday's

Radisson Hotel and Suites on Town Lake

© Permenter and Bigley

restaurant. All rooms have hair dryers, coffeemakers, and irons with ironing boards. Guests also receive complimentary newspapers on weekdays. Ninety-two guest rooms are two-room suites, and a concierge level is also available. This hotel is especially convenient for those looking to unwind on Town Lake's hike and bike trail. & (Downtown Austin)

SHERATON AUSTIN HOTEL
500 N. I-35
Austin
512/480-8181 or 800/325-3535
$$$$
The 254-room hotel has meeting space, a health club, a pool, and a Jacuzzi that holds 25 people, as well as a restaurant on the 18th floor with a view of Austin. The spacious guest rooms are furnished in Drexel Heritage and are complete with coffeemakers, hair dryers, makeup mirrors, and ironing boards and irons. This hotel is a good choice for those interested in spending time on Sixth Street. & (Downtown Austin)

Motels

LA QUINTA AT THE CAPITOL
300 E. 11th St.
Austin
512/476-1166 or 800/687-6667
$$
The motel's "Gold Medal Rooms" all have 25-inch TVs and speaker phones. Complimentary breakfast and free local calls are offered. & (Downtown Austin)

Bed-and-Breakfasts

SOUTHARD HOUSE
908 Blanco St.
Austin
512/474-4731

www.austin360.com
$$–$$$$
Southard House is popular with intellectuals visiting the University of Texas, as well as architects, lawyers, and international visitors. The large map of the world is dotted with colored pins showing the home cities of Southard House guests. Airport pickup, business calls for guests, accommodation of special diets, and other amenities are offered in this restored and convenient Victorian Greek Revival house in Clarksville, a few blocks from the restaurants and shops of West Sixth Street. (Downtown Austin)

NORTH AUSTIN

Hotels

AUSTIN NORTH HILTON AND TOWERS
6000 Middle Fiskville Rd.
Austin
512/451-5757, 800/347-0330, or 800/HILTONS
$$$–$$$$
Austin North Hilton welcomes guests to the Hill Country with a Western-motif lobby of stenciled walls, an antler chandelier, and a reception desk made of native Texas limestone. The 332 guest rooms each have an oversized desk, two phones, and an overstuffed chair with ottoman. The pool is surrounded by lush landscaping, and the Cabana Club offers refreshments. The concierge level, with 18 meeting rooms, offers complimentary continental breakfast and afternoon hors d'oeuvres. No charge for children staying in the same room as their parents. & (North Austin)

BEST WESTERN ATRIUM NORTH
7928 Gessner Dr.

NORTH AUSTIN

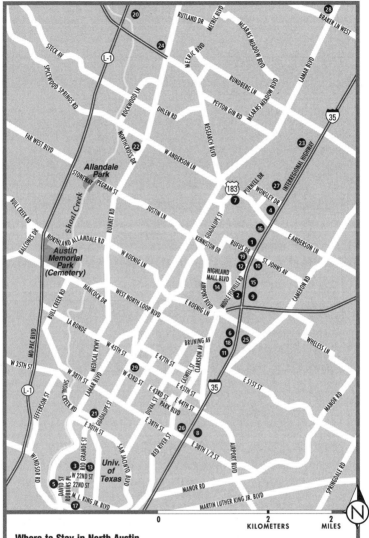

Where to Stay in North Austin

1 Austin Chariot Resort Inn & Conference Center
2 Austin North Hilton and Towers
3 Austin's Wildflower Inn
4 Best Western Atrium North
5 Carrington's Bluff Bed & Breakfast
6 Courtyard by Marriott Austin
7 Days Inn North
8 Days Inn University
9 Doubletree Hotel Austin
10 Drury Inn and Suites North
11 Fairfield Inn by Marriott Austin
12 Four Points Hotel by ITT Sheraton
13 Governor's Inn
14 Habitat Suites Hotel
15 Hampton Inn Austin North
16 Holiday Inn Express
17 Inn at Pearl Street
18 La Quinta Inn/Suites Highland Mall
19 La Quinta Inn/Suites North
20 La Quinta Inn/Suites-Mo-Pac
21 McCallum House
22 Northpark Executive Suite Hotel
23 Park Inn International
24 Ramada Limited
25 Ramada Limited Airport North
26 Rodeway Inn–University
27 Travel Lodge Suites Austin
28 Walnut Forest Motel
29 Woodburn House

Austin
512/339-7311 or 800/468-3708
$$

Located one block west of I-35, this property is built around an enclosed atrium that boasts a heated swimming pool and dry sauna. Some rooms feature Jacuzzi tubs; environmentally friendly "green" rooms are also available. Continental breakfast and complimentary newspaper are included in the daily rate for guests. Guest facilities include a business center, laundry services, and restaurant and bar adjacent to the property. Kids under age 18 stay free. Local calls, cable TV, and in-room movies round out the amenities. & (North Austin)

DOUBLETREE HOTEL AUSTIN
6505 N. I-35

Austin
512/454-3737 or 800/222-8733
$$–$$$$

Located north of the airport along I-35 at U.S. 290, this hotel, with its Spanish Colonial architecture, is a local landmark. Amenities include 350 guest rooms with generous work areas. The Courtyard Cafe overlooks a multilevel courtyard with greenery and waterscapes. The exercise facility includes a swimming pool and a volleyball court. & (North Austin)

FAIRFIELD INN BY MARRIOTT AUSTIN
959 Reinli St.
Austin
512/302-5550 or 800/228-2800
$$–$$$

Located off I-35 and U.S. 290, three

The Historic Driskill Hotel

The Driskill Hotel opened in 1886 with a grandeur that was a rarity on the Texas frontier. Before the Driskill came along, travelers to Austin reported being forced to lodge in establishments with dirty rooms, and even being forced to share their quarters with other travelers. The names of such establishments have not come down to us, a small loss. But with the Driskill, Austin had something to brag about. The four-story L-shaped building had three grand entrances and such architectural details as arched windows, balconies, columns, corbels, and gargoyles. Wide corridors paved with black slate and marble led from the entrances, merging in a magnificent lobby underneath a four-story sky-lit rotunda. President Lyndon B. Johnson and Lady Bird always stayed at the Driskill; they had their own suite. The hotel has hosted other heads of state, legislators, lobbyists, aspiring and "arrived" socialites, honeymooners, and, of course, visitors to the capital.

miles from the University of Texas and four miles from downtown, the inn boasts famous Marriott hospitality with down-to-earth prices. In addition to 63 bright and attractive guest rooms, the hotel offers "spa rooms" with personal spas and king-size beds. Complimentary continental breakfast, a heated indoor pool and exercise room, free movie channel, and local phone calls are offered; vending machines and fax and copy services are available. & (North Austin)

FOUR POINTS HOTEL BY ITT SHERATON
7800 N. I-35
Austin
512/836-8520 or 800/325-3535
$$$
Formerly the Howard Johnson, this 188-room property is located at the intersection of U.S. 183 and I-35, convenient to many stops in far north Austin. Guests enjoy complimentary breakfast and an outdoor swimming pool. Facilities include a restaurant, bar, fitness center, cable TV, room service, and modem lines. All rooms include a refrigerator and three telephones. & (North Austin)

HABITAT SUITES HOTEL
500 Highland Mall Blvd.
Austin
512/467-6000 or 800/535-4663
$$$–$$$$
Travelers who want a "green" environment that utilizes recycled materials, natural products, and no unnecessary chemicals will appreciate this hotel. The eco-friendly property boasts an ionized pool and hot tubs, water and energy conservation measures throughout, with many recycled materials used in the construction. Both one- and two-bedroom suites are available, each with cof-

feemakers. A full buffet breakfast is served daily, and evening hospitality is offered Monday through Saturday from 5 to 7. & (North Austin)

HAMPTON INN AUSTIN NORTH
7619 N. I-35
Austin
512/452-3300 or 800-HAMPTON
$$$
Complimentary continental breakfast, free local calls, and cable television with in-room movies are standard features at this property. Also offered: a heated swimming pool and an exercise facility. & (North Austin)

HOLIDAY INN EXPRESS
7622 N. I-35
Austin
512/467-1701 or 800/HOLIDAY
$$
With indoor corridors, the Holiday Inn Express has the feel of a hotel at motel prices. Guests are offered a complimentary continental breakfast and use of an outdoor pool. & (North Austin)

NORTHPARK EXECUTIVE SUITE HOTEL
7685 Northcross Dr.
Austin
512/452-9391 or 800/851-9111
$$–$$$$
A property that includes a full buffet breakfast and social hour for guests, as well as in-room VCRs and complimentary movie rental. Visitors can use the facilities at a local health club. One- and two-bedroom suites are offered in this hotel near Northcross Mall. & (North Austin)

Motels

AUSTIN CHARIOT RESORT INN & CONFERENCE CENTER

7300 N. I-35
Austin
512/452-9371 or 800/432-9202
$$

Chariot Resort Inn offers a convenient, inexpensive room. The hotel includes a restaurant and bar, and an outdoor pool. Rooms are simple but clean in this conveniently located property. ঙ (North Austin)

**COURTYARD
BY MARRIOTT AUSTIN**
5660 N. I-35
Austin
512/458-2340 or 800/321-2211
$$

Guests can enjoy in-room movies, an outdoor pool and whirlpool, and a small health club. Room service available. ঙ (North Austin)

DAYS INN NORTH
820 E. Anderson Ln.
Austin
512/835-4311 or 800/725-ROOM
$$

This basic accommodation offers standard motel rooms as well as an outdoor swimming pool. Chili's restaurant is located nearby. ঙ (North Austin)

DAYS INN UNIVERSITY
3105 N. I-35
Austin
512/478-1631 or 800/725-ROOM
$$

A no-frills property offering inexpensive accommodations in the area of the University of Texas campus. Guests have use of an outdoor swimming pool; a café is located next door. Local calls are free, as is a daily continental breakfast. ঙ (North Austin)

DRURY INN AND SUITES NORTH
I-35 and St. Johns
Austin

512/467-9500 or 800/325-8300
$$$

Visitors enjoy a buffet breakfast and cocktail hour Monday through Thursday; rooms include coffeemakers. Guests can work out the kinks in the outdoor pool or purchase a daily membership to a local health club for $5. ঙ (North Austin)

**LA QUINTA INN/SUITES
HIGHLAND MALL**
5812 N. I-35
Austin
512/459-4381 or 800/687-6667
$$

Along with clean, family-friendly rooms, the hotel offers free local calls and a complimentary breakfast. ঙ (North Austin)

LA QUINTA INN/SUITES NORTH
7100 N. I-35
Austin
512/452-9401 or 800/687-6667
$$

Rooms boast oversized desks (some also have recliners) and dataport phones with computer hookups; microwaves and refrigerators can be rented in your room. Complimentary breakfast and a swimming pool round out the amenities. Children under age 18 are free in parents' room. ঙ (North Austin)

LA QUINTA INN/SUITES-MO-PAC
11901 N. Mo-Pac Expwy.
Austin
512/832-2121
$$

Like other La Quinta Inns, this location offers family-friendly accommodations. Children under age 18 are free in parents' room. ঙ (North Austin)

PARK INN INTERNATIONAL
9220 N. I-35

Lake Austin Spa Resort

Perched in the rolling hills on a quiet shore of Lake Austin, the Lake Austin Spa Resort combines spa luxury with the rustic atmosphere of a lake retreat. With healthy dining, exercise programs, spa treatments, and many activities, the resort is casual elegance at its best.

Activites range from aerobics classes on a suspended wood floor to tennis, dancing, mountain biking, and even sculling on the lake's calm waters. Guests can try a massage, a facial, a manicure, an aloe vera body mask, an invigorating sea salt scrub, or an aromatherapy scalp conditioning.

Accommodations include 40 cottage rooms with saltillo tile floors, private baths, central air and heat, telephones, cable TV, and king, double, or queen beds. Guests have use of an outdoor pool, an indoor water-aerobics pool, a sauna, a steam and Jacuzzi, training room, a walking trail, and tennis courts. Ten cottages were recently renovated; these suites include a meditation garden, deluxe soaking tub, and a terrace.

The resort is located at 1705 South Quinlan Park Road. Call 512/372-7360 or 800/847-5637 for more information; check out the Web site at www.lakeaustin.com.

Austin
512/837-7372
$
Located near the intersection of I-35 and U.S. 183, this hotel includes free HBO, 30-channel cable TV, free local calls, king-size beds in the single rooms, and free continental breakfast. Some rooms include refrigerators. ⅙ (North Austin)

RAMADA LIMITED
9102 Burnet Rd.
Austin
512/835-7070 or 800/880-0709

$$
Free continental breakfast is offered at this property near the intersection of U.S. 183 and Burnet Road. Standard room features include HBO, color TVs, whirlpool baths, and small refrigerators. ⅙ (North Austin)

RAMADA LIMITED
AIRPORT NORTH
5526 N. I-35
Austin
512/451-7001 or 800/880-0709
$
With a free shuttle service to the bus

station, this property also includes a complimentary extended continental breakfast daily from 6 a.m. to 10 a.m. with bagels, waffles, and cereal. ও (North Austin)

RODEWAY INN–UNIVERSITY
2900 N. I-35
Austin
512/477-6395 or 800/228-2000
$$
Guests at this 50-room motel in the University of Texas campus area have use of an outdoor swimming pool. Rooms are simple but comfortable and include coffeemakers, free local calls, cable TV, and free continental breakfast. ও (North Austin)

TRAVEL LODGE SUITES AUSTIN NORTH
8300 N. I-35

Austin
512/835-5050 or 800/578-7878
$–$$
A three-story all-suites property offering one- and two-bedroom accommodations. Suites include kitchenettes with microwaves, refrigerators, and coffeemakers. Free breakfast is available daily; a laundry room and outdoor pool are also offered. ও (North Austin)

WALNUT FOREST MOTEL
11506 N. I-35
Austin
512/835-0864
$
This motel is tucked off busy I-35 under a grove of trees. The simple rooms are clean and comfortable in this property, which harks back to the early days of motel travel. Weekly rates are available. ও (North Austin)

Top Ten Must-See Things in Austin
by Nancy and Roger Danley, innkeepers, McCallum House Bed-and-Breakfast

1. The **Texas Capitol** building and Capitol extension.
2. The **UT Tower**, campus, and "The Drag."
3. The **LBJ Library**, especially the model of the Oval Office.
4. **Town Lake**, especially the hike and bike trail.
5. **Zilker Park**; don't miss Barton Springs and the gardens.
6. **Central Market**, the most fascinating market this side of Istanbul.
7. Bats leaving **Congress Avenue Bridge** at dusk (spring, summer, and early fall).
8. The view from **Mount Bonnell**.
9. The **Sixth Street** nightlife scene.
10. The **Lady Bird Johnson Wildflower Research Center** (spring is best).

© Permenter and Bigley

Renaissance Austin Hotel, p. 39

Bed-and-Breakfasts

AUSTIN'S WILDFLOWER INN
1200 W. 22nd-½ St.
Austin
512/477-9639
kjackson
@austinwildflowerinn.com
$$

Innkeeper Kay celebrates the Hill Country's famously beautiful spring wildflowers with bright flowers leading up the path to this pretty white clapboard house. Inside you'll find stenciled flowers brightening up the walls and the stairs. Lace curtains let in lots of sunshine, and the four guest rooms (two with private baths) are light and bright. Kay holds the record for variety breakfasts: A guest from Britain stayed almost six weeks, and not one menu was repeated. (North Austin)

CARRINGTON'S BLUFF BED & BREAKFAST
1900 David St.
Austin
512/479-0638

www.citysearch.com/aus /carringtonbluff
$$–$$$

Bordering Shoal Creek, this estate dates back over 100 years. Located just seven blocks from the University of Texas campus and nine from the state capitol, the six-room inn offers TV in some rooms and phones in all rooms; two rooms share a bath. No smoking indoors and no children under the age of 10. (North Austin)

GOVERNOR'S INN
611 W. 22nd St.
Austin
512/477-0711
www.citysearch.com/aus /carringtonbluff
(same owner as above)
$$–$$$

Built in 1897, this impressive mansion is just two blocks from the University of Texas campus. The neoclassical Victorian house, with high ceilings, lots of white paneling, and several porches, once served time as a fraternity house. Now the wrought-iron gates lead to comfortable rooms named for Texas governors—appropriate since the Texas Governor's Mansion is just around the corner on 11th Street. The sound of university students passing by, laughing and happy, adds to the warm and youthful atmosphere of the Governor's Inn. (North Austin)

INN AT PEARL STREET
809 W. Martin Luther King Blvd.
at Pearl St.
Austin
512/477-2233 or 800/494-2203
$$$–$$$$

This turn-of-the-century Greek Revival mansion is the newest kid on the block of downtown bed-and-breakfast establishments. Four eclectic guest rooms (and more in the works) are decorated in imaginative styles; the choices are the French Room, the European Room, the Far East Room, and the Gothic Suite, all with private baths. The inn, once selected as Austin's Symphony Designer Showhouse, is surrounded by porches and has a large deck shaded by massive trees. It offers old-world ambience right in the heart of downtown. On weekdays a continental breakfast is served; on weekends it's a full breakfast complete with champagne and dessert. (North Austin)

MCCALLUM HOUSE
613 W. 32nd St.
Austin
512/451-6744
mccallum@austintex.net
$$–$$$
Not only do innkeepers Nancy and Roger Danley welcome all their guests, they make the inn a comfortable home-away-from-home for many visiting professors, which makes for lively breakfast conversation. This bed-and-breakfast inn is ¾ mile from the University of Texas. The five guest rooms and suites all have private baths and kitchens; four have private porches. The house has a huge screened-in porch with inviting, white wicker furniture. Jane Y. McCallum, an early suffragette, once lived here with her husband and her five children. The year the house was built, 1927, McCallum began fighting for women's right to vote. A wonderful banner on the wall of the landing proclaims just that. (North Austin)

WOODBURN HOUSE
4401 Ave. D
Austin
512/458-4335
www.woodburnhouse.com

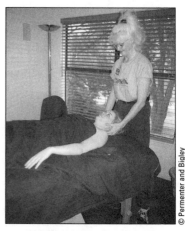

Lake Austin Spa Resort, p. 35

© Permenter and Bigley

$$
This bed-and-breakfast is in Austin's Hyde Park neighborhood, an area filled with lovely old homes. (The Austin Visitors Center recommends this neighborhood for touring.) Woodburn House was named for a former occupant, Bessie Hamilton Woodburn, daughter of a Texas provisional governor after the Civil War. The spacious mansion has porches both upstairs and down, and four guest rooms, all with private baths and lace curtains covering their long windows. (North Austin)

NORTHWEST AUSTIN

Hotels

COURTYARD BY MARRIOTT AUSTIN NORTHWEST
9409 Stonelake Blvd.
Austin
512/502-8100 or 800/321-2211
$$–$$$
This hotel is convenient to the Great Hills area and shopping at the Arboretum. Irons and ironing boards, and cof-

feemakers are standard in all rooms, as are oversized desk/work areas. Executive rooms include king-size beds, refrigerators, and microwaves; "spa king rooms" also include full-size Jacuzzis. ♿ (Northwest Austin)

HAMPTON INN HOTEL AUSTIN NORTHWEST ARBORETUM
3908 W. Braker Ln.
Austin
512/349-9898 or 800/HAMPTON
$$$

Located at the intersection of Mo-Pac Expressway (Loop 1) and Braker Lane, this 123-room hotel includes 25-inch televisions, coffeemakers, irons, and complimentary HBO. Guests have use of an outdoor pool and an exercise room; a range of dining choices are located about a mile away in the Arboretum area. ♿ (Northwest Austin)

HOLIDAY INN NORTHWEST PLAZA
8901 Business Park Dr.
Austin
512/343-0888 or 800/HOLIDAY
$$$

Tucked just off U.S. 183 and Mo-Pac Expressway (Loop 1), this large hotel offers standard rooms with coffeemakers, hair dryers, and Nintendo video games. Guests also have use of an indoor/outdoor heated pool and an exercise room with sauna and whirlpool. Other facilities include a garden atrium restaurant and a sports bar with a 10-foot big-screen TV. ♿ (Northwest Austin)

RENAISSANCE AUSTIN HOTEL
9721 Arboretum Blvd.
Austin
512/343-2626 or 800/HOTELS-1
$$$$

Formerly the Stouffer Renaissance Hotel, this elegant accommodation is located in the upscale Arboretum shopping area, with restaurants, boutique shopping, and movie theaters within walking distance. Visitors also have use of a full health club including an indoor/outdoor pool. The hotel offers three restaurants, 24-hour room service, a lobby bar, and an adjacent nightclub, Tangerines. ♿ (Northwest Austin)

Motels

CORPORATE LODGING SUITES
4815 W. Braker Ln., #516
Austin
512/345-8822 or 800/845-6343
www.corporatelodging.com
$$–$$$

This unique service links travelers with apartments for as little as a one-night stay. The seven apartment communities are located in far northwest Austin near the Arboretum. Apartments are either one or two bedrooms. Some properties include fireplaces; all are fully furnished and include washers and dryers, TVs, VCRs, and daily maid service. (Northwest Austin)

Campgrounds

EMMA LONG METROPOLITAN PARK
6.5 miles off RR 2222 on
City Park Rd.
512/346-1831
$

There are 20 three-way hookups available here, as well as tent sites and all facilities. Camping is $6 per night for a site without utilities (plus a first-day entry fee of $3 per vehicle Mon–Thu or $5 Fri–Sat). Sites with utilities cost $10 per day plus the first-day entry fee. (Northwest Austin)

SOUTHWEST AUSTIN

Hotels

**MELBOURNE HOTEL
& CONFERENCE CENTER**
4611 Bee Caves Rd.
Austin
512/328-4000
$$–$$$
The Melbourne is a quiet haven in Westlake Hills, a pleasant suburb of Austin. The setting combines the quiet of Hill Country with big-city conveniences. Each of the 55 guest rooms includes a small refrigerator; there is a gazebo in the garden, and conference rooms can accommodate from 5 to 100 people. ♿ (Southwest Austin)

Motels

HEART OF TEXAS MOTEL
5303 U.S. Hwy. 290 West
Austin
512/892-0644
$–$$
For a small place, this 30-room motel offers some nice amenities. In addition to king-size beds and recliners, guest rooms have refrigerators and microwaves, cable TV with HBO, remote controls, and free local calls. Along with a swimming pool, guests can enjoy a putting green and horseshoe facilities. (Southwest Austin)

SOUTH AUSTIN

Hotels

EMBASSY SUITES
300 S. Congress Ave.
Austin
512/469-9000 or 800/EMBASSY
$$$$
Located just south of the river on the corner of Barton Springs Road, the Embassy has 262 suites, both smoking and nonsmoking, opening directly onto a plant-filled, sky-lit atrium. Each suite contains two TVs, two telephones, wet bar, microwave, refrigerator, coffeemaker, ironing board and iron, and hair dryer. Children under age 12 stay free in same suite as parents. ♿ (South Austin)

HOLIDAY INN SOUTH
3401 S. I-35
Austin
512/448-2444 or 800/HOLIDAY
$$$
Every convenience is provided at this recently redecorated luxury hotel. Each of the 190 oversized rooms and 20 elegant suites features a desk area, telephone, modem hookup, a refrigerator, a freezer, a coffeemaker, remote-control color TV, HBO, and pay-per-view movies. To further add to guest comforts, the Country Kitchen Restaurant, a lobby lounge, and a swimming pool, as well as complimentary airport transportation, free parking, room and valet service, and on-site laundry facilities are available. ♿ (South Austin)

HYATT REGENCY AUSTIN
208 Barton Springs Rd.
Austin
512/477-1234 or 800/233-1234
$$$$
The 446-room hotel, which includes 18 suites, is located on the south shores of Town Lake, close to Palmer Auditorium and right on Austin's nine-mile hike and bike trail. It's also convenient to the Austin Convention Center, the Capitol, the University of Texas, and Sixth Street, Austin's famed nightlife district. The hotel has two restaurants and two lounges, a fully

equipped health club, and an outdoor pool and whirlpool, as well as complete conference, meeting, and banquet facilities. Guest rooms have hair dryers, irons and ironing boards, and voice mail. ⅋ (South Austin)

OMNI AUSTIN SOUTHPARK
4140 Governor's Row
Austin
512/448-2222
$$$$
Until recently this was a Wyndham Hotel. On the east side of I-35, it offers meeting space, a restaurant, health club and pool, and free parking, and it's in a prime location, close to downtown. ⅋ (South Austin)

Motels

AUSTIN MOTEL
1220 S. Congress Ave.
Austin
512/441-1157
$–$$$
This historic motel rises above the category of "motel" thanks to beautiful Spanish styling and a pool. It offers free HBO and free coffee and is located just over a mile south of Town Lake, close to historic Sixth Street attractions. There are both budget and luxury rooms with Jacuzzi tubs. (South Austin)

BEST WESTERN SEVILLE PLAZA INN
4323 S. I-35
Austin
512/447-5511 or 800/528-1234
$$
Local telephone calls are free at this motel, which also has guest laundry and in-room coffee. Amenities include HBO, a pool, and continental breakfast. The motel is on the interstate near Ben White Boulevard close to

U.S. 90 and U.S. 71. Conveniently located on the north-south interstate through town. ⅋ (South Austin)

DAYS INN SOUTH
4220 S. I-35
Austin
512/441-9242 or 800/325-2525
$$–$$$
No swimming pool here, but there are Jacuzzi jets in the bathtubs. Rooms also have mini-refrigerators; 25-inch TVs with HBO, cable, and remote control; and free local telephone calls. A complimentary continental breakfast is served in the lobby. ⅋ (South Austin)

EXEL INN OF AUSTIN SOUTH
2711 S. I-35
Austin
512/462-9201 or 800/356-8013
$
Guest rooms have remote-control TVs and clock/radios, and local calls are free. Laundry facilities, a pool, and a complimentary continental breakfast are also offered. The motel is conveniently located on I-35, the north-south interstate through town. ⅋ (South Austin)

FAIRFIELD INN SOUTH
4525 S. I-35
Austin
512/707-8899 or 800/228-2800
$$
Located off I-35 South, the inn boasts famous Marriott hospitality with down-to-earth prices. In addition to bright and attractive guest rooms, the hotel offers spa rooms with personal spas and king-size beds, plus complimentary continental breakfast, a heated indoor pool and exercise room, a free movie channel, and free local phone calls. Fax and copy services are available. ⅋ (South Austin)

GREATER AUSTIN

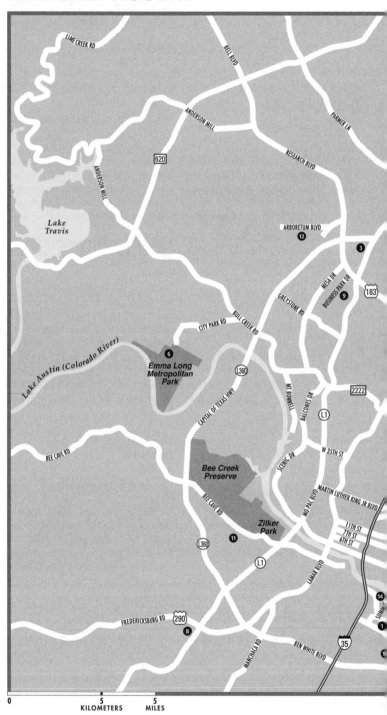

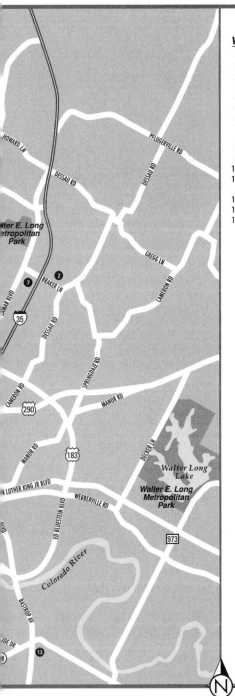

Where to Stay in Greater Austin

1 Citiview Bed and Breakfast (EA)
2 Corporate Lodging Suites (NW)
3 Courtyard by Marriott Austin Northwest (NW)
4 Econolodge (EA)
5 Embassy Suites (EA)
6 Emma Long Metropolitan Park (NW)
7 Hampton Inn Hotel Austin Northwest Arboretum (NW)
8 Heart of Texas Motel (SW)
9 Holiday Inn Northwest Plaza (NW)
10 La Quinta Inns/Oltorf (EA)
11 Melbourne Hotel and Conference Center (SW)
12 Renaissance Austin Hotel (NW)
13 Royal Palm RV (EA)
14 Summit House Bed and Breakfast (EA)

HAWTHORNE SUITES SOUTH
4020 S. I-35
Austin
512/440-7722 or 800/527-1133
$$$–$$$$

These suites come with fully equipped kitchens and irons and ironing boards. Complimentary breakfast and a social hour are offered. Choose an "open-air" suite, with no divisions between the rooms, or a two-story suite. In addition you'll have swimming pool, hot tub, sport court, and health club access. ♿ (South Austin)

INN HOME AMERICA
1001 S. I-35
Austin
512/326-0100
$$$$

All guest rooms and suites have fully equipped kitchens to make you feel at home. Phone numbers are private, local calls are free, and there is voice mail, too. Suites are rented by the day, the week, or the month, with weekly maid service. Ask for a room with a view of downtown along the lake. ♿ (South Austin)

LA QUINTA BEN WHITE
4200 S. I-35
Austin
512/443-1774 or 800/531-5900
$$

Gold Medal Rooms feature fresh decor with rich wood furniture, expanded bathrooms, and more. A complimentary breakfast includes cereal, fresh fruit, pastries, bagels, juice, milk, and coffee. Local calls are free, as are Expanded Free TV channels, movies, and video games. ♿ (South Austin)

LA QUINTA INNS/OLTORF
1603 Oltorf
Austin

Driskill Hotel, p. 27

© Eleanor S. Morris

512/447-6661 or 800/531-5900
$$

La Quinta's fresh new look includes a crisp white exterior with teal trim. Guests are offered a complimentary light breakfast and free local calls, as well as free TV channels, movies, and video games. ♿ (South Austin)

MOTEL 6 SOUTH
2707 S. I-35
Austin
512/444-5882 or 800/440-6000
$

Located about 2½ miles south of downtown, the Motel 6 South has 109 guest rooms, a swimming pool, and TV with cable and HBO. There's coffee in the lobby every morning at 7, and a convenient Kettle Restaurant on the premises. ♿ (South Austin)

QUALITY INN SOUTH
2200 S. I-35
Austin
512/444-0561 or 800/228-5151
$$

SOUTH AUSTIN

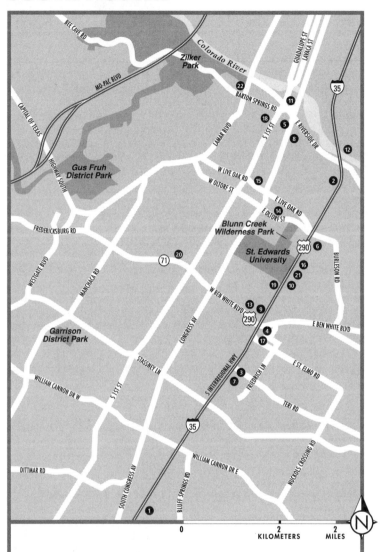

Where to Stay in South Austin

1 Austin Capitol KOA
2 Austin Motel
3 Best Western Seville Plaza Inn
4 Days Inn South
5 Embassy Suites
6 Exel Inn of Austin South
7 Fairfield Inn South

8 Fairview Inn
9 Hawthorne Suites South
10 Holiday Inn South
11 Hyatt Regency Austin
12 Inn Home America
13 La Quinta Ben White
14 La Quinta Inns/Oltorf
15 Lazy Oak Inn

16 Motel 6 South
17 Omni Austin Southpark
18 Pecan Grove RV Park
19 Quality Inn South
20 Ramada Inn South
21 Ramada Limited Town Lake
22 Shady Grove RV Park

Minutes from downtown, the state capitol, and Sixth Street. Amenities include a swimming pool and hot tub, a fitness room, complimentary continental breakfast in the lobby, and the Marco Polo restaurant next door. You'll also have in-room coffee, movies, and a refrigerator, free cable, and free local calls. ♿ (South Austin)

RAMADA INN SOUTH
1212 W. Ben White Blvd.
Austin
512/447-0151 or 800/228-2828
$$–$$$
The Ramada offers both standard rooms and suites. The suites have full-size Jacuzzi tubs in the center of the rooms. Along with a swimming pool, cable TV, and HBO, the Ramada Inn South offers guests a full all-you-can-eat breakfast of eggs, pancakes, fruit—the works. ♿ (South Austin)

RAMADA LIMITED TOWN LAKE
2915 S. I-35
Austin
512/444-8432
$
This motel, about two miles south of downtown, has 58 rooms with TV and HBO, and a pool. A complimentary continental breakfast is offered in the front lobby each morning, as well as free shuttles, free local phone calls, and a restaurant and bar next door. ♿ (South Austin)

Bed-and-Breakfasts

FAIRVIEW INN
1304 Newning Ave.
Austin
512/444-4746 or 800/310-4746
www.fairview-bnb.com
$$$
Built in 1910 and set in large, well-

landscaped grounds off the street and shaded by old oak trees, this Texas Colonial Revival mansion in historic Travis Heights is barely a mile from busy downtown. The lovingly restored home, an Austin landmark, received an Austin Heritage Award for historic preservation. Famous Texans were entertained in the mansion in the past. All the rooms are Texas-size: There are four guest rooms in the big house and two suites in the carriage house in the rear, all of which have private baths. (South Austin)

LAZY OAK INN
211 W. Live Oak
Austin
512/447-8873
www.austin360.com
$$$
This plantation-style farmhouse, built circa 1911, is barely six minutes from downtown and is within walking distance to the shops and restaurants on South Congress Avenue. Relax on the front porch or by the backyard fish pond. The Lazy Oak Inn's rate includes a continental breakfast. (South Austin)

Campgrounds

AUSTIN CAPITOL KOA
7009 S. I-35
Austin
512/444-6322 or 800/284-0206
Daily, weekly, and monthly rates. The campgrounds have 132 three-way hookups, a tent village, eight cabins, and all facilities. (South Austin)

PECAN GROVE RV PARK
1518 Barton Springs Rd.
Austin
512/472-1067
$
Self-contained RVs only at 13 three-

way hookups. The park offers laundry and shower facilities as well as daily, weekly, and monthly rates. It's a 2-minute walk to the hike and bike trail and the funky Barton Springs restaurants, and a 10-minute walk to Barton Springs. 🚹 (South Austin)

SHADY GROVE RV PARK
1600 Barton Springs Rd.
Austin
512/499-8432
$
This RV park in a beautiful pecan grove in the heart of town offers 50 three-way hookups; electric, water, and cable are included in the price, and most pets are OK. (South Austin)

EAST AUSTIN

Hotels

EMBASSY SUITES
5901 N. I-35
Austin
512/454-8004 or 800/EMBASSY
$$$
The complimentary amenities of this all-suites property include a full breakfast and a manager's reception in the evenings with snacks and both alcoholic and nonalcoholic beverages. The hotel includes an indoor pool and exercise facility. 🚹 (East Austin)

Motels

ECONOLODGE
6201 U.S. Hwy. 290 East
Austin
512/458-4759 or 800/553-2666
$$
Located at the intersection of I-35 and U.S. 290, this basic but comfortable chain motel includes a complimentary continental breakfast for guests, as well as access to an outdoor swimming pool. There are non-smoking rooms, in-room microwaves and refrigerators, free HBO and cable, and a restaurant. 🚹 (East Austin)

LA QUINTA INNS/OLTORF
1603 Oltorf
Austin
512/447-6661 or 800/531-5900
$$
A swimming pool, complimentary breakfast, oversize desks, dataport phones with computer hookups, and microwave/refrigerators are available for guests. 🚹 (East Austin)

Bed-and-Breakfasts

CITIVIEW BED & BREAKFAST
1405 E. Riverside Dr.
Austin
512/441-2606
$$$–$$$$
This Frank Lloyd Wright–style home from the 1950s is built high on a hill, with picture windows framing a panoramic view of downtown to the north. The decor is art deco, of course, and there's lots of land surrounding the inn. (East Austin)

SUMMIT HOUSE BED & BREAKFAST
1204 Summit St.
Austin
512/445-5304
$$
There are four comfortable guest rooms in this bed-and-breakfast on top of a hill—hence the name. The house and herb garden are situated on an old Indian campground under 100-year-old oak trees, just minutes from downtown. There are chickens roaming freely and laying fresh eggs for the filling down-home breakfast served every morning. (East Austin)

Campgrounds

ROYAL PALM RV
7901 E. Ben White Blvd.
Austin
512/385-2211
$
There are 32 three-way hookups here along with all facilities—but no tents. Other facilities include a pool, club-house, playground, and laundry. (East Austin)

© Permenter and Bigley

4

Austin boasts fine restaurants serving haute cuisine and continental fare, but real Texas dining lies in the small-town diners, the neighborhood cafés, and the smoky barbecue pits across the state.

Cattle rule in Texas, and beef, from T-bone to ground, makes an appearance on most menus and at backyard cookouts. The early cowboy cooks knew that not all meat was like steak; some of it was tough and even stringy. They used Western ingenuity to turn what could have been waste into dishes that award-winning restaurants are now proud to serve. Chicken-fried steak is such a dish, using one of the toughest cuts of meat: the round steak. It's tenderized (the cook just beats the meat into submission), then dipped in an egg and milk batter, floured, and fried to a golden crisp.

Fajitas are a favorite "trash to treasure" Tex-Mex treat. Fajitas were created by chuckwagon cooks who learned that marinating the tough skirt steak in lime juice broke down the meat into chewable consistency. Sliced in narrow strips and grilled, it is now served with cheese, salsa, and guacamole, and rolled into a flour tortilla. Restaurants like to toss the meat onto a hot metal platter with a squirt of lime juice, sending up enough fragrant fajita smoke to make everyone around wish they had ordered this spicy concoction.

The following list of restaurants is just a sampling of what we think are some of the best dining establishments in Austin, a city with hundreds of eateries. The cost rating guide is based upon an appetizer, entrée, and dessert for one person. Wheelchair accessibility is indicated by the ♿ symbol.

Price rating symbols:
$ **Under $10**
$$ **$11 to $20**
$$$ **$21 and up**

American

Central Market Cafe (NA), p. 62
East Side Cafe (EA), p. 77
Good Eats Cafe (NA), p. 64
Green Pastures (SA), p. 74
Hut's Hamburgers (DA), p. 56
Hyde Park Bar & Grill (NA), p. 64
Kerbey Lane Cafe (NA, NWA, SA),
  p. 64, 70, 75
The Lodge at Lakeview (NWA), p. 70
Ma Ferguson's (NA), p. 65
Old Pecan Street Cafe (DA), p. 60
Shady Grove (SA), p. 76
Threadgill's (NA), p. 66
Waterloo Ice House (DA), p. 61

Asian

Chinatown (NWA, SWA), p. 67, 71
Hunan Lion (SA), p. 75
Korean Garden Restaurant (NA), p. 65
Mongolian BBQ (DA, NA), p. 59, 65
Seoul Sushi Bar and Restaurant
  (SA), p. 76
Tien Jin Chinese Restaurant
(SA), p.77

Barbecue

Artz Rib House (SA), p. 72
The County Line on the Lake
  (NWA), p. 67
Five Star Smokehouse (SWA), p. 72
Green Mesquite (SA), p. 74
Iron Works Barbecue (DA), p. 57
Pok-E-Jo's Smokehouse (NWA), p. 70
Rudy's Country Store and Bar-B-Q
  (NWA), p. 71
Sam's Bar-B-Cue (EA), p. 78
Stubb's Bar-B-Q (DA), p. 60–61

Best Breakfast

Cisco's Restaurant, Bakery & Bar
  (EA), p. 77
Nau Enfield Drug (DA), p. 60–61
Trudy's Texas Star (NA), p. 66

Delicatessen

Katz's Deli and Bar (DA), p. 58

Fine Dining

The Bitter End Bistro and Brewery
  (DA), p. 51
Jeffrey's (DA), p. 58
Mezzaluna (DA), p. 59
The Paggi House (SA), p. 76

German

Scholz Garten (NA), p. 65–66

International

Belgian Restaurant (SWA),
  p. 71
Castle Hill Cafe (DA), p. 53
Chez Nous (DA), p. 54
Gilligan's Restaurant and Bar
  (DA), p. 56
Granite Cafe (DA), p. 64
Hula Hut (NWA), p. 67
Jean-Pierre's Upstairs (NA),
  p. 64
Louie's 106 (DA), p. 58
Mirabelle (NWA), p. 70

Italian

Aldo's Northwest (NWA), p. 66
Brick Oven (DA), p. 53
Carmelo's Italian Restaurant
  (DA), p. 53

Seafood

The Boiling Pot (DA), p. 51–53
Catfish Parlour (NWA), p. 66
Cherry Creek Catfish Co.
  (SA), p. 72
City Grille (DA), p. 55
Gilligan's Restaurant and Bar
  (DA), p. 56
Shoreline Grill (DA), p. 60

Southwestern

Canyon Cafe (SWA), p. 71
Granite Cafe (DA), p. 64
Z Tejas Grill (DA), p. 61

Steaks

Austin Land and Cattle Company
  (DA), p. 51

Dan McKlusky's (DA, NWA),
  p. 56, 67
The Hoffbrau (DA), p. 56

Tex-Mex

Casita Jorge's (NA), p. 62
Chuy's (SA), p. 72–74
El Arroyo (DA), p. 56
El Sol y La Luna (SA), p. 74
Fonda San Miguel (NA), p.62– 64
Jalisco Bar (SA), p. 75
La Palapa (EA), p. 77
Las Manitas Avenue Cafe (DA),
  p. 58
Las Palomas (SWA), p. 72
Manuel's Downtown (DA), p. 58
Matt's El Rancho (SA), p. 75–76
Mesa Hills Cafe (NWA), p. 70
Mexico Tipico Restaurante
  (EA), p. 78
Ninfa's Mexican Restaurant
  (NA), p. 65
Nuevo Leon (EA), p. 78
Rosie's Tamale House (NWA), p. 71
Texas Chili Parlor (DA), p. 61
Trudy's Texas Star (NA), p. 66

Vegetarian

Mr. Natural (EA), p. 78
West Lynn Cafe (DA), p. 61

DOWNTOWN AUSTIN

**AUSTIN LAND AND CATTLE
COMPANY
1205 N. Lamar Blvd.**

**Austin
512/472-1813
$$$**

Here, steaks are hand-cut, aged properly, and seasoned with a secret family recipe. Start with a salad, escargot, Texas sweet onion pie, or mushrooms battered with Shiner Bock, then move on to favorites like filet mignon, rib eye, or New York strip. Other popular dishes include New Zealand lamb chops with jalapeño or mint sauce, sauteed mahimahi, yellowfin tuna, grilled chicken, and vegetable lasagna. Dinner daily. Reservations recommended. & (Downtown Austin)

**THE BITTER END BISTRO AND
BREWERY
311 Colorado St.
Austin
512/478-2337
$$$**

Its name may include the word "brewery," but don't look for pub grub in this elegant eatery. One of Austin's most lauded restaurants, The Bitter End serves up surprising dishes such as grilled lamb loin with mint harissa, capellini with sun-dried tomatoes, and roasted duck breast with potato pancakes. Lunch Mon–Fri; dinner only Sat–Sun. & (Downtown Austin)

**THE BOILING POT
700 E. Sixth St.
Austin**

T I P

Incidentally (or not so incidentally), all of Austin's restaurants are nonsmoking. This caused quite a flap when the law was passed, but things have settled down considerably, and folks seem to eat out as often as before.

DOWNTOWN AUSTIN

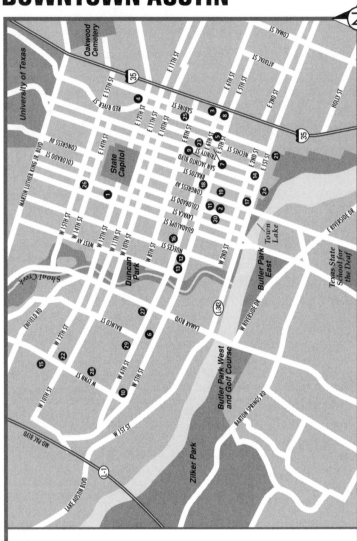

Where to Eat in Downtown Austin
1 Austin Land and Cattle Company
2 The Bitter End Bistro and Brewery
3 The Boiling Pot
4 Brick Oven
5 Carmelo's Italian Restaurant
6 Castle Hill Cafe
7 Chez Nous
8 City Grille
9 Dan McKlusky's
10 El Arroyo
11 Gilligan's Restaurant and Bar
12 The Hoffbrau
13 Hut's Hamburgers
14 Iron Works Barbecue
15 Jeffrey's
16 Katz's Deli and Bar
17 Las Manitas Avenue Cafe
18 Louie's 106
19 Manuel's Downtown
20 Mezzaluna
21 Mongolian BBQ
22 Nau Enfield Drug
23 Old Pecan Street Cafe
24 Shoreline Grill
25 Stubb's Bar-B-Q
26 Texas Chili Parlor
27 Waterloo Ice House
28 West Lynn Cafe
29 Z Tejas Grill

512/472-0985

$$

Don't wear your white shirts to this down-and-dirty seafood joint. Your waitress will robe you up with a plastic bib and hand you a wooden mallet, then set before you your task: a pan filled with spicy boiled shrimp, crab claws, sausage, corn on the cob, and potatoes, all spilled out on the white butcher paper tablecloth. Lunch and dinner Fri–Sun; dinner only Mon–Thu. & (Downtown Austin)

BRICK OVEN
1209 Red River St.
Austin
512/477-7006
www.austin360.com
/eats/brickoven
$

For over a decade and a half, the Brick Oven has offered some of Austin's finest pizza, elevating itself above the fast-food genre to become a city tradition. Today three locations (the others are in northwest Austin on Research Boulevard and in north Austin on West 35th Street) provide diners with real oven-baked pizza as well as other Italian favorites. Lunch and dinner Mon–Sat; dinner only Sun. & (Downtown Austin)

CARMELO'S ITALIAN RESTAURANT
504 E. Fifth St.
Austin
512/477-7497
www.austin360.com/eats
/carmelos
$$$

Traditional Southern Italian cuisine is served here, as are delicious veal parmesan and veal marsala, seafood, and chicken. Lunch and dinner Mon–Fri. Reservations recommended. & (Downtown Austin)

CASTLE HILL CAFE
1101 W. Fifth St.
Austin
$$

This Austin classic is brilliantly decorated with wonderful hand-carved and brightly painted Mexican animals from the state of Oaxaca, which are becoming collector's items. And the menu is almost as creative with starters like Mushroom with Basil Ajoli. Entrées include Grilled Shrimp served on a corn tamale with sauteed spinach and Navajo Crusted Pork Tenderloin. Served with these plates is a salad of crisp greens, cucumber slices, tomato wedge, and shredded carrots and cabbage. The sesame-ginger dressing is unusual and good.

Cathy Dailey, one of the founders of this deservedly popular restaurant, has opened another upscale restaurant, Mirabelle, in Northwest Austin. Castle Hill Cafe is open for lunch Mon–Fri 11 a.m.–2:30 p.m.; for dinner Mon–Sat 6–10 p.m. (Downtown Austin)

Katz's Deli and Bar, p. 58

© Permenter and Bigley

Texas Barbecue

Barbecue ranks with state politics when it comes to provoking heated discussion between Texans. One barbecue joint has a sign over its counter that says it best: "Bar-b-que, sex and death are subjects that provoke intense speculation in most Texans. Out of the three, probably bar-b-que is taken most seriously." You'll find that's true when you ask any Texan for a favorite smokehouse or, heaven forbid, you ask a pit owner for a barbecue recipe. The smoky meats are cooked according to secret methods that many pit masters plan to take to their graves with them, but most recipes call for slow cooking (sometimes 20 hours for brisket) over oak, hickory, or mesquite. The meat is rubbed with dry spices and finished off with a tomato-based sauce. Beef rules most of the Texas barbecue pits in the form of brisket, ribs, and sausage.

Glossary of Texas Barbecue

Mosey up to the counter and order up some barbecue, one of the stars of the Austin culinary world. Here's a little cheat sheet to help you decipher the local barbecue lingo:

Baby back ribs—Ribs from a young hog; usually the most tender of the rib cuts.

Barbacoa—The Spanish took the Indian word barbacoa to describe the smoky meat, the basis for our own word barbecue. You will find barbacoa on the menu in many South Texas restaurants, especially Tex-Mex. It refers to special type of barbecue: the head of a cow wrapped in cheesecloth and burlap, slow smoked in a pit.

CHEZ NOUS
510 Neches St.
Austin
512/473-2413
$$

This personable, small French bistro just around the corner from Sixth Street serves delicious, authentic French cuisine. The *prix fixe menu du jour* includes a choice of soup, appetizer or salad, entrée, and dessert. The simple decor is enlivened by a mural of Montmartre on one wall, lace curtains in the windows, flowers (not real) in aperitif bottles, and lots of French posters on other walls. Background music is soft; service is friendly and attentive. Lunch and

Beef clod—Part of the shoulder or the neck near the shoulder; used like brisket.

Brisket—Chest muscle of a cow. This typically tough cut requires a long, slow cooking period to break down to fibrous meat. When many Texans say they're eating barbecue, they mean brisket. Every joint probably serves up this barbecue dish of Texas.

Cabrito—Young goat.

Country-style pork ribs—Backbone of a hog. These ribs contain large chunks of meat and sometimes resemble a pork chop.

Marinade—A seasoned liquid mixture in which meat is soaked prior to cooking. Acidic marinades such as those containing lime juice help tenderize meat. (Note: Acidic marinades should never be used in aluminum containers.)

Rub—Dry ingredients rubbed onto meat to season it during cooking.

Sauce—The flavored liquid used as a condiment after the meat has cooked. In Texas, most sauces are tomato-based.

Skirt steak—Diaphragm muscle of a cow. This tough cut is usually used for fajitas after marinating.

Slab of ribs—A whole side of the rib cage.

Smoke ring—The tell-tale pink ring in meat that authenticates it as barbecue.

Sop—A basting sauce applied during the barbecuing process.

Spare ribs—The lower portion of a hog's rib.

Texas hibachi—A 55-gallon drum used as a barbecue cooker.

dinner Tue–Fri; Sat–Sun dinner only. (Downtown Austin)

CITY GRILLE
401 Sabine
Austin
512/479-0817
$$$
You'll find the City Grille, specializing in mesquite-grilled steaks and seafood, located in a refurbished warehouse from the 1890s. Old wooden floors and a beamed ceiling contrast with the elegance of candlelight and linen tablecloths. The beef is certain to be tender and the grilled fish moist and tasty, all in line with the restaurant's popular reputation. Dinner seven days a

TRIVIA

Austin is known as "River City," which aptly describes its longtime connection with the Colorado River. Thanks to dams along the river, Austin enjoys two back-to-back lakes located within city limits.

week. Reservations recommended. & (Downtown Austin)

DAN MCKLUSKY'S
301 E. Sixth St.
Austin
512/473-8924
www.austin360.com/eats
/danmckluskys
$$$

This is a steak-lover's mecca, where wait staff serve up consistently tender steaks. Also, "custom combinations" can be ordered: steak and chicken, steak and seafood, steak and lamb, even steak and quail. All served with a generous house salad and your choice of baked or fried potatoes, rice pilaf, or the fresh vegetable of the day. Lunch Mon–Fri; dinner seven days a week. & (Downtown Austin)

EL ARROYO
1624 W. Fifth St.
Austin
512/474-1222
$–$$

Named for the dry arroyo that carves through the lot, El Arroyo serves up popular Tex-Mex dishes, killer margaritas, and Mexican brews. You can dine indoors or outside in this eatery that's a favorite with many longtime

Austinites. Lunch and dinner daily. & (Downtown Austin)

GILLIGAN'S RESTAURANT AND BAR
407 Colorado St.
Austin
512/474-7474
www.austin360.com/eats
/gilligans
$$–$$$

With a name like Gilligan's, you'd expect island cuisine, and that's just what you get at this casually elegant eatery. Don't expect the fun atmosphere of joints like the Hula Hut, however; Gilligan's serves up its island fare atop white tablecloths. Check out the Jamaican jerk or favorites like coconut shrimp. The nightly fare is accompanied by an extensive wine list and, on many nights, live music. Dinner daily. & (Downtown Austin)

THE HOFFBRAU
613 W. Sixth St.
Austin
512/472-0822
$–$$

Since 1934, butter-grilled steaks and chicken have satisfied hungry downtown employees at this casual eatery. Lunch and dinner Mon–Fri. (Downtown Austin)

HUT'S HAMBURGERS
807 W. Sixth St.
Austin
512/472-0693
$

Since 1939 this hip-hopping joint has been serving up some of Austin's most popular burgers. Over 20 types of burgers—from the Wolfman Jack to the Big Bopper—appear on the menu, which also includes chicken-fried steak, salads, and a daily blue-plate special. Save room for the

Tex-Mex

The designation "Tex-Mex" refers to the particular style of Mexican food found in the Lone Star State. Unlike New Mexico's Mexican food, which might include blue corn tortillas, or California's Mexican food, which relies on avocados and black olives, Tex-Mex uses a lot of ground beef, cheese, and chile sauce. You can find great chicken enchiladas with a flavorful verde tomatillo sauce, vegetarian dishes, or even shrimp enchiladas. But the real Tex-Mex favorite, known affectionately as Regular Plate No. 1, is an order of beef enchiladas, refried beans, and Spanish rice. If you're lucky, leche quemada, a sugary pecan praline, will be brought out with your check.

Tamales, both mild and spicy varieties, are also found on every Tex-Mex menu, but they're most popular during the Christmas season. Some stores like Austin's Green and White Grocery sell tamales by the dozen during the holidays when it's popular to take them to office parties and home get-togethers. Making tamales at home is a time-consuming job, traditionally tackled by large families. Tamales start with the preparation of a hog's head, boiled with garlic, spices, peppers, and cilantro. After cooking, the meat is ground and then simmered with spices. As the filling is prepared, other family members ready the hojas (corn husks) used to wrap the tamale. Others prepare the masa, cornmeal worked with lard and seasonings, that is spread thinly on the shucks before filling with meat. Finally, the tamales are steamed in huge pots.

Texas-size onion rings. Lunch and dinner daily. ⅊ (Downtown Austin)

IRON WORKS BARBECUE
100 Red River St.
Austin
512/478-4855
$
The Iron Works for years was just that, an ironworks. The rustic building that housed the Weigel Iron-works now cooks up delicious brisket, chicken, sausage, and ribs near the Convention Center. The classic barbecue plate comes with a choice of two out of three side dishes: beans, potato salad, and cole slaw. Top this off with a slice of pecan, apple, or cherry pie, or peach cobbler, while you enjoy deciphering the dozens of brands burned into the wooden siding. Lunch and dinner

Mon–Fri; lunch only Sat. (Downtown Austin)

JEFFREY'S
1204 West Lynn St.
Austin
512/477-5584
$$$

Chef David Garrido, recently acclaimed by the James Beard Foundation, makes magic with an amazing array of flavors. For adventurous cuisine, this fine dining establishment in the historic Clarksville neighborhood takes high honors indeed. For starters, Chef Garrido suggests shredded goose on a small blue corn taco sauced with fresh mango puree. Oysters are a specialty, served crispy on root chips (sea sprouts) with *habañero* honey aioli. Sturgeon, pecan-wood-smoked for sweetness and served in an orange champagne sauce, is accompanied by a black Oregon truffle in a wine/butter/shallot sauce. Exotic dishes like elk, served with hazelnut wild rice and huckleberry thyme sauce, are also on the menu. But be sure to leave room for desserts, too. Dinner only, Mon–Sat. Reservations recommended. ♿ (Downtown Austin)

KATZ'S DELI AND BAR
618 W. Sixth St.
Austin
512/472-2037
$–$$

"We never klose" is the boast of this restaurant, open 24 hours a day. This is where Austinites have been getting their kosher-style deli fix since 1979, when Katz's introduced "bagel" and "deli" to the Texas vocabulary. Bagels range from toasted with butter for $1.95 to the legendary cream cheese–slathered roll, thick with lox and green lettuce, for $8.50. Chicken

soup comes with both noodles and matzoh balls, and homemade blintzes come in a choice of cheese, apple, or blueberry. To top it all off, there's Top of the Marc (see Nightlife) with music and dancing nightly: jazz, rock, and blues. Breakfast, lunch, and dinner seven days a week. ♿ (Downtown Austin)

LAS MANITAS AVENUE CAFE
211 Congress Ave.
Austin
512/472-9357
$–$$

Grab a booth up front, take a stool at the counter, or head to the back (walk right on through the kitchen) to the covered patio for some good downtown Tex-Mex. Check out the chalupas, tacos, or enchiladas, or start your morning with breakfast in either American or Tex-Mex style. Breakfast and lunch daily. ♿ (Downtown Austin)

LOUIE'S 106
106 E. Sixth St.
Austin
512/476-2010
$$$

Tapas, those delicious appetizers from Spain, are a specialty here, as are pastas, risottos, bouillabaisse, paella, and special meats from the rotisserie. Lunch Mon–Fri; dinner seven days a week. ♿ (Downtown Austin)

MANUEL'S DOWNTOWN
310 Congress Ave.
Austin
512/472-7555
$$$

Manuel's offers interesting variations of such favorites as grilled (not fried) flautas filled with your choice of shredded beef, pork, chicken, or, for vegetarians, black beans and cheese

Top Ten Places to Power Lunch in Austin

by Barbara Redding, Executive Editor of *Ports of Call*, a publication of Weissmann Travel Reports

1. **The Café at the Four Seasons Hotel**, 98 San Jacinto Blvd., 512/685-8300.
2. **Mezzaluna**, 310 Colorado St., 512/472-6770.
3. **Castle Hill Cafe**, 1101 West Fifth St., 512/476-0728.
4. **Gilligan's Restaurant and Bar**, Fourth and Colorado Sts., 512/474-7474.
5. **West Lynn Cafe**, 1110 West Lynn, 512/482-0950.
6. **Manuel's Downtown**, 310 Congress Ave., 512/472-7555.
7. **Fonda San Miguel**, 2330 West Loop Blvd., 512/459-4121.
8. **Lupin**, 3300 West Anderson Ln., 512/454-6054.
9. **Green Pastures**, 811 West Live Oak, 512/441-1888.
10. **The Paggi House**, 200 Lee Barton Dr., 512/478-1121.

or mushrooms. The chile rellenos are poblano peppers stuffed with sweet corn, cilantro, and cheese. No lard and no preservatives go into anything cooked and served at this lively spot. Lunch and dinner Mon–Fri; brunch and dinner Sat–Sun. ♿ (Downtown Austin)

MEZZALUNA
310 Colorado St.
Austin
512/472-6770
$$–$$$
This fine Italian restaurant offers a variety of pasta dishes. Lunch and dinner Mon–Fri; dinner only Sat–Sun. Reservations recommended. ♿ (Downtown Austin)

MONGOLIAN BBQ
117 San Jacinto Blvd.
Austin
512/476-3938
www.austin360.com/eats /mongolianbbq
$
With more than 15 fresh vegetables and three choices of meat, you can create the stir-fry of your dreams in this large and rustic eatery on the corner of San Jacinto and Second. After dousing the heaping plateful of raw comestibles with a variety of sauces, watch it sizzle on a Mongolian grill right before your eyes. Downstairs from the grill, eat on a picnic-style table in a large room with a mirrored wall. Lunch and dinner daily. ♿ (Downtown Austin)

NAU ENFIELD DRUG
1115 West Lynn St.
Austin
512/476-1221
$

This old-fashioned drug store is a long-time favorite with locals. Belly up to the counter or take a booth and enjoy a taste of a real drugstore malt, burger, or sandwich. Breakfasts are very popular as well, when the grill serves up omelets, huevos rancheros, and so many types of breakfast tacos they have a poster listing possible combinations. Try anything from chorizo and potato to egg and cheese. Breakfast and lunch daily. 🜸 (Downtown Austin)

OLD PECAN STREET CAFE
310 E. Sixth St.
Austin
512/478-2491
$–$$

Pecan Street serves continental food, with an emphasis on grilled fish, in a historic building on Sixth Street. In 1871 the Platt-Simpson building was part of a livery stable; in 1901 it became a hardware store. Inside there are original stone walls and wooden floors; outside on the red brick wall is a plaque telling the building's history. The restaurant is easy to spot; the win-

dows are shaded by bright blue awnings. In addition to offering a nice variety of meals, the menu lists certain favorites each night, so if you find something you really like, you can count on it being there. That the pecan pie is a perennial favorite goes without saying. Lunch and dinner Mon–Sat; Sunday brunch. 🜸 (Downtown Austin)

SHORELINE GRILL
98 San Jacinto Blvd.
Austin
512/477-3300
$$$

For a ringside seat to see the bats fly out from under the Congress Avenue Bridge, this elegant Four Seasons Hotel restaurant is the place. Especially when you can enjoy a memorable seafood or prime rib meal while overlooking Town Lake. Lunch Mon–Fri; dinner daily. Reservations recommended. 🜸 (Downtown Austin)

STUBB'S BAR-B-Q
801 Red River St.
Austin

Old Pecan Street Cafe

© Eleanor S. Morris

512/480-8341
www.austin360.com/eats
/stubbsbbq
$

Stubb's is well-known for both its barbecue and its blues, with a long history of featuring both smokin' musicians and slow-cooked meats. Try Stubb's beef and pork link sausage, beef brisket, and either beef or pork spare ribs. Plates are served heaped with traditional side orders such as potato salad, coleslaw, beans, yellow squash, corn on the cob, green beans, stewed tomatoes and okra, country greens, and more. If barbecue's not your thing, you'll find a catch of the day on the menu as well as chicken-fried steak, marinated chicken breast, and other dishes prepared away from the smoker. Lunch and dinner are served daily; open until 2 a.m. ♿ (Downtown Austin)

TEXAS CHILI PARLOR
1409 Lavaca
Austin
512/472-2828
$

When out-of-state visitors come to Austin, they look for a real taste of the Lone Star State. And they find it at the Texas Chili Parlor, a funky restaurant that's within walking distance of the Capitol. Saunter up to a bowl of red. . . and make that "XXX" chili if you're feeling especially brave. Other dishes include Tex-Mex favorites and burgers. Lunch and dinner daily; late-night hours Thu–Sat. ♿ (Downtown Austin)

WATERLOO ICE HOUSE
600 N. Lamar Blvd.
Austin
512/472-5400
$

Burgers, fries, tacos, nachos, chicken, chicken-fried steak, and once-in-a-while specials are on the menu at this informal eatery where everything is prepared from scratch. Waterloo also boasts an extensive beer selection. Lunch and dinner daily. ♿ (Downtown Austin)

WEST LYNN CAFE
1110 West Lynn St.
Austin
512/482-0950
$

The innovative menu of this vegetarian restaurant includes such dishes as spanokopita, a classic Greek dish of flaky phyllo dough layered with spinach, eggs, and sliced almonds and topped with fresh dill and oregano and ricotta and feta cheeses. Some dishes on the menu can be prepared cholesterol-free and nondairy if you wish. Sandwiches, salads, smoothies, fresh juices, and natural sodas are also on the menu in this attractive café, where you can eat outdoors under an arbor. Lunch and dinner daily; Sunday brunch. ♿ (Downtown Austin)

Z TEJAS GRILL
1110 W. Sixth St.
Austin
512/478-5355
$–$$

This restaurant is perched atop a flight of outdoor stairs, leading up to both outdoor and indoor dining. The grill is affiliated with Brio's Restaurant next door and shares the same enthusiasm for innovative cuisine with unusual food blends. Crunchy catfish beignets are served with jalapeño tartar sauce, and the chicken and sausage gumbo ya-ya is as tasty as its name is enthusiastic. Voodoo tuna is served with black peppercorn vinaigrette and soy

What a choice! Austin has more restaurants and bars per capita than any other city in the United States, and Austinites eat out more often than do residents of any other Texas city, including Dallas, Houston, and San Antonio.

mustard sauce, and z'green salad, of mixed greens with Roma tomatoes and colored peppers, comes with a sun-dried tomato and basil dressing. Breakfast, lunch, and dinner daily. ＆ (Downtown Austin)

NORTH AUSTIN

CASITA JORGE'S
2203 Hancock Dr.
Austin
512/454-1980
www.austin360.com/eats
/casitajorges
$$
If you bring along the kids, ask for a table near the aquariums; otherwise opt for patio dining on a nice day. This lively restaurant serves up top-rate Tex-Mex, with popular dishes includ-ing enchiladas, fajitas, tacos, and all the usual, dished out with rice and beans. The margaritas are hefty, so take it easy. Lunch and dinner daily. ＆ (North Austin)

CENTRAL MARKET CAFE
4001 N. Lamar Blvd.
Austin
512/206-1000
$
Central Market has been called "the best market this side of Istan-bul," so it stands to reason that the market's café is a very popular spot. You can eat either indoors or outside on the deck under the tall oak trees. Breakfast, 7 to 11 daily, features the Taco Bar, a delicious build-your-own buffet. You can wrap fresh Central Market tortillas around a choice of creamy eggs, bacon, sausage, black beans, and potatoes. Or indulge in French Grid-dle Toast or a Belgian Waffle, either by itself or Supreme. And there's healthy oatmeal, Scotch oats cooked fresh every morning, with milk, raisins, brown sugar—add a banana if you like.

For lunch and dinner, line up at The Bistro counter for delicious daily soups, gourmet sandwiches and sal-ads, The Grill for burgers, platters of chicken or roast beef, or fresh fish dishes (salmon, mahimahi, catfish, trout). If you prefer, there's lasagna and calzone at the Brick Oven along with other pastas and pizzas.

Weekends you can enjoy live music with featured Austin artists, on the deck and the patio, along with your meal. Each month brings a new selection, and you can pick up a monthly calendar as you walk in the door of the café. Open 7 a.m. to 10 p.m. daily. (North Austin)

FONDA SAN MIGUEL
2330 W. North Loop
Austin
512/459-4121
$$$
Fonda's hacienda Sunday brunch is

NORTH AUSTIN

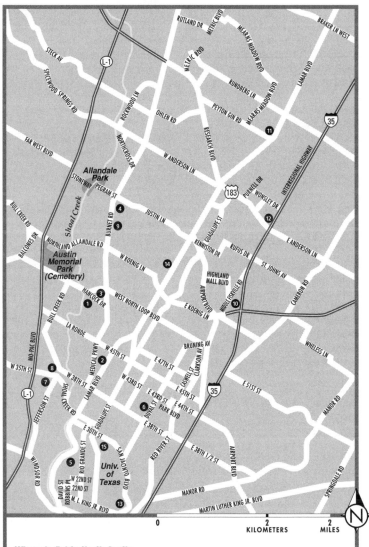

Where to Eat in North Austin

1 Casita Jorge's
2 Central Market Cafe
3 Fonda San Miguel
4 Good Eats Cafe
5 Granite Café
6 Hyde Park Bar & Grill

7 Jean-Pierre's Upstairs
8 Kerbey Lane Cafe
9 Korean Garden Restaurant
10 Ma Ferguson's
11 Mongolian BBQ

12 Ninfa's Mexican
   Restaurant
13 Scholz Garten
14 Threadgill's
15 Trudy's Texas Star

an Austin treat, as is the classic Mexican cuisine on the regular menu. Here you'll find a beautiful setting of Mexican tiles and artifacts and a plant-filled bar serving unique drinks. Dinner Mon–Sun; brunch Sun 11:30 a.m.–2 p.m. Reservations recommended. & (North Austin)

GOOD EATS CAFE
6801 Burnet Rd.
Austin
512/451-2560
$

Good Eats can be counted on for both grilled and lean, fried and steamed food to suit all-American palates, whether you're looking for chicken-fried steak or a heaping plate of steamed vegetables. When Good Eats fries, it's with canola oil only; and on the healthy side of the menu you'll find high-fiber, low-fat, nutrient-dense choices. Daily specials are posted on the chalkboard in this informal café with a roadside-diner atmosphere and friendly, laid-back help. Breakfast, lunch, and dinner. & (North Austin)

GRANITE CAFE
2905 San Gabriel St.
Austin
512/472-6483
$$$

For a decade, the owners of two other popular Austin eateries, Mezzaluna and The Bitter End, have also operated the Granite Cafe. This innovative restaurant offers dishes with a Southwest flair such as Southwestern rubbed Texas rib eye, and chicken quesadillas with sour cream and smoked tomato salsa. Open for lunch and dinner daily. & (Downtown Austin)

HYDE PARK BAR & GRILL
4206 Duval St.
Austin

512/458-3168
$–$$

Hyde Park Grill, a very informal all-American eatery, has super lentil soup on the menu daily, and there's also a soup of the day if you want a change. "We" like their stir-fry and the Asian chicken salad, but the spinach salad is delicious, too. Lunch and dinner daily. & (North Austin)

JEAN-PIERRE'S UPSTAIRS
3500 Jefferson, Second Level
Austin
512/454-4811
$$$

The menu blends continental and Southwest in such dishes as grilled salmon wrapped in apple-smoked bacon and served with a key lime port sauce; and tequila beef tenderloin with a burgundy peppercorn sauce, accompanied by tender julienne vegetables.

But be sure to save some room for the famous dessert soufflés; so far Jean-Pierre's is the only restaurant in town to serve them. Open for lunch Mon–Fri; dinner Mon–Sat. Reservations recommended. (North Austin)

KERBEY LANE CAFE
3704 Kerbey Ln.
Austin
512/451-1436
www.austin360.com/eats
/kerbeyland
$$$

Start your day right with Kerbey Lane's pancakes, sandwiches, crisp salads, and all sorts of imaginative specials. The migas (eggs scrambled with crispy tortilla bits) with spicy red sauce are as good as can be found anywhere. The service is friendly and snappy. Breakfast, lunch, and dinner daily. & (North Austin)

Just beyond the city limits on the shores of Lake Travis stands what's termed the "sunset capital of Texas," the Oasis Cantina del Lago (6500 Comanche Trail, 512/266-2442). Austinites flock to the multiple decks of this restaurant and bar to watch an unparalleled sunset and to enjoy a Tex-Mex dinner, a tangy margarita, and an end to another central Texas day.

KOREAN GARDEN RESTAURANT
6519 N. Lamar Blvd.
Austin
512/302-3149
$$

This restaurant offers Korean and Japanese cuisine, including a new sushi bar. Korean dishes include *cho ki gui*, smoked yellow fish; *kal bi tang*, a traditional Korean cow bone broth with noodles; and kimchi soup with pork. Japanese dishes range from *u-dong* (a thick noodle soup) to chicken teriyaki to chicken curry with *yakimandoo*, a spicy dish. Lunch and dinner daily. (North Austin)

MA FERGUSON'S
6000 Middle Fiskville Rd.
Austin
512/206-3030
www.austin360.com/eats
/mafergusons
$$$

Ready for a taste of Texas home-cookin'? You'll find it at this restaurant that's named for Miriam Ferguson, the first woman governor of Texas. Go for the chicken-fried steak, fried catfish, German sausage, barbecue brisket, tequila shrimp, or seafood lasagne. Breakfast, lunch, and dinner daily; closed 2–5 p.m. daily. & (North Austin)

MONGOLIAN BBQ
9200 N. Lamar Blvd.
Austin
512/837-4898
www.austin360.com/eats
/mongolianbbq
$

Like its sister restaurant on San Jacinto, grilled veggies are the specialty of the day in this eatery that's a far cry from a typical "BBQ" joint. Lunch and dinner daily. & (North Austin)

NINFA'S MEXICAN RESTAURANT
214 E. Anderson Ln.
Austin
512/832-1833
$–$$

Come early for a table on peak Friday and Saturday nights at this popular Tex-Mex hangout. The food is plentiful and mighty tasty and includes all the typical fare from enchiladas to tacos. Don't miss the terrific green salsa served with chips; it's good enough to make a meal itself. Save room for the flour tortillas, made right in the restaurant in view of diners. Lunch and dinner daily. & (North Austin)

SCHOLZ GARTEN
1607 San Jacinto Blvd.
Austin
512/474-1958

www.austin360.com/eats
/scholzgarten
$$

Since 1866 this restaurant and pub, just up the street from the Capitol, has been privy to many "real deals" put together by the state's movers and shakers. University of Texas students, and their visiting parents, too, have enjoyed the menu mix of bratwurst, sauerkraut, and down-home staples like chicken-fried steak. Lunch and dinner Mon–Sat; closed Sun. ♿ (North Austin)

THREADGILL'S
6416 N. Lamar Blvd.
Austin
512/451-5440
www.threadgills.com
$

Threadgill's is an Austin institution, the place where Janis Joplin got her break, and you can get tried-and-true chicken-fried steak and cream gravy on homemade biscuits. It's hard to believe that Threadgill's began life as a gas station back in the thirties. Some local pickers started playing outside, crowds came, and the owners began serving beer. Soon food followed, and good-bye gas pumps. You'll find plenty of neon signs and old beer clocks hangin' on the walls to transport you back in time while you chow down on pork roast, liver, and chicken and dumplings with black-eyed peas and okra. Whatever you order, expect huge portions, great vegetables, and fresh home-cooking. For downtown diners, a new Threadgill's is now open at 301 W. Riverside Dr. Lunch and dinner daily. ♿ (North Austin)

TRUDY'S TEXAS STAR
409 W. 30th St.
Austin

512/477-2935
$$

This UT-area eatery has more atmosphere than its younger siblings in north and south Austin. The green chicken enchiladas, served in all their gooey goodness with rice and beans and flour tortillas, are always popular fare. Breakfast here includes both American and Tex-Mex dishes; especially good are the migas, scrambled eggs cooked up with strips of corn tortillas and bits of tomato. Breakfast, lunch, and dinner daily; open until 2 a.m. Fri–Sat. ♿ (North Austin)

NORTHWEST AUSTIN

ALDO'S NORTHWEST
12233 N. FM 620
Austin
512/331-6400
$$

Although it's located in a strip center, this restaurant is an excellent choice for a quiet, intimate dinner for two. Start with a wine selected from an extensive wine list; follow up with Italian favorites served by an attentive waitstaff. Lunch and dinner Tue–Sun; closed Mon. (Northwest Austin)

CATFISH PARLOUR
11910 Research Blvd.
Austin
512/258-1853
www.austin360.com/eats
/catfishparlour
$$

Wear an adjustable belt to this all-you-can-eat restaurant: The boneless catfish, mouthwatering hush puppies, pinto beans, and coleslaw will have you going back for more. Lunch and dinner Mon–Sat; closed Sun. ♿ (Northwest Austin)

CHINATOWN
3407 Greystone Dr.
Austin
512/343-9307
$$

Located right on the corner of Greystone and Mo-Pac, Chinatown has an elegant air, with white linen tablecloths, attentive waitpersons, and the feel of a restaurant designed to celebrate special events with special dishes. Lunch and dinner daily. & (Northwest Austin)

THE COUNTY LINE ON THE LAKE
5204 FM 2222
Austin
512/346-3664
$$

Always popular, you may have to wait, but the wait will be made easier by the beautiful Hill Country view. Continue to enjoy it by eating outdoors if the weather's nice (which is most of the time in the Hill Country!). Enjoy the view from the hill while digging into the big meaty ribs, lean brisket, and special sausage The County Line is famous for throughout the Southwest. The atmosphere is upscale roadhouse. You can watch Bull Creek as it runs into Lake Austin while drinking iced-down beer and frozen margaritas in the Longneck Bar. For dessert, the Kahlua pecan brownie is a must. Lunch and dinner daily. & (Northwest Austin)

DAN MCKLUSKY'S
10000 Research Blvd.
Austin
512/346-0780
www.austin360.com/eats
/danmckluskys
$$$

Like its downtown cousin, this Arboretum steakhouse serves up corn-fed Omaha steaks in a casually elegant atmosphere. Chicken, seafood, lamb, shrimp, and lobster round out the selections. Lunch weekdays and dinner daily; brunch on Sunday only. & (Northwest Austin)

HULA HUT
3826 Lake Austin Blvd.
Austin
512/476-4852
$$

The blend of Tex-Mex and Hawaiian is intriguing, made especially tasty when you choose to dine out over the lake, where boaters tie up their boats by the giant fish sculpture guarding the pier bar. (There's indoor dining, too, if you prefer.) The restaurant looks like a bit of Hawaii, thatched roof and all, and the food is delicious and served in generous portions. As an introduction to the mixed cuisine, the thin, crispy taco chips are served with a spicy pineapple and tomato salsa. The Chicken/Guacamole Tubular is enough for two. The taco is more like a burrito, drizzled with red chili sauce and sour cream, served with beans and rice. Filled with hot grilled chicken, creamy guacamole, and both Monterey Jack cheese and cream cheese flavored with roasted garlic and cilantro, it's very filling. One of the Hawaiian touches, the Polynesian Pu Pu Platter, also more than enough for two, is a delicious medley of coconut-crusted large shrimp, shrimp flautas, and other seafood delicacies. The menu lists barbecue ribs and chicken tacos, grilled chicken nachos, chicken flautas, and chile con queso along with Hawaiian grilled chicken and grilled fresh-fish tacos stuffed with char-grilled mahi-mahi, red cabbage, cilantro, and jalapeño-lime sauce. A Texas dessert treat is fried ice cream, here served

GREATER AUSTIN

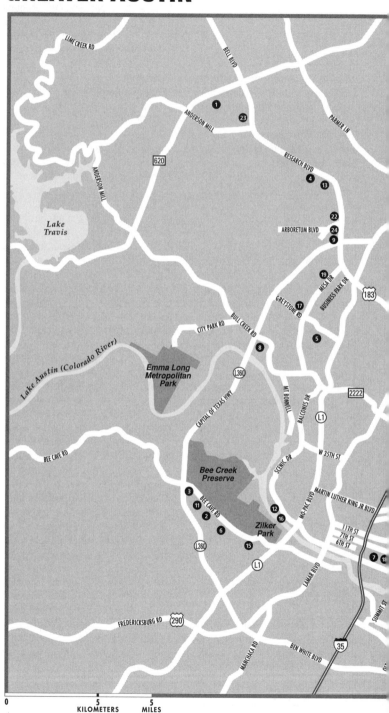

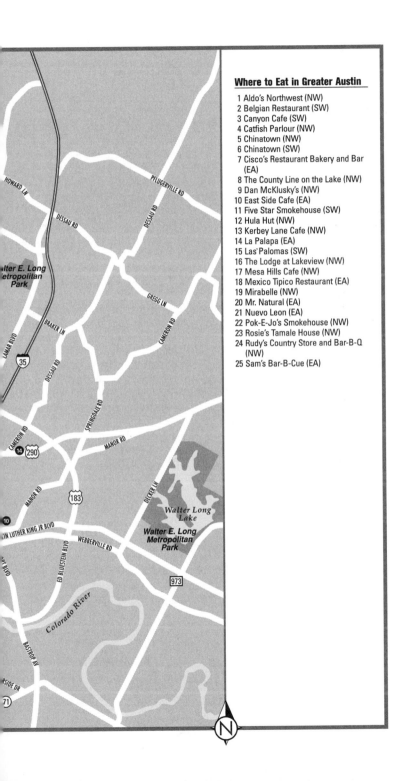

Where to Eat in Greater Austin

1 Aldo's Northwest (NW)
2 Belgian Restaurant (SW)
3 Canyon Cafe (SW)
4 Catfish Parlour (NW)
5 Chinatown (NW)
6 Chinatown (SW)
7 Cisco's Restaurant Bakery and Bar (EA)
8 The County Line on the Lake (NW)
9 Dan McKlusky's (NW)
10 East Side Cafe (EA)
11 Five Star Smokehouse (SW)
12 Hula Hut (NW)
13 Kerbey Lane Cafe (NW)
14 La Palapa (EA)
15 Las Palomas (SW)
16 The Lodge at Lakeview (NW)
17 Mesa Hills Cafe (NW)
18 Mexico Tipico Restaurant (EA)
19 Mirabelle (NW)
20 Mr. Natural (EA)
21 Nuevo Leon (EA)
22 Pok-E-Jo's Smokehouse (NW)
23 Rosie's Tamale House (NW)
24 Rudy's Country Store and Bar-B-Q (NW)
25 Sam's Bar-B-Cue (EA)

with a coconut and cornflake crust, floating in a pool of hot fudge sauce. Lunch and dinner daily. & (Northwest Austin)

KERBEY LANE CAFE
12602 Research Blvd.
Austin
512/258-7757
www.austin360.com/eats
/kerbeylane
$–$$
Just off bustling U.S. 183 you'll find a quiet oasis in this café, which offers the same seriously good meals found at the other two Kerbey Lane locations. Breakfast, lunch, and dinner daily; open 24 hours. & (Northwest Austin)

THE LODGE AT LAKEVIEW
3826-B Lake Austin Blvd.
Austin
512/476-7372
$$$
Perched right on the edge of Lake Austin, this casually elegant eatery offers a much calmer atmosphere than its neighbor, the Hula Hut. The Lodge, much as its name suggests, exudes a mountain lodge atmosphere, a theme carried out in the menu, which includes steaks, seafood, pasta, and burgers. Lunch and dinner are served daily; Sunday brunch is also offered. & (Northwest Austin)

MESA HILLS CAFE
3435 Greystone Dr.
Austin
512/345-7423
$–$$
Dine inside or out, taking in an exalted view of downtown Austin while perched high above Mo-Pac on the café's pleasant covered patio. Luncheon is served 11–5 with a choice of a dozen platefuls accompanied by

rice, beans, and a taco. Lunch and dinner daily. & (Northwest Austin)

MIRABELLE
8127 Mesa Dr.
Austin
512/346-7900
$$
Mirabelle has been called a "clone" of the very popular Castle Hill Cafe in downtown Austin, which can hardly be a bad thing. Although the decor is different, pleasing with golden walls, with dark wood and glass dividers breaking the large room into smaller, more intimate dining places, the menu is pretty much the same, having been transferred almost intact. Which is not surprising, since this, like the Castle Hill Cafe, is the creation of Cathy Dailey, one of the founders. Particularly tasty is the Wild Mushroom Risotto with Basil Ajoli: four croquettes, served with a fresh green salad with a champagne vinaigrette dressing. For dessert, the New Orleans-style Bread Pudding, served with a caramel and bourbon sauce, was a sweet taste treat.

Open for lunch Mon–Fri 11 a.m.–2 p.m.; for dinner Mon–Thu 5:30–9:30 p.m.; for dinner Fri–Sat 5:30–10 p.m. (Northwest Austin)

POK-E-JO'S SMOKEHOUSE
9828 Great Hills Tr.
Austin
512/338-1990
$
Deciding to eat at Pok-E-Jo's is simple; the hard part lies in whether to order the smoky beef ribs the size of nightsticks, the tender pork ribs, the juicy brisket, or the mild or spicy sausage. There's even pork loin, chicken, ham, and sometimes turkey to make your decision that much tougher. Smoked 16 to 20 hours over

green mesquite, every choice is a winner. Lunch and dinner are served daily. & (Northwest Austin)

ROSIE'S TAMALE HOUSE
13776 Research Blvd.
Austin
512/219-7793
$

The plates here are simple Tex-Mex choices: enchiladas, tacos, quesadillas, flautas, and, you guessed it, tamales. This popular eatery is located in a strip center, but its cuisine is straight out of a typical South Texas home kitchen. Year-round Christmas decorations give this eatery a festive flair. Open for lunch and dinner daily. & (Northwest Austin)

RUDY'S COUNTRY STORE AND BAR-B-Q
11570 Research Blvd.
Austin
512/418-9898
www.austin360.com/eats
/rudysbbq
$

Rudy's calls itself "the worst barbecue in Texas," but you sure wouldn't know that from the taste of its barbecue or the size of the crowds that flock to this popular eatery. Rudy's has an extensive menu: pork, baby back, St. Louis, and beef short ribs, plus chicken, prime rib, pork loin, chopped beef, sausage, turkey, and brisket. Start the day with breakfast tacos until 11 a.m. Breakfast, lunch, and dinner daily. & (Northwest Austin)

SOUTHWEST AUSTIN

BELGIAN RESTAURANT
3520 Bee Caves Rd.
Austin
512/328-0580

$$$
While deciding between duck in cherry sauce, dover sole in lemon sauce, or chicken tenders topped with scallops and sage in a white cream sauce, be sure to save room for dessert. The dessert menu includes Belgian chocolate mousse and a Belgian ice-cream sundae with chocolate sauce. Lunch and dinner Mon–Fri; dinner Sat–Sun. Reservations recommended. & (Southwest Austin)

CANYON CAFE
Loop 360 (Capital of Texas Hwy.)
and Bee Caves Rd.
Austin
512/329-0400
$$$

With the atmosphere of a North Woods lodge, this restaurant is housed in a circular building warm with the glow of log pillars, railings, and ceiling. The menu boasts many Southwestern dishes, from quesadillas to tacos with shrimp. Don't expect fast-food service or prices, however; this is nouvelle Southwestern cuisine, with menu surprises like chile-rubbed tuna and tequila chicken pasta. Open for lunch and dinner daily; brunch served on Sunday. (Southwest Austin)

CHINATOWN
3300 Bee Caves Rd.
Austin
512/327-6588
$–$$

Chinatown has moved a few blocks west, into the shopping center at Walsh Tarleton, but all 77 items on the menu are the same as before. Shrimp, beef, chicken, and pork, all in rich sauces and in a myriad of combinations, are prepared by the same chef. Lunch and dinner daily. & (Southwest Austin)

© Permenter and Bigley

*Oasis Cantina del Lago
at Lake Travis, p. 65*

For Tex-Mex lovers, some popular favorites are available as well. Don't miss the live mariachi music on Friday night. Lunch and dinner. க் (Southwest Austin)

SOUTH AUSTIN

ARTZ RIB HOUSE
2330 S. Lamar Blvd.
Austin
512/442-8283
$–$$
Wrap your hands around either pork or beef ribs at this eatery. Can't decide? Select a combination plate and sample the baby backs, country-style pork ribs, or meaty beef ribs. Other barbecued items include brisket, smoked chicken, sausage (Austin's own Smoky Denmarks), and skewered char-grilled shrimp. The plates are piled high with potato salad, crispy coleslaw, and pinto beans. Lunch and dinner daily. க் (South Austin)

FIVE STAR SMOKEHOUSE
3638 Bee Caves Rd.
Austin
512/328-1800
$
This restaurant boasts an extensive menu. Take your pick from brisket, baby back ribs, pork loin, smoked ham, smoked chicken, smoked turkey, and sausage. Many meats are smoked 12 to 15 hours to reach barbecued bliss. Plates are served with an excellent potato salad, beans, and bread. Save room for the home-baked pies—apple, chocolate, chocolate pecan, buttermilk, Toll House, and key lime—or a piece of old-fashioned peach cobbler. Lunch and dinner daily. க் (Southwest Austin)

CHERRY CREEK CATFISH CO.
5712 Manchaca at Stassney
Austin
512/440-8810
$$
Although it specializes in seafood, you'll find just a little of everything on this eclectic menu. Start with anything from shrimp gumbo to fried green tomatoes to jalapeño peppers, then work your way to blackened catfish, chicken-fried steak, frog legs, barbecue ribs, or a po'boy sandwich. If you're on your way home, Cherry Creek also offers carryout family packs featuring catfish, shrimp, or ribs. Lunch and dinner daily. க் (South Austin)

LAS PALOMAS
3201 Bee Caves Rd.
Austin
512/327-9889
$$–$$$
Check out the traditional Mexican fare at this eatery: chicken mole, pork pibil Veracruz-style dishes, and more.

CHUY'S
1728 Barton Springs Rd.

SOUTH AUSTIN

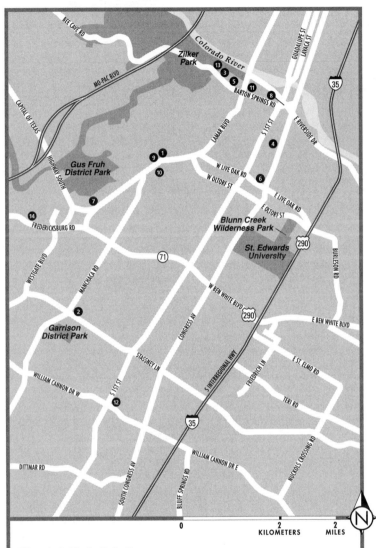

Where to Eat in South Austin

1 Artz Rib House
2 Cherry Creek Catfish Co.
3 Chuy's
4 El Sol Y La Luna
5 Green Mesquite
6 Green Pastures

7 Hunan Lion
8 Jalisco Bar
9 Kerbey Lane Cafe
10 Matt's El Rancho
11 The Paggi House

12 Seoul Sushi Bar and
   Restaurant
13 Shady Grove
14 Tien Jin Chinese
   Restaurant

Austin
512/474-4452
$

Chuy's is Austin at its most funky! With 1,000 wooden fish dangling from the ceiling of the bar and hubcaps covering the ceiling of the dining room, the result is hilarious. Walls are painted Mexican pink and green, and piñatas dangle invitingly, just waiting for someone to smack them open. There's a memorial altar to Elvis at the front door, and the crowd most nights testifies to the great taste of the Tex-Mex fare. The menu may be limited but regulars favor the taco salad, the blue corn tortillas, the barbecued chicken tacos, the chips, and the salsa. Lunch and dinner daily. & (South Austin)

EL SOL Y LA LUNA
1224 S. Congress St.
Austin
512/444-7770
$

Bright and cheery with Mexican decor featuring, of course, El Sol (The Sun) and La Luna (The Moon), El Sol Y La Luna has been named one of the best Hispanic restaurants in the country by *Hispanic Magazine*. Not only do they serve up great food, they also have live Latin American music on weekends, along with that Mexican specialty, pozole (pork and garbanzo beans), so tasty you'll think you're in Acapulco. Try all the enchiladas, especially the enchiladas zacatecaños, creamy with avocado sauce. A very popular specialty on Tuesdays are the four-cheese gorditos, and they're snatched up in a hurry. Breakfast, lunch, and dinner Wed–Sat; breakfast and lunch only Sun–Tue. (South Austin)

GREEN MESQUITE
1400 Barton Springs Rd.

Austin
512/479-0485
$

This rustic and homey Austin tradition serves up music on weekends, with local bands playing. Gosh, there's chicken-fried steak, catfish, jambalaya, and bubba tacos—soft, flour tortillas stuffed with your choice of barbecued beef, turkey, or chicken; topped to the gills with lettuce, tomato, and shredded cheddar cheese; and served with a homemade salsa and a choice of two sides: beans, Cajun rice, big chunky coleslaw, or potato salad. The po'boy sandwiches are as authentic as any you'll get in New Orleans, and of course all the pies are homemade. Lunch and dinner daily. & (South Austin)

GREEN PASTURES
811 W. Live Oak
Austin
512/444-4747
$$$

Shades of the Old South! This white mansion, surrounded by manicured grounds and strutting peacocks, is instant Scarlet O'Hara–Rhett Butler ambience. Retro Southern gentility and the best Sunday brunch in Texas make this an Austin classic. What everybody likes is not only the good taste of the food, but the sheer abundance of the spread. There's always a large assortment of cheeses and fruits, shrimp, salads, maybe a choice between prime rib and grilled blue marlin tampico (tomato, green pepper, and onion sauce), three or four vegetables, and at least four desserts. The peach and plum strudel is special, and the Green Pastures bread pudding is a must. Lunch and dinner daily; Sunday buffet. Reservations recommended. & (South Austin)

Jalisco Bar

HUNAN LION
4006 S. Lamar Blvd.
Austin
512/447-3388
$$–$$$
A statue of a happy Buddha greets you at the entrance to this pretty restaurant with flowered booths, etched glass dividers, and four fish tanks to set a relaxing mood. The Seven Star Platter will do that, too, with Alaskan king crab legs, shrimp, scallops, roast pork, and boneless fried chicken, all stir-fried with mixed vegetables. Other specialties of this four-star Mandarin-style restaurant are sesame chicken and Beijing duck. Lunch, dinner. & (South Austin)

JALISCO BAR
414 Barton Springs Rd.
Austin
512/476-4838
$
Warm up a chilly day with a bowl of tortilla soup or add some heat to any day with spicy enchiladas, tacos, or fajitas. If you order a slammer, it will be brought to you by a howling waiter, slammed on the table with a flourish, drawing the attention of the entire restaurant. Brace yourself. Lunch, dinner daily. (South Austin)

KERBEY LANE CAFE
2700 S. Lamar Blvd.
Austin
512/445-4451
$$
Austin couldn't get along without its supply of wholesome food available any hour of the day or night. Healthy meals featuring fresh, locally grown produce are served round-the-clock daily in this light, bright restaurant. A bucolic mural of hills and a plowed green field on one wall is attractive, and the wait staff wear whatever they're comfortable in. Breakfast, lunch, and dinner daily. & (South Austin)

MATT'S EL RANCHO
2613 S. Lamar Blvd.

Austin
512/462-9333
$–$$

This is Tex-Mex Austin-style, evolved from grandfather Delphino Martinez's first restaurant in 1925. It's a family restaurant, with longtime employees that are like family, too. In addition to dishes like the enchilada plate (with a sauce of chile con carne), you can try seafood and steak. But chile rellenos are also pretty special, with raisins and pecans part of the filling. Everything is handmade—tortillas, tostadas, even the praline candy—and all the meat is premium. Lunch and dinner daily except Tue. & (South Austin)

THE PAGGI HOUSE
200 Lee Barton Dr.
Austin
512/478-1121
$$$

Built in the 1840s, the Paggi House has been many different things over the years. At first it served as Colonel Sterling Goodrich's plantation house and between 1860 and 1875 it served as an inn. In 1884, Michael Paggi, a Texas businessman, purchased the house and expanded it to its present size. Today it is a restaurant that serves fine continental food. Lunch Mon–Fri; dinner Mon–Sat. Reservations recommended. & (South Austin)

SEOUL SUSHI BAR
AND RESTAURANT
6400 S. First St.
Austin
512/326-5807
$$

The decor is spare and Japanese, with shoji screens offering table privacy. The food is a nice mix of Japanese and Korean. The two cuisines go together very well, neither being greasy like some other Asian styles. A soup dinner comes with Korean kimchi (spicy pickled cabbage), and seasoned bean sprouts. A popular dish is *bul gal*, tender barbecued ribs marinated in a special sauce. And of course there's sushi: crab, octopus, flounder, tuna, red snapper, squid, shrimp, smoked salmon, salmon roe—the list goes on and on. Lunch and dinner daily. & (South Austin)

SHADY GROVE
1624 Barton Springs Rd.
Austin
512/474-9991
$–$$

Relaxed dining is the rule here in yet another laid-back Austin-style eatery where you can dine indoors or out under the pecan trees. Shady Grove is set in a real grove in what was once a trailer park; in fact, the trailer at the end of the patio is put to use as rest rooms. Try the special Hippie Sandwich for a real taste treat of grilled zucchini, eggplant, mushrooms, roasted bell peppers, tomato, and arugula on a seven-grain wheat bun dressed with melted mozzarella and pesto mayonnaise. Indoors there's a full bar, rock walls, stone pillars, and a cozy fireplace. Thursday night during the summer there's music under the pecan trees, with local talent like Asleep at the Wheel and the Bad Livers. Lunch and dinner daily. & (South Austin)

TIEN JIN CHINESE RESTAURANT
4601 S. Lamar Blvd., #105
Austin
512/892-6699
$–$$

Cantonese and Szechwan are the styles at this popular Chinese restaurant, with specialties like orange beef, General Tso's chicken, and sesame

El Sol Y La Luna, p. 74

chicken with the subtitle "Return of the Phoenix."

Other menu options include Three Delicacies—fresh shrimp, chicken, and scallops with broccoli, baby corn and snow peas; or the Happy Family—shrimp, chicken, and pork with vegetables. Lunch and dinner daily. &. (South Austin)

EAST AUSTIN

CISCO'S RESTAURANT, BAKERY & BAR
1511 E. Sixth St.
Austin
512/478-2420
$

Rudy "Cisco" Cisneros was the man who made migas and huevos rancheros famous. The restaurant has been serving migas (tortilla chips fried with onion, tomatos, scrambled eggs, melted cheese, sausage, and beans) for years. This Austin favorite—a bakery, bar, and restaurant—is a family business that has operated under

various guises since 1929. Breakfast and lunch daily. &. (East Austin)

EAST SIDE CAFE
2113 Manor Rd.
Austin
512/476-5858
$$

Dine in any of the several rooms in this 1920s home, which sits on a third of an acre where East Side's herbs and vegetables are grown. "Some restaurants talk about fresh food," they say. "We grow it." Chipotle pecan soup, artichoke manicotti, wild mushroom crepes—the menu is eclectic and delicious. Lunch and dinner daily; brunch Sat–Sun. Reservations accepted. &. (East Austin)

LA PALAPA
U.S. Hwy. 290 E. at Cameron Rd.
Austin
512/459-8729
$–$$

With its distinctive thatched palm palapa roof, this restaurant is tough to miss. Tex-Mex favorites such as fajitas and enchiladas top the menu. Lunch and dinner daily. ♿ (East Austin)

MEXICO TIPICO RESTAURANTE
1707 E. Sixth St.
Austin
512/472-3222
$–$$

Known for cabrito (goat), fajitas, and caldos (thick soups), Mexico Tipico has mariachi music on Friday and Saturday. Tamales and corn tortillas are handmade; the vegetarian enchiladas are delicious. Breakfast and lunch Tue–Thu; breakfast, lunch, and dinner Fri–Sun; closed Monday. ♿ (East Austin)

MR. NATURAL
1901 E. Cesar Chavez St.
Austin
512/477-5228
$–$$

Tex-Mex and health food don't generally go hand in hand, but at Mr. Natural you'll find favorite foods with a vegetarian twist. Veggie fajitas, enchiladas, chile rellenos, tamales, and salads are offered; vegan dishes are available. Breakfast, lunch, and dinner; closed Sun. ♿ (East Austin)

NUEVO LEON
1209 E. Seventh St.
Austin
512/479-0097
$–$$

Although the name makes you think that you're about to sample the cuisine of the northern Mexican state of Nuevo León, it applies to the cartoon character on the cover of the bright pink menu, a lion juggling a tray of glasses. The cuisine is Tex-Mex, and the Wednesday special (there's a special daily), the Nuevo Leon Burrito, is a winner—a giant flour tortilla stuffed with beef and smothered in Nuevo Leon's chile con carne. It's more than a meal. Lunch and dinner Mon–Fri; breakfast, lunch, and dinner Sat–Sun. ♿ (East Austin)

SAM'S BAR-B-CUE
2000 E. 12th St.
Austin
512/478-0378
$

Go to Sam's with a big appetite. Plates include ribs, brisket, chicken, spicy sausage, and even mutton. Side dishes include fiery beans spiced with plenty of black pepper, and potato salad. You can take out or dine in the small dining room decorated with newspaper clippings featuring the late Stevie Ray Vaughan. The Austin blues musician was a devoted Sam's customer, even making some long-distance call-in orders for Sam's specialties when he was on the road. Lunch and dinner daily. No credit cards. ♿ (East Austin)

© Permenter and Bigley

5

SIGHTS AND ATTRACTIONS

There's no denying that touring Austin's many diverse attractions is a capital idea. Regardless of your interest, you'll find plenty of sights not only indoors, but also out, given Austin's average of 300 sunny days a year. From historic sites to nature sites, from ice-skating on a hot summer day to strutting with peacocks at a historic park, from canoeing on Town Lake to shopping in the West End, there are more than 101 things to see and do. Along the way be sure to notice Austin's art in public places (see page 95 for more information). For an overall view of Austin and its offerings, try a city tour (see page 100). Note: Maps in this chapter show locations of sights and attractions only.

DOWNTOWN AUSTIN

AUSTIN HISTORY CENTER
810 Guadalupe St.
Austin
512/499-7480
This beautifully restored 1930s art deco building houses print and photo materials relating to Austin's history. Exhibits of archival photographs in the entrance corridor change regularly. Hours: Mon–Thu 9–9, Fri–Sat 9–6, Sun 12–6. Free. (Downtown Austin)

AUSTIN PUBLIC LIBRARY
800 Guadalupe St.

Austin
512/499-7301
The main branch of the Austin library system offers not only books but business information, children's programs and services, and consumer services. Notice the Art in Public Places piece, *Eagle II*, of Cor-Ten steel by David L. Deming (1976) out in front. Hours: Mon–Thu 9–9, Fri–Sat 9–6, Sun 12–6. Free. (Downtown Austin)

AUSTIN'S BAT COLONY
Congress Avenue Bridge
at Town Lake

DOWNTOWN AUSTIN

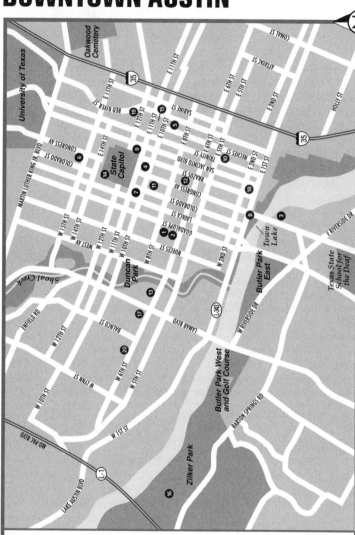

Sights in Downtown Austin

1 Austin History Center
2 Austin Public Library
3 Austin's Bat Colony
4 Capitol Complex Visitors Center
5 German Free School
6 Gethsemane Lutheran Church
7 Governor's Mansion
8 Lone Star Riverboat
9 Lorenzo de Zavala State Archives
  and Library
10 O. Henry Home and Museum
11 Old Bakery and Emporium
12 Paramount Theatre
13 Sixth Street
14 State Capitol
15 Symphony Square
16 Town Lake Greenbelt
17 Treaty Oak
18 Visitor Information Center
19 Waller Creek Walkway
20 West End

Austin
512/478-0098
Austin has received international attention for its colony of up to 1.5 million Mexican free-tailed bats that reside under the Congress Avenue Bridge during the summer months. Every night at sundown, the bats fly out to feast on Hill Country mosquitoes. The best viewing is from the hike and bike trail, the bridge, or a free bat-viewing area in the parking lot of the *Austin American-Statesman* (305 S. Congress Ave.). The best viewing months are July and August. For more on the bats, check out the information kiosks at the Four Seasons Hotel (98 San Jacinto Blvd.) and the *Austin American-Statesman* parking lot. (Downtown Austin)

CAPITOL COMPLEX VISITORS CENTER
E. 11th and Brazos Sts.
Austin
512/305-8400
Formerly this 1857 building on the Capitol grounds served as the General Land Office; it holds the title as the oldest government office building in the state. Once the workplace of short story writer O. Henry, this building now operates as a visitors center and Texas History Museum, with displays and exhibits about the center of Texas government. Hours: Tue–Fri 9–5, Sat 10–5. Free. (Downtown Austin)

GERMAN FREE SCHOOL
507 E. 10th St.
Austin
512/482-0927
Just off the banks of Waller Creek, this school was constructed by German immigrants in 1857. The building, constructed using a rammed-earth technique, includes two large rooms, a gym, and playgrounds. Today the school is used by the German-Texan Heritage Society and the German Free School Guild and hosts educational programs. Genealogists can use the family history research materials as well. Hours: Thu 1–4. Free. (Downtown Austin)

GETHSEMANE LUTHERAN CHURCH
1510 Congress Ave.
Austin
512/463-6092
This Gothic Revival–style church was built in 1882 and stands as a reminder of Austin's first Swedish settlers. Today the church serves as a library of the Texas Historical Commission and is open to the public (although you must enter through the back door). Hours: Mon–Fri 8–5. Free. (Downtown Austin)

GOVERNOR'S MANSION
1010 Colorado St.
Austin
512/463-5516
For over 130 years, Texas governors

T I P

For a romantic look at downtown Austin, hop aboard a horse-drawn carriage. Call the Austin Carriage Service, 512/243-0044, or Die Gelbe Rose, 512/477-8824.

have enjoyed the opulence of this grand home. Tours (scheduled every 20 minutes Mon–Fri from 10 a.m. to noon) take visitors past the main staircase, through the formal parlor, and finally into the dining room. Call to check the status of tours; the home is sometimes closed because of incoming dignitaries. At press time, the mansion was under renovation. Free. (Downtown Austin)

LONE STAR RIVERBOAT
Congress Ave. and S. First St.
Austin
512/327-1388
Enjoy a 90-minute excursion on Town Lake aboard this double paddle-wheeler for an unbeatable view of the lake and the city skyline. The cruises depart from the dock west of the Hyatt Regency on Town Lake. The riverboat also offers bat-watching cruises to view Town Lake's colony of Mexican free-tailed bats. Public cruises are available Mar–Oct. Hours vary depending on season. $9 adults, $7 seniors, $6 children under 12. (Downtown Austin)

LORENZO DE ZAVALA STATE ARCHIVES AND LIBRARY
1201 Brazos St.
Austin
512/463-5455
Located just east of the Capitol, this building houses the archives of state government, including important genealogical records. Stop by the public areas on the first floor for a look at historic documents or to trace your family's roots in the Lone Star State. Hours: Library, Mon–Fri 8–5 p.m.; Genealogy, Tue–Sat 8–5. Free. (Downtown Austin)

O. HENRY HOME AND MUSEUM
409 E. Fifth St.

TRIVIA

In 1885 Austin installed the first of 27 Moonlight Towers, tall streetlights that bathed the city in "artificial moonlight." Today, 17 of the original towers still stand, one of them at Ninth and Guadalupe downtown. At 165 feet, they are the city's tallest streetlights.

Austin
512/472-1903
This modest house, built in 1891, was the home of William Sidney Porter, better known as short story writer O. Henry, from 1893 to 1895. Today the cottage, recently renovated, contains the writer's personal belongings. Hours: Wed–Sun 12–5. Free; donations appreciated. (Downtown Austin)

OLD BAKERY AND EMPORIUM
1006 Congress Ave.
Austin
512/477-5961
You'll find everything from bread to knitted breadwarmers in this historic structure, which first opened in 1876. Notice the limestone eagle by John Didelot, on top of the building, installed in 1876. Downstairs, the bakery offers fresh-out-of-the-oven treats; upstairs, senior citizens sell their handcrafted wares. Hours: Mon–Fri 9–4, Sat hours vary. Free. (Downtown Austin)

PARAMOUNT THEATRE
713 Congress Ave.

Austin
512/472-5411

This neoclassical movie palace, built in 1915, has been expertly restored and is used primarily for the performing arts (with the exception of a classic movie now and then). The box office is open Mon–Fri 12–5:30; weekends if a performance is scheduled. (Downtown Austin)

SIXTH STREET
Sixth St. from I-35 to Congress Ave.
Austin

Known for both its historic architecture and its nationally recognized nightlife, this stretch of Sixth Street constitutes Austin's nightlife district. Daytime visitors come to shop its eclectic boutiques, view historic buildings on self-guided tours, and dine in its popular restaurants; night owls enjoy the bars with live music, where the late-night revelry lasts until 2 a.m. (Downtown Austin)

STATE CAPITOL
11th St. and Congress Ave.
Austin
512/463-0063

You might think that Texas' motto is "The bigger, the better," especially after a visit to the state capitol. Taller than its national counterpart, the pink granite building houses the governor's office, the Texas legislature, and several other executive state agencies. Hours: Mon–Fri 8:30–4:30, Sat 9:30–4:30, Sun 12:30–4:30. Free. (Downtown Austin)

SYMPHONY SQUARE
Red River St. at 11th St.
Austin

The state gave the area to the city in 1982. Waller Creek turns subterranean under the square where there are four restored more-than-a-century-old buildings. The Jeremiah Hamilton home is the only original one—the other three were moved from other locations. Jeremiah Hamilton had been the slave of A.J. Hamilton, a carpenter and a governor during Reconstruction. Hamilton built this limestone, two-story house, making it triangular to wedge it into the odd-shaped lot bordered by Waller Creek, Red River, and 11th Street. The other three houses date from 1870 (old Wilson Mercantile), 1880 (Doyle House), and 1887 (Hardeman House). (Downtown Austin)

TOWN LAKE GREENBELT
Loop 1, Mo-Pac Bridge to
South First St.
Austin

A popular trail lines the scenic shores on the north and south sides of Town Lake. Austinites come to walk, jog, and enjoy the beauty of the city. The best view of the downtown skyline can be seen from the south side of Town Lake. (Downtown Austin)

TREATY OAK
503 Baylor St.
Austin

This 500- to 600-year-old oak captured the nation's attention in 1989, when it was deliberately poisoned

TRIVIA

The Texas State Capitol is seven feet taller than the United States Capitol.

and well-wishers from Austin and around the nation brought offerings and prayers. Today one-third of the original tree, once called the finest example of a tree in North America, is gone, but Austinites are grateful for how much has been saved from the malicious herbicide poisoning. Free. (Downtown Austin)

VISITOR INFORMATION CENTER
201 E. Second St.
Austin
512/478-0098 or 800/926-2282
Stop here for brochures and information on attractions, trolley and bus routes, dining, and entertainment. Call for a menu of information choices. Hours: Mon–Fri 8:30–5, Sat 9–5, Sun 12–5. (Downtown Austin)

WALLER CREEK WALKWAY
15th St. to Cesar Chavez St.
Austin
This 1.8-mile trail of gravel and concrete follows Waller Creek from 15th Street on the north to Cesar Chavez Street on the south. The trail passes along Symphony Square while the creek passes under it. There are ongoing works of art to be seen along the walkway at 500 East Cesar Chavez Street: untitled relief carvings in limestone by David Santos, Ramon Maldonado, Alejandro Bernal, and Tecolete. (Downtown Austin)

WEST END
Sixth St. between Lamar Blvd. and West Lynn St.
Austin
This enclave of eclectic shops and restaurants is a favorite stop with downtown workers for a quiet lunch or some unique shops. The district is also home to the headquarters of the Austin Lyric Opera, the Austin Independent School District, the Austin Writer's League, the Austin Children's Museum, and Women and their Work Gallery. (Downtown Austin)

NORTH AUSTIN

CENTER FOR AMERICAN HISTORY AT THE UNIVERSITY OF TEXAS
Sid Richardson Hall
23rd and Red River Sts.
Austin
512/495-4515
Located next to the LBJ Library on the University of Texas campus, this extensive library houses over 120,000 volumes dealing with the history of the Lone Star State. The stacks are closed, but the materials are available to researchers. Includes the Barker Collection. Hours: Mon–Sat 9–5. Free. (North Austin)

THE DRAG
Guadalupe St. from 21st to 25th Sts.

Austin's Sixth Street entertainment district, p. 83

© Eleanor S. Morris

NORTH AUSTIN

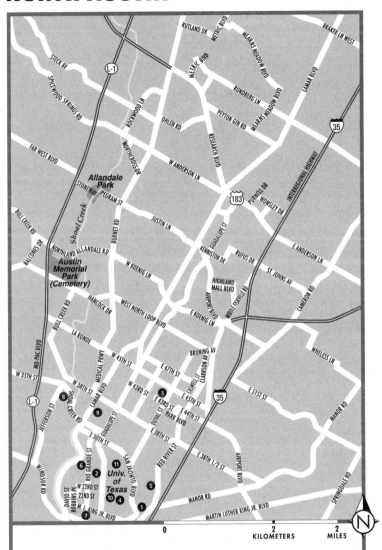

Sight in North Austin

1 Center For American
History
2 The Drag
3 Elisabet Ney Museum
4 Littlefield Fountain

5 Lyndon B. Johnson
Presidential Library and
Museum
6 Neill-Cochran Museum
House

7 Santa Rita No. 1
8 Senior Activity Center
9 Shoal Creek Greenbelt
10 University of Texas
11 University of Texas Tower

TRIVIA

The General Land Office was the scene of a comic-opera war back when President Sam Houston and Vice President Mirabeau Lamar were fighting over the site of the state capital. Lamar wanted Austin to be the capital, and the 1839 Capital Commission so named it. Houston wanted it either in his namesake, Houston, or in Washington-on-the-Brazos. When the Mexicans invaded Texas in 1842, President Houston sent a small company to seize the republic's archives, housed in the General Land Office. But he was thwarted by the patriotic efforts of one Angelina Eberly, owner of a nearby boarding house. She sounded a warning by setting off a cannon that was usually employed to warn the populace of Indian raids. Houston's men were routed and the archives remained safely stashed away in the Eberly boarding house. This little standoff has gone down in local history as the "Archives War."

Austin

This funky strip across the street from the University of Texas campus is always rowdy and a good place to people-watch. You'll find the university bookstore, a Barnes and Noble, unique shops, trendy coffeehouses, food carts, occasional panhandlers, and more. Hours: Vary by store; peak days Mon–Fri. (North Austin)

ELISABET NEY MUSEUM
304 E. 44th St.
Austin
512/458-2255
Sculptor Elisabet Ney was one of Texas' most colorful characters. Her restored home and studio exhibits the work and some of the personal belongings of the first prominent sculptor in Texas. The first floor contains two large rooms filled with her sculptures of famous Texans, a small entranceway, and a parlor. Ney's bedroom, which was seldom used (she usually slept outside in a hammock), is on the second floor. A third-floor tower room,

reached by a spiral staircase, was the study of Dr. Montgomery, Ney's husband, who made his home near Houston. With its tower and stone columns, you may think this studio resembles a tiny European castle, but throughout the building are many Texas touches: bronze stars decorating the balcony balustrade, cedar rails on the banister, and walls of native limestone. Hours: Wed–Sat 10–5, Sun 12–5. Free. (North Austin)

LITTLEFIELD FOUNTAIN
University of Texas campus
South Mall
21st St. between Guadalupe St.
and Speedway
Austin
This bronze by Pompeo Coppini was commissioned by Major George Washington Littlefield in honor of those of the university who gave their lives in World War I. The three-tiered fountain represents the Navy on one side, the Army on the other; and in the center a ship is led by three sea-

Hill Country Flyer

Just outside the northwest boundaries of the city in the community of Cedar Park, the Hill Country Flyer offers visitors a look at the Hill Country aboard restored passenger cars that recall the early days of Austin transportation. The Hill Country Flyer transports visitors on a round-trip excursion through the oak- and cedar-dotted hills to the town of Burnet. The 143-ton engine that powers the tourist train once powered both passenger and freight trains, chugging through Texas and Louisiana. In 1956 the mighty engine was retired and donated to the City of Austin as a park display for three decades.

Today five coach cars plus three air-conditioned/heated lounge cars give passengers a chance to travel in style. Once the train is loaded, a loud blow on the steam whistle signals the start of the journey as the train departs Cedar Park. The locomotive heads north along U.S. 183, veering west as it crosses the South San Gabriel. Listen for the clatter of the wheels as the train crosses the river on an old-fashioned wooden trestle.

From the river valley, the train climbs 500 feet as it journeys westward into the Hill Country. It was along this route that granite was hauled from Marble Falls to Austin for the construction of the Capitol. The pink stone was mined from Granite Mountain and loaded on this line. Some of this stone, stacked to capacity on the cars, never made it to the capital city: Chunks of pink granite still lie along the tracks where they fell from the train over a century ago.

Arrival in the town of Burnet is a weekly event enjoyed by the townspeople. Many come out to meet the train and the visitors who enjoy a three-hour stop in their town. Stroll to downtown Burnet, where members of the local gunfighters association perform a Wild West gunfight in Town Square for guests. For information, call 512/477-8468.

Your look at the LBJ Library begins with a 20-minute presentation on the President's early years in the Hill Country, political life in the House and Senate, and finally the White House years.

The first two floors offer films on Johnson's life and career, as well as exhibits featuring jeweled gifts from foreign dignitaries and simpler handmade tokens from appreciative Americans. Visitors also can take in special displays of political, civil rights, and educational memorabilia. The second floor also has a special area for changing exhibits, and the First Lady Theater, where you can take a look at the many contributions made by Lady Bird Johnson.

Don't miss the short elevator ride up to the eighth floor with a reproduction of LBJ's White House Oval Office furnished as it was during his term. Here, too, color transparencies give you a peek into some of the public and private rooms of the White House.

horses, two ridden by Tritons. (North Austin)

LYNDON B. JOHNSON PRESIDENTIAL LIBRARY AND MUSEUM
2313 Red River St.
Austin
www.lbjlib.utexas.edu
512/916-5136

No visit to Austin would be complete without a stop at the LBJ Library and Museum. Located on the campus of the University of Texas, this impressive facility serves as a reminder of the Hill Country's most famous resident. The eight-story library, constructed of travertine marble, is the repository for all 35 million documents produced during the LBJ administration. The files, housed in red, acid-free boxes stamped with the gold presidential seal, are open only to scholars and researchers. But a wealth of other exhibits and displays are open to the public on the three museum floors of the library: floors one, two, and eight. They contain over 35,000 historical objects ranging from a ship's passport signed by Thomas Jefferson to a moon rock. Other objects pertain to the Johnson family, foreign affairs, and gifts from other countries. Hours: Daily 9–5. Free. (North Austin)

NEILL-COCHRAN MUSEUM HOUSE
2310 San Gabriel
Austin
512/478-2335

Built around 1853, this Greek Revival home was designed by Abner Cook, the builder of the Governor's Mansion. Today the Colonial Dames of America operate the grand home and conduct tours. Hours: Wed–Sun 2–5. $2. (North Austin)

SANTA RITA NO. 1
Corner of Martin Luther King Blvd. and Trinity St.
Austin

This oil rig, named for Santa Rita, the saint of the impossible, is in a way the patron saint of the University of Texas, or at least of the university's exchequer. The rig was in the business of pumping oil for 19 years, beginning in 1923 when an oil well in West Texas finally blew in, justifying the faith of a group of investors who gave the claim the name. Oil royalties have been flowing into the Permanent University Fund ever since, and the derrick has been standing on the corner as a memorial, set in motion only for state occasions. (North Austin)

University of Texas Tower

SENIOR ACTIVITY CENTER
2874 Shoal Creek
Austin
512/474-5921

A variety of programs and services are available here for persons 50 or older. Besides workshops, table games, physical fitness classes, tours, and special events, such services as health screening and tax assistance are offered. (North Austin)

SHOAL CREEK GREENBELT
North side of Town Lake between Guadalupe St. and Lamar Blvd.
Austin

This three-mile granite, crushed limestone, and concrete trail winds along Shoal Creek north to 38th Street, passing through Duncan Park, Pease Park, and Bailey Park, winding up at Seider's Spring Park. (North Austin)

UNIVERSITY OF TEXAS
I-35 and Martin Luther King Blvd.
Austin
512/471-3434

Start your visit to the sprawling 357-acre UT campus at the visitor information center located in the Arno Nowotny Building, a historic structure built in 1859. The building was formerly an asylum for the blind. Prior to that, the building was once occupied by General George Custer. Tours of the campus are offered Jun–Nov Mon–Fri 11 and 2, Sat 2 only; Dec–May Mon–Sat 2 only. (North Austin)

UNIVERSITY OF TEXAS TOWER
Between 21st and 24th Sts.
Austin
512/475-7348

This tower drew national attention on August 1, 1966, when Charles Whitman opened fire from its balcony, killing over a dozen pedestrians blocks away and wounding 31. Today the tower houses administration offices; at press time the balcony was under renovation and would, for the first time in nearly three decades, soon open to the public for guided tours. (North Austin)

NORTHWEST AUSTIN

CAMP MABRY NATIONAL GUARD
West 35th St. and Loop 1 (Mo-Pac)
Austin
512/465-5059
Home of both the Army and Air National Guard, this historic post dates back to 1892 as a summer base for the Texas Volunteer Guard. Today the base includes the Texas Military Forces Museum, an outdoor collection of military artifacts, and a mile-long jogging trail that's popular with locals. Two pieces of sculpture grace the grounds among the artillery: *Audie L. Murphy*, a bronze by Bill Leftwich in Building No. 82; the metal *Salute* by Simon G. Michael in Building No. 1. Hours: Wed–Sun 2–6, Thu 10–4. Free; donations accepted. (Northwest Austin)

MAYFIELD PARK
3505 W. 35th St.
Austin
512/327-5437
Take a walk with the peacocks that wander at will in this park on 22 acres of Barrow Creek Cove on Lake Austin. (Northwest Austin)

MOUNT BONNELL
3800 Mount Bonnell Rd.
Austin
If you're looking for a scenic overlook of the Hill Country and Lake Austin, here it is. Wear walking shoes for the many steps up to the lookout, where you'll find a view that's well worth the climb. The overlook is located one mile past the west end of West 35th Street. Hours: Daily 5–10. Free. (Northwest Austin)

SOUTHWEST AUSTIN

LADY BIRD JOHNSON WILDFLOWER RESEARCH CENTER
4801 La Crosse Ave.
Austin
512/292-4100
Established by Lady Bird Johnson, this center was founded to research, promote, and preserve native plants. A popular springtime stop for Austinites, the center has fields that

O. Henry Home and Museum, p. 82

© J. Griffis Smith/Austin CVB

bloom with color during peak months. Volunteers and docents are on hand to tell you how to utilize wildflowers in your own landscaping. Hours: Grounds Tue–Sun 9–5:30; Visitors Gallery Tue–Sat 9–4, Sun 1–4; Wild Ideas: The Store Sat 9–5:30, Sun 1–4; Wildflower Cafe Tue–Sat 9–4, Sun 11–4. $3.50 adults, $2 students and seniors, $1 children 18 months to 5 years. (Southwest Austin)

SCENIC OVERLOOK
Capital of Texas Hwy.
Austin
Just north of Wild Basin Preserve at 805 N. Loop 360. Park your car and look at the Austin skyline far to the east over the hills. (Southwest Austin)

SCENIC VIEW
Pennybacker Bridge
Capital of Texas Hwy.
Austin
Enjoy the view over Lake Austin from this breathtaking suspension bridge. (Southwest Austin)

TOM MILLER DAM
Red Bud Trail at Lake Austin
Austin
800/776-5272
Tom Miller Dam is just south of the Walsh Boat Landing, with four acres for day-use only, providing picnicking, boat ramps, and access to Lake Austin. It's illegal to climb on the dam, but you can fish in the lake below it. Fishermen park along Red Bud Trail and walk down to the shore to cast their lines, hoping to catch catfish and bass. (Southwest Austin)

WILD BASIN WILDERNESS PRESERVE
805 N. Loop 360
Capital of Texas Hwy.
Austin

512/327-7622
For a close look at the terrain, flora, and fauna of the Hill Country, step out of the city at this wilderness preserve located just minutes from downtown. The 220-acre sanctuary includes 2.5 miles of trails that wind through the brush; an easy-access trail is also available. Hours: Daily dawn to dusk; tours Sat and Sun. $1 adults, 50 cents ages 5–12. (Southwest Austin)

SOUTH AUSTIN

BARTON CREEK GREENBELT
Scottish Woods Trail
Capital of Texas Hwy.
Austin
512/327-5478
From Scottish Woods Trail, off Loop 360 a mile north of Mo-Pac, walk down to this 7.5-mile hiking trail. The natural surface is rocky in spots. Be sure to bring water as there are no drinking fountains on the trail. Call for trail conditions in bad weather. (South Austin)

BARTON SPRINGS POOL
2201-½ Barton Springs Rd.
Austin
512/867-3080
Even if you don't want to take a dip, stop by for a look at these pristine springs. Year-round, a flow of 68-degree water from the Edwards Aquifer fills this 1,000-foot-long pool, and no matter what the month you'll find some brave souls swimming laps in its chilly depths. Truly a symbol of Austin, this swimming pool is dear to the hearts of Austinites. The pool is usually open from 5 a.m. to 10 p.m., but call for hours since it sometimes closes for cleaning. $2.50 adults, 25 cents children. (South Austin)

GREATER AUSTIN

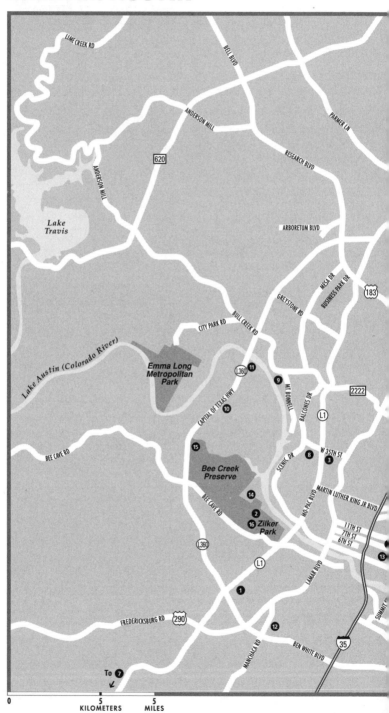

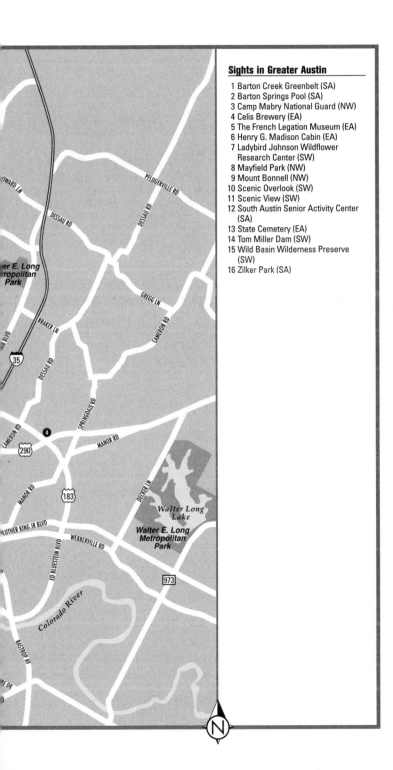

Sights in Greater Austin

1 Barton Creek Greenbelt (SA)
2 Barton Springs Pool (SA)
3 Camp Mabry National Guard (NW)
4 Celis Brewery (EA)
5 The French Legation Museum (EA)
6 Henry G. Madison Cabin (EA)
7 Ladybird Johnson Wildflower
Research Center (SW)
8 Mayfield Park (NW)
9 Mount Bonnell (NW)
10 Scenic Overlook (SW)
11 Scenic View (SW)
12 South Austin Senior Activity Center
(SA)
13 State Cemetery (EA)
14 Tom Miller Dam (SW)
15 Wild Basin Wilderness Preserve
(SW)
16 Zilker Park (SA)

SOUTH AUSTIN SENIOR ACTIVITY CENTER
3911 Manchaca Rd.
Austin
512/448-0787

A variety of programs and services are available here for persons 50 years of age or older. Besides recreational activities like workshops, table games, physical fitness classes, tours, and special events, such services as health screening and tax assistance are also offered. Take a look at the tile mosaic and broken china artwork by Jill Bedgood and Steve Wiman in the lobby and the multipurpose room here. Titled *Community Quilt,* the work is part of the city's Art in Public Places program. (South Austin)

ZILKER PARK
2100 Barton Springs Rd.
Austin
512/478-0098

This 400-acre downtown park is where Austinites come to play—whether that means enjoying a game of rugby, flying a kite, playing with the dog, savoring gardens, or having a picnic. You can also hike, bike, jog, and fish. It's been a city park since 1917, when the initial acreage was donated by Colonel A.J. Zilker. Throughout the park you'll find picnic tables, playgrounds, ball fields, and group shelters; there is a miniature train, and along Town Lake you can rent rowboats and canoes. (South Austin)

EAST AUSTIN

CELIS BREWERY
2431 Forbes Dr.
Austin
512/835-0884

Take a tour of a brewery with a huge, shiny, bright copper fermenting tank

Lyndon B. Johnson Presidential Library and Museum at the University of Texas, p. 88

© Permenter and Bigley

sitting in the window. Tours are offered Tue–Sat at 2 and 4, Fri at 5:30. Free. (East Austin)

THE FRENCH LEGATION MUSEUM
802 San Marcos St.
Austin
512/472-8180

This Greek Revival–style residence is the only foreign legation in the country ever built outside of Washington, D.C. The home has a breezeway, with doors at either end to cool the house on hot Texas days. Downstairs there are four rooms, whose most notable characteristics are their bright and varied colors. Paint experts were consulted when the house was renovated, and paint chips were analyzed to arrive at the colors you see today. Apparently *charge d'affaires* Alphonse Dubois de Saligny enjoyed variety— you'll see mustard green walls, pink banisters, and pink baseboards! Behind the house stands a separate kitchen, the only authentic freestanding French Creole kitchen in the United States. The kitchen is filled with French kitchen utensils and furniture dated before 1845, including a hand-carved rosewood cabinet built to cool bread when it was removed from the oven, hung from the walls out of the reach of rodents. A French prayer chair sits meditatively in one corner, near a wedding cake mold, a lacemaker's lamp, and a French butter churn. Tours are conducted Tue–Sat 1–5, and there's a bang-up Bastille Day celebration every July 14. Hours: Tue–Sun 1–5. $3 adults, $1 children 11–18, 50 cents children under 10. (East Austin)

HENRY G. MADISON CABIN
2300 Rosewood
Austin
512/472-6838
The African American heritage of Austin is the focus of this 1863 cabin. It's amazing to learn that 10 people— two parents and eight children— once lived in this one-room home. Inside there are historic artifacts. Hours: Daily 8–6; call for free tour. (East Austin)

STATE CEMETERY
E. Seventh St. at Comal St.
Austin
512/478-8930
This last resting place of many well-known Texans is known as the "Arlington Cemetery of Texas." Graves include those of Stephen F. Austin, father of Texas, as well as eight former governors. (East Austin)

PUBLIC ART

In 1985 the Art in Public Places (AIPP) ordinance was established to preserve and encourage the unique artistic qualities that make Austin special. The ordinance sets aside 1 percent of the total construction cost for all new or remodeled public buildings, parks, parking facilities, and decorative or commemorative structures for the commission, purchase, and installation of art.

A second way in which Austin celebrates and promotes the arts is in the awarding of Cultural Contracts. These contracts allow local nonprofit, tax-exempt cultural arts organizations to apply for funding from the city. The categories that qualify for funding include dance, theater, literature, visual and mixed arts, and music. Thus, for more than a decade, Art in Public Places has made it possible for talented artists known both locally and nationally to enhance public spaces throughout the city. Works of art range from murals and outdoor sculptures to functional works integrated into architecture.

Recommendations are made by an Art in Public Places panel, composed of seven respected local design and visual arts professionals. The panel

TRIVIA

Wondering why a foreign legation (an official residence and office of a foreign diplomat) was built in Austin? Don't forget: Texas was once a separate country, complete with its own foreign ambassadors!

Camp Mabry National Guard, p. 90

© Permenter and Bigley

works closely with project architects and city department and community representatives to secure works of high quality that represent a broad range of media, styles, and cultural sensibilities. Artists have incorporated traditions and objects to create cultural landmarks for all of Austin.

DOWNTOWN AUSTIN

On the south edge of the Congress Avenue Bridge, there's a tribute to Austin's bats: an original artwork by Austin's Dale Whistler, a sculpture of a bat in flight. Titled Nightwing, the piece is designed to move with the wind.

On the north shores of Town Lake, look for the futuristic Lone Star Gazebo, made of steel by Rodolfo Ybarra (1995). It's on Cesar Chavez Street just west of Congress at Colorado Street, adjacent to Buford Tower, a memorial to Captain James Buford.

Also on Cesar Chavez Street, west of Lamar Boulevard, is the iron and

cast concrete piece, Opossum Temple and Voodoo Pew (1993), by Lars Stanley, Robert Phillips, and T. Paul Hernandez. Another work, at 800 Cesar Chavez Street, is the Seaholm Power Plant metal signage, which was dedicated in 1951.

Heading north and west of Congress Avenue along Fourth Street, you'll find Untitled (1978), a Cor-Ten steel work by Jerry Hartung at 208 W. Fourth; Bus Stop (1986), two long-legged two-dimensional aluminum figures by William King, at Fourth and Colorado Streets; and Prelude by Itzik Ben Shalom, a bronze in Republic Square Park at Fourth and Guadalupe. On the north side of the park is Taylor Fountain, dedicated in 1988. The designer of the limestone work was James A. Turner.

Moving to Austin's famous Sixth Street scene, cast your eyes up to the architecture atop the Driskill Hotel (604 Brazos Street on the corner of Sixth Street). There you'll see the limestone likenesses of both Colonel Jesse L. Driskill and J.W. Driskill, along with longhorn steer heads and gargoyles. All were completed (with the building) in 1886.

Along 10th Street there are several works of art. Over the Top, a bronze by Waldine Tauch (dedicated 1971) is at the American Legion Department of Texas, 709 E. 10th Street. The Source by John Christiansen, a 1994 bronze, graces Waller Creek Center, 625 E. 10th, while at the State Treasury Building, 200 E. 10th, you'll find Charles Umlauf's bronze, The American Eagle. The noted Austin sculptor also sculpted Abstraction, Form Vii, to be seen at the Teacher Retirement System of Texas' building at 10000 Red River Street.

The memorial to World War II dead on West 11th and Colorado Streets depicts a lone soldier atop a rock, with a tree on his right and flowers on his left, and a panel inscribed with names behind him.

Austin's famous sculptor Elisabet Ney did the bronze of Dr. David Thomas Inglehart in 1903. It stands at 11th and Red River Streets. Big Rock, a 1990 limestone by David Santos, can be seen in Waterloo Park at 12th and Red River Streets. On 12th Street between Lavaca and Colorado there is the Memorial to the Builders of the Great State of Texas, a bronze by Hugo Villa (1938). Charles Umlauf has a work on 12th Street, too. His 1970 bronze Symbol of Education graces the Texas State Teacher's Association Building at 316 W. 12th.

CAPITOL GROUNDS

Nine memorable works of art are on the Capitol grounds, beginning with the Goddess of Liberty. Although she is an aluminum replica of the original, she stands just as tall atop the Capitol dome. The original statue (now in the Texas Memorial Museum) was dedicated in 1886, the replica in 1986. The Hiker, a bronze by Theo Alice Ruggles Kitson (1951), and The Cowboy (1921), an action bronze of a cowboy on a bronco leaping over a tall cactus, by Constance Whitney Warren, are testimonies to the Texas lifestyle; the remaining five are testimonies to Texas heroes. Heroes of the Alamo, a bronze by Crohl Smith, was erected in 1901. The Confederate Monument, a bronze by Pompeo Coppini, was dedicated in 1903. Terry's Texas Rangers, another bronze by Pompeo Coppini, was dedicated in 1907, while even earlier, a Volunteer Fireman's Monument was dedicated in 1896. It was replaced by a bronze by J. Segesman, of a fireman holding a small child in his arms, and was rededicated in 1905. Monument to Memory of Hood's Brigade, also a bronze work by Pompeo Coppini, was dedicated in 1910.

NORTH AUSTIN

There are 25 pieces of sculpture on the campus of the University of Texas. Both Littlefield Fountain and Alexander Phimister Proctor's Mustangs are among the best known, but all are interesting. Charles Umlauf is responsible for several, such as The Torchbearers, a bronze in front of the Undergraduate Library on West Mall at Guadalupe and 23rd Streets; Muse, a bronze on the fourth floor terrace opening off the President's Office in the main building, 2400 Inner Campus Drive; The Family, a 1962 bronze at the George Kozmetsky Center For Business Education, 21st Street and Speedway; Seated Bather II, a 1965 bronze in the courtyard of the Huntington Art Building at 23rd and San Jacinto

Streets; and a 1962 bronze The Three Muses, in Centennial Park on 15th and Red River Streets.

Pompeo Coppini was a prolific sculptor for Austin, too, with eight historical figures such as Robert Lee, Albert Sidney Johnston, Jefferson Davis, Woodrow Wilson, and James Stephen Hogg, all in 1933; and George Washington, South Mall at 21st Street between Guadalupe and Speedway. Other interesting works are Monument Holistic IX (1981) of cold rolled steel by Betty Gold, at Trinity Street north of 23rd Street; and Stonelith #136, a limestone and glass piece in the courtyard of the Huntington Art Building at 23rd and San Jacinto Streets. And don't miss the two longhorns, Texas Longhorn by Jim Hamilton (1992) at the Alumni Center, San Jacinto Street south of 23rd Street; and The Texas Longhorn by Duke Sundt, a 1983 bronze in front of the Frank Erwin Center at Red River Street just south of Martin Luther King Jr. Boulevard.

Unusual is Merlin the Magical Sage, carved from a large oak tree stump by David Kestenbaum. You'll find it at Eastwoods Park–Harris Park Boulevard north of 26th Street. There's a Charles Umlauf sculpture at Austin Community College's Northridge Campus, 11928 Stonehollow Drive. The bronze is titled Prometheus (1990). Las Mesas Inner Column (1986), of granite by Jesus Batista Moroles, is in Century Park at 13521 Burnet Road.

NORTHWEST AUSTIN

Up at the Arboretum shopping center you'll find two interesting pieces of sculpture. The Arboretum Cows, of marble by Harold Clay, are adja-cent to the food court at the mall, 9722 Great Hills Trail. Untitled, a metal piece by Tom Torrens, is at Clarksville Pottery, 9722 Great Hills Trail, #380. Along the Capitol of Texas Highway at #8911 you'll find The Red Check in steel by Bernar Venet (1986); and at the University of Texas at Austin, Balcones Research Center at Read Granberry and Neils Thompson Drives, there is David Slivka's Machu Picchu (1974) in wood, nylon webbing, and plaster. Sanctuary of the Tribal Alligator (1988) can be found at Hill Elementary School, 8607 Tallwood Drive. Of cast concrete, it's by T. Paul Hernandez.

SOUTH AUSTIN

In addition to the Umlauf Sculpture Garden (see Chapter 6, Museums and Galleries), there are four public works of art in South Austin. Take a look at the steel architecture details (1991) by Lars Stanley ornamenting Fire Station #17, at 4128 South First Street. Partners (1994), a bronze by Robert E. Coffee, is at the Sheriff's Association of Texas, 1601 South I-35. An unusual Wall of Hands (1994) covers the wall of the St. Elmo Service Center at 4411 Meinardus Drive. The cast ceramic tiles are by Tre Arenz. There's a bronze statue of Jimmy Clay (1994) at the Jimmy Clay Golf Course, 5411 Jimmy Clay, done by Daniel Hawkins. Also enjoyable is an outdoor sculpture tour of Town Lake and Zilker Park, starting on the south shores of the lake.

In Zilker Park, before you enter the Zilker Botanical Gardens at 2220 Barton Springs Road, notice the main entrance gates (1995). The steel gates, by Lars Stanley and Louis Herrera Jr., are a garden in themselves, of graceful wrought-steel leaves and vines. Over by Barton Springs Pool, 2201 Barton Springs Road, there are three figures in bronze by Glenna Goodacre called the Philosophers' Rock *(1994).* The philosophers are J. Frank Dobie, Walter Prescott Webb, and Roy Bedichek. Nearby is the Zilker Park Playscape, also at 2201 Barton Springs Road. The Phantom Ship, *of cast concrete by Jill Bedgood (1991), seems to be a happy dolphin-type fish among the seaweed.*

There are some interesting works along the Town Lake hike and bike trail. At Lou Neff Point, at the confluence of Town Lake and Barton Creek, you'll find the Lou Neff Point Gazebo *(1993)* of iron and steel by David Santos and Joe Perez. At Butler Shores on the Town Lake hike and bike trail at Riverside Drive just west of the Lamar Boulevard Bridge, Untitled *(Chris Kerns Memorial, 1992) is of limestone, granite, and found objects by Paul Siebenaler.*

At Auditorium Shores, between South First Street and Lamar Boulevard, is the Stevie Ray Vaughan Memorial *(1993),* a bronze by Ralph Helmick. At the Auditorium Shores intersection of South First Street and Riverside Drive is the Bicentennial Fountain *(1976)* of granite and Cor-Ten steel, by Ken Fowlet.

Moving over to the Dougherty Cultural Arts Center, 1110 Barton Springs Road, you'll find another Untitled *(1980), a limestone, steel, and wood sculpture by David Ellis.* The Gargoyles *(1990),* at the Zachary Scott Theater Center, 1510 Toomey Road, is made of fiberglass and clay by Stephen Ray.

EAST AUSTIN

Along the Holly Street Power Plant (2401 Holly Street west of Congress) is the Big Arch *(1992)* of limestone and iron by David Santos and Joe Perez.

Central Access Television Station at 1143 Northwestern Avenue has two works of art: Outdoor Studio *(1990)* is of metal, cinderblock, and concrete by Laurel Butler and Rita Starpattern; and Snake Culvert *(1990)* of cast concrete is by T. Paul Hernandez. A bright artwork is Color At Play *by Mary Visser, a fantasy piece of concrete and ceramic tile at University Hills Library, 4721 Loyola Lane.*

BREMOND BLOCK
Between Seventh and Ninth
Guadalupe and San Antonio Sts.
Austin
This historic block includes nine registered landmarks, beautiful homes constructed at this site from 1850 to

T I P

Parking in the Capitol and downtown area comes at a premium. The best way to explore this area is aboard the 'Dillo, the trolley service that starts at the Coliseum's free parking lot at the intersection of West Riverside Drive and Bouldin Avenue. These green trolleys travel up and down the streets from the river to the university.

1877. The Austin Convention and Visitors Bureau offers tours of the block departing from the steps of the Capitol Sat–Sun at 11 a.m. Free. (Downtown Austin)

CAPITOL GROUNDS TOUR
South steps of Capitol
Austin
512/478-0098
Tour the grounds of this stately building for a look at its statues and for tales of its fascinating history. One-hour walking tours depart promptly at the designated hour from the south steps of the Capitol. Hours: Mar–Nov Sat 2 p.m., Sun 9 a.m. Free. (Downtown Austin)

CONGRESS AVENUE/EAST SIXTH STREET WALKING TOURS
South steps of Capitol
Austin
512/478-0098
Enjoy a guided walking tour with a look at historic sites such as the 1915 Paramount Theatre, the 1876 Walter Tips Building, and the 1886 Driskill Hotel. Hours: Thu–Sat 9 a.m., Sun. 2 p.m. Free. (Downtown Austin)

© Eleanor S. Morris

6

MUSEUMS AND GALLERIES

There's not a dull museum in lively Austin. Among them are a museum covering the 10-year span of the Republic of Texas, a museum in the house where humorist O. Henry lived, and a museum housing a rare and treasured copy of the Gutenberg Bible. One museum features locally found dinosaur bones; another celebrates the ethnicity of the city. Visual arts by both local and national artists are vibrantly represented in numerous galleries around downtown, north, and south Austin. (Many are located downtown, along Third, Fourth, and Sixth Streets.) At present two vital city museums, the Austin Museum of Art and the George Washington Carver Museum have come together to plan for a future 86,000-square-foot facility in downtown Austin. While the project builds, visit the three fine museums—and others—at their present locations.

ART MUSEUMS

**AUSTIN MUSEUM OF ART
AT LAGUNA GLORIA
3809 W. 35th St.
Austin
512/458-8191**
Located in a Mediterranean-style villa built in 1916 and now listed on the National Register of Historical Places, the museum is set on 12 green acres of lovely grounds once owned by Stephen F. Austin, who purchased the land in 1832 but died

before he could build on it. The museum has become nationally known for its art exhibits, sculpture gardens, and educational programs. The museum building was once the home of Clara Driskill Servier, who is considered a Texas heroine for her work in preserving the Alamo for posterity. The estate was deeded to the Texas Fine Arts Commission in 1943. The grounds, near the middle of the city, are secluded, shady, and spacious, with wandering walks, sunken sculpture gardens, and rock terraces that lead down to the shores of Lake Austin. The museum specializes in twentieth-century American art, serving as a showcase for modern painters, sculptors, photographers, and architects. There's a museum shop located downtown at 107 W. Sixth Street, 512/477-0766. Hours: Tue–Wed and Fri–Sat 10–5, Thu 1–5, Sun 12–5. $2 adults, $1 children. (Northwest Austin)

AUSTIN MUSEUM OF ART DOWNTOWN
823 Congress Ave.
Austin
512/495-9224
The Museum of Art Downtown features traveling exhibits of paintings, drawings, poetry, and text. It's mission: to provide dynamic exhibitions focusing on American art of the U.S., Mexico, and the Caribbean.

Top Ten Artists' Studios and Galleries
by Jane Steig Parsons, chairman of Gallery Galavanteurs, the University of Texas Ladies Club

1. **Umlauf Sculpture Gardens and Museum** (130 Charles Umlauf sculptures), 605 Robert E. Lee Rd., 512/445-5582.

2. **Gustav Likan Studio** (colorist; "Father of acrylics"), 1407 Ridgecrest, 512/327-2591.

3. **Dan Pogue Studio** (bronze casting and stone sculpture), Cedar Park. By appointment only, 512/441-6717.

4. **Michael Frary Studio** (watercolor landscapes and oil abstractions), 3409 Spanish Oak. By appointment only, 512/453-0544.

5. **Don Herron Clay Works** (functional art and utilitarian pottery), 555 Guinevere Ln. By appointment only, 512/328-1043.

6. **Terra Rosa Studio** (Tim High's fine art prints, drawings, and paintings), 2308 Lawnmont Ave. By appointment only, 512/451-1923.

7. **Spicewood Gallery** (original paintings, sculpture, glass, porcelain, and jewelry), 1206 W. 38th St., 512/458-6575.

8. **Warren Cullar Studio** (abstract watercolors and acrylics), 12102 Conrad Rd. By appointment only, 512/250-8868.

9. **Spirit Echoes Gallery** (exhibiting fine art from 60 artists), 701 Brazos St., 512/320-1492.

10. **David Deming Studio** (sculptures in bronze and steel), Dripping Springs. By appointment only, 512/441-6717.

In 1997, construction of a new home for the museum began. Designed by architect Robert Venturi, the four-story, 86,000-square-foot facility will provide generous gallery space, modern classrooms, and a 300-seat, performance-quality auditorium, giving art lovers across Texas a world-class visual arts center. The new building, located at Third and Guadalupe Streets, should be open by the year 2002. Hours: Tue–Sat 10–6; Thu 10–8; Sun 12–5; closed Mon. $3 adults, $2 students and seniors, free to children under 12; Thu is $1 day. (Downtown Austin)

ELISABET NEY MUSEUM
304 E. 44th St.
Austin
512/458-2255
This small museum houses the works of sculptor Elisabet Ney in her former house and studio, a limestone building tucked into a quiet corner of the historic Hyde Park neighborhood. Although she was born in Munster, Germany, in 1833, Ney was famous well before she settled in Austin in 1892. The first woman to be accepted into the Munich Art Academy, she sculpted such notables as Bismarck, Garibaldi, and Ludwig II of Bavaria, whose life-size likenesses can be seen in the museum today. She and her Scots husband, Dr. Edmund Montgomery, moved to the United States to avoid the Franco-Prussian War. After a 20-year hiatus, she resumed her career in 1892, when she received commissions to model Sam Houston and Stephen F. Austin for the Colombian Exposition in Chicago. Today these marble sculptures are in the capitol, but the plaster models are in the museum. A plaster model of Lady Macbeth, which Ney considered her masterpiece, stands in the full light of the large studio window. (The original is in the Smithsonian in Washington, D.C.) Hours: Wed–Sat 10–5, Sun 12–5. Free. (North Austin)

HARRY RANSOM HUMANITIES RESEARCH CENTER
University of Texas campus
21st and Guadalupe Sts.
Austin

Austin Museum of Art at Laguna Gloria, p. 101

© Eleanor S. Morris

512/471-8944

Exhibits of twentieth-century American, British, and French literary materials, photography, film, theater arts, and visual arts are displayed on the fourth and seventh floors of the center, and in Leeds Gallery in Flawn Academic Center west of the UT Tower. One of only 48 copies worldwide of the Gutenberg Bible (1449–1450) is on exhibit on the first floor of the Harry Ransom Center. Hours: Mon–Wed and Fri 9–4:30, Thu 9–7. Additional hours for the Bible: Sat 9–5, Sun 1–5. Leeds Gallery hours: Mon–Fri 9–4:30. Free. (North Austin)

JACK S. BLANTON MUSEUM OF ART
University of Texas Art Building
23rd and San Jacinto Blvd.
University of Texas campus
Austin
512/471-7324

Considered one of the top 10 university art galleries in the country, the museum is housed in two separate facilities on the university campus. The permanent collections are in the Harry Ransom Humanities Research Center, at 21st and Guadalupe Streets, where more than 9,000 works range from ancient to contemporary art from Australia, Europe, Latin America, and the United States. The art galleries are home to twentieth-century artwork as well as popular culture from the late nineteenth and early twentieth centuries. Works from Mexican artists are also on display. There is a gift shop. Hours: Mon–Sat 10–6. Free; suggested donation of $2. (North Austin)

UMLAUF SCULPTURE GARDEN AND MUSEUM
605 Robert E. Lee Rd.
Austin

512/445-5582

The museum was built with private funds and contains more than 200 sculptures by internationally known sculptor Charles Umlauf. Charles and Angeline Umlauf gave their home, studio, and work to the City of Austin in 1985. The works are displayed by rotation on six acres of xeriscaped gardens. The setting is lovely, with a waterfall, streams, and ponds under tall cedar and oak trees. The works are executed in diverse materials, from exotic woods to terra cotta, rich bronzes, and alabasters; they range from detailed realism to lyrical abstractions. There is a 10-minute video in which the artist tells about his work and philosophy and describes his methodology. Hours: Wed–Fri 10–4:30; Sat and Sun 1–4:30; closed Mon and Tue. $3 adults, $2 seniors, $1 students, free children under 6. (South Austin)

SCIENCE AND HISTORY MUSEUMS

AUSTIN HISTORY CENTER
810 Guadalupe St.
Austin
512/499-7480

Everything ever printed or recorded about Austin and Travis County is zealously collected and protected within the walls of the Austin History Center. The center is housed in another of Austin's historical buildings, a beautiful art deco interpretation of Renaissance Revival style. It was built in the 1930s as the main library and is still fondly referred to as "Old Main." (The new building, ultramodern glass and cement, is right next door.) The exhibit of archival photographs changes. The library is run by a very helpful and friendly staff.

TRIVIA

Austin has the sixth-highest number of artists per capita in the U.S.

Hours: Mon–Thu 9–9, Fri–Sat 9–6, Sun 12–6. Free. (Downtown Austin)

CAPITOL COMPLEX VISITORS CENTER
112 E. 11th St.
Austin
512/305-8400
The General Land Office, the oldest government building in Texas, has permanent and changing exhibits, information on tours, informative brochures, and a gift shop. Hours: Tue–Fri 9–5, Sat 10–5. Free. (Downtown Austin)

CENTER FOR AMERICAN HISTORY AT THE UNIVERSITY OF TEXAS
Sid Richardson Hall
23rd and Red River Sts.
Austin
512/495-4515
The Texas Collection here has 120,000 volumes of Texana alone. Stephen F. Austin's papers and those of his father, Moses Austin, are here, as well as the Bexar Archives and other important historical materials dealing with the settling of the state. A closed-stack library, it's open for research to anyone abiding by the rules. Hours: Mon–Sat 9–5. Free. (North Austin)

THE FRENCH LEGATION MUSEUM
802 San Marcos St.
Austin
512/472-8180
Austin's oldest standing building, this Greek Revival bayou-style mansion, built in 1841, is preserved by the Daughters of the Republic of Texas. It was built by Alphonse Dubois de Saligny, named *charge d'affaires* to the Republic of Texas when Louis Philippe of France recognized the republic in 1839. The parlor contains some furnishings that belonged to Saligny, while others are pieces of the period. The legation's kitchen is the only authentic reproduction of an early Creole kitchen in the United States. Tours are conducted Tue–Sat 1–5, and there's a bang-up Bastille Day celebration every July 14. Hours: Tue–Sun 1–5. $3 adults, $1 children 11–18, 50 cents children under 10. (East Austin)

GEORGE WASHINGTON CARVER MUSEUM
1165 Angelina
Austin

The French Legation Museum

© Permenter and Bigley

Charles Umlauf's works can also be seen in public institutions across the United States, such as the Smithsonian Institution in Washington, D.C., and the Metropolitan Museum of Art in New York City. In Texas, his works can be seen in public places from Abilene to Waco.

512/472-4809

Texas' first African American neighborhood history museum displays artifacts, videos, oral histories, community-related photographs, and other archival material depicting the local, regional, and national history of African Americans. The museum documents the significant contribution blacks have made on both city and country levels. The facility includes art exhibits relating to African American culture and heritage. Hours: Tue–Thu 10–6, Fri–Sat 12–5. (East Austin)

LORENZO DE ZAVALA STATE ARCHIVES AND LIBRARY
1201 Brazos St.
Austin
512/463-5455

Some of Texas' most important historic documents and collections are housed here in the Texas State Library, including genealogy records. The library is named for an elected interim vice president of the Texas Republic. The large lobby mural, painted by Peter Rogers in collaboration with Peter Hurd, depicts events and personages of the republic. Also in the lobby are exhibits displaying artifacts of the Texas Republic, and on the second floor there is a colorful display of every flag that played a part in Texas history. A large statue of Sam Hous-

ton stands at the entrance to the building. Hours: Mon–Fri 8–5; Genealogy Tue–Sat 8–5. Free. (Downtown Austin)

LYNDON B. JOHNSON PRESIDENTIAL LIBRARY AND MUSEUM
2313 Red River St.
Austin
512/916-5136

The library houses 40 million pages from the entire public career of Lyndon Baines Johnson and also those of close associates (used primarily by scholars). Year-round public viewing of the permanent historical and cultural exhibits includes gifts from foreign heads of state, a moon rock, and a replica of the Oval Office. Hours: Daily 9–5 except Christmas. Free. (North Austin)

NEILL-COCHRAN MUSEUM HOUSE
2310 San Gabriel
Austin
512/478-2335

A blend of Greek Revival architecture and native Texas materials makes this mansion a truly unique Austin landmark. Abner Cook, the master builder who also built the Governor's Mansion used native limestone and pine from Bastrop to construct this home in 1855 for Washington L. Hill. It served as a family home to a succession of owners (during the Civil War Federal soldiers were hospitalized here, and some are buried near the house) until it was purchased in 1958 by the Colonial Dames of America. Hours: Wed–Sun 2–5. $2. (North Austin)

O. HENRY HOME AND MUSEUM
409 E. Fifth St.
Austin
512/472-1903
Austin is proud to boast that William Sydney Porter, otherwise known as short story master O. Henry, once lived in Austin, and his Victorian cottage, built circa 1892, contains his desk, writing materials, and other period furnishings. On the first weekend in May, the museum sponsors the O. Henry Pun-Off competition. It's open to the public and adds up to a lot of fun. It's held in the backyard, where both a book fair and country western music are going on at the same time. All three trophies—first, second, and third place—are of "the rear end of a horse." Hours: Wed–Sun 12–5. Free. (Downtown Austin)

REPUBLIC OF TEXAS MUSEUM
510 E. Anderson Ln.
Austin
512/339-1997
This collection of the Daughters of the Republic of Texas focuses on the 10 years of the republic, from 1836 to

Statue of King Ludwig II at the Elisabet Ney Museum, p. 103

© Permenter and Bigley

1846. Hours: Mon–Fri 10–4. $2 adults, $1 children. (North Austin)

TEXAS MEMORIAL MUSEUM
2400 Trinity St.
Austin
512/471-1604
The museum offers an eclectic mixture of both Texas and natural history, including paleontology, antique firearms, wildlife dioramas, Indian artifacts, rare gems and minerals, and the original Goddess of Liberty statue removed from the capitol dome during recent restoration (and replaced with a safer replica). The museum has a gift shop. Hours: Mon–Fri 9–5, Sat 10–5, Sun 1–5. Free. (North Austin)

Alphonse Dubois de Saligny, French *charge d'affaires* to the Republic of Texas, never occupied the French Legation; he left in a huff because of the "Pig War." The pigs on a neighboring site ate Saligny's corn, and perhaps even worse, chewed on some table linens that he had purchased in New Orleans on his way to this outpost of civilization. His servant shot the pigs, the animals' owner beat the servant, and the "war" was on.

GALLERIES

Art exhibits are held in galleries throughout the city as well as in more informal venues such as restaurants and cafés. Exhibits in both types of venues are listed in the Austin Chronicle, *and the* Austin American-Statesman *lists these in its Thursday* XLent *entertainment section.*

THE ARBORETUM
10000 Research Blvd.
Austin
512/345-3001
Features various three-dimensional media, with contemporary handmade fine crafted glass, metal, wood, and wire. Hours: Mon–Wed and Fri–Sat 10–6, Thu 10–8, Sun 1–5. (Northwest Austin)

ARTSPACE GALLERY
403 Baylor St.
Austin
512/474-7799
The Artist's Coalition of Austin features work by coalition members. There's a changing exhibit every month, and you might find paintings, sculpture, wood constructions, mixed media—the works. The next-door space is rented to local artists who want to have their own shows, so there's always plenty of interest to see in both galleries. Hours: Tue 3–6, Thu 3–8 or by appointment. Open meetings on Mon at 6:30. (Downtown Austin)

ARTWORKS GALLERY
1214 Sixth St.
Austin
512/472-1550
Original serigraphs, original watercolors, classical oils by national and international artists, and Bedermier-style furniture are on display. Hours: Mon–Sat 10–6, Sun 1–5. (Downtown Austin)

CLARKSVILLE POTTERY AND GALLERIES
4001 Lamar Blvd.
Austin
512/794-8580
This fine crafts gallery represents 300 artists, about a third of them Texans, the rest out of state. The gallery features wooden ware such as boxes and clocks, pottery, blown glass, and gold and silver jewelry. Hours: Mon–Sat 10–6, Thu 10–8, Sun 12–6. Additional location is at 9722 Great Hills Tr., 512/454-9079. (Northwest Austin)

DOUGHERTY ARTS CENTER GALLERY
1110 Barton Springs Rd.

T I P

The Dougherty Arts Center is under the aegis of the Austin Parks and Recreation Department and as such offers the after-school Isely Artists and Creativity Club programs for youngsters. The staff works hard to plan a fun-filled creative arts curriculum that will expand imagination and encourage interest in both visual and performing arts.

Los Días de los Muertos

Austin's Mexic-Arte Museum celebrates Los Días de los Muertos, the Days of the Dead, with an exhibition, usually the last weekend in October into the first of November. A Mexican celebration since prehistoric times, Days of the Dead is a joyous event in which the living place objects for the soul to take along on its journey to the next world. Nowadays in Hispanic culture it's celebrated by communing with departed relatives and friends by sharing food with them, decorating their graves, burning copal, and toasting them. Yellow marigolds, candles, toys, personal mementos, and photographs are placed on an altar, graves are cleaned and weeded, and relatives lay their offerings on the graves. Children make masks of skulls decorated with butterflies and flowers because in Mexican culture, death is not considered scary.

Austin
512/397-1472
Exhibits here run the gamut of the art world, featuring local, national, and international artists. You'll find watercolor exhibits, sculpture, student art, faculty art, international children's art, multidisplays of world cultures—even a working metalsmith. Call to see what's on each month. Hours: Mon–Thu 9–9:30, Fri 9–5:30, Sat 10–2. Free. (South Austin)

ECLECTIC ETHNOGRAPHIC ART GALLERY
916 W. 12th St.
Austin
512/477-1816
International folk art, furnishings, and colorful furniture by Texas artists. You'll find hand-painted furniture, pre-Colombian artifacts, African art, and etched glass. Hours: Mon–Sat 10–6, Sun 12–6. (Downtown Austin)

FIRE ISLAND HOT GLASS STUDIO
3401 E. Fourth St.
Austin
512/389-1100
All sorts of hand-blown glass is for sale here, and you can watch it being blown. Paperweights, vases, perfume bottles, oil lamps, drinking glasses, Christmas ornaments, glass bead jewelry, fish—even refrigerator magnets. Demonstrations offered every Saturday. Hours: Mon–Fri 8–5, Sat 9–1. (East Austin)

FLATBED PRESS AND GALLERY
912 W. Third St.
Austin
512/477-9328
Master printers Katherine Brimberry and Gerald Manson specialize in intaglio, relief, and monotype prints in this print gallery and publishing workshop. Hours: Mon–Fri 9:30–5, Sat 11–3 or by appointment. (Downtown Austin)

GALERIA SIN FRONTERAS
1701 Guadalupe St.
Austin
512/478-9448
You'll find contemporary Latino art—paintings, prints, photographs, mixed media, all mediums; primarily the works of local artists—in this gallery "without boundaries." Hours: Tue–Sat 11–6. (North Austin)

GRAPHIC CONCERN
1202 W. Sixth St.
Austin
512/472-7428
Featured are original works by many Austin artists, including pastels, photography, glass, and paintings. Hours: Mon–Sat 10–5. (Downtown Austin)

HEARTLAND GALLERY
4006 S. Lamar Blvd., Suite 950
Brodie Oaks Center
Austin
512/447-1171
Specializing in local talent, the gallery sells a wide selection of fine contemporary work by more than 200 artists. Treasures include pottery, raku, jewelry, blown glass, stained glass, metal, wood, and fiber. Hours: Mon–Wed and Fri–Sat 10–6, Thu 10–9, Sun 12–5. (South Austin)

IMAGES OF AUSTIN AND THE SOUTHWEST
4612 Burnet Rd.
Austin
512/451-1229
Paintings, sculpture, furniture, and jewelry with Texas and Southwestern themes are showcased here. Hours: Mon–Sat 10–6. (North Austin)

SGRAFFITO STUDIO AND GALLERY

809 W. 12th St.
Austin
512/708-9000
This is a do-it-yourself art place: Make your mark on coffee mugs, platters, dog dishes, and more at this ceramics studio. Then the studio applies clear glaze and fires your finished work. In four days it's ready to take home. Hours: Tue–Fri 11–8, Sat 11–6, Sun 12–6. (Downtown Austin)

SPIRIT ECHOES ART GALLERY
701 Brazos St., Suite 120
Austin
512/320-1492
The gallery has a wide selection of paintings, monotypes, collage, and prints by more than 60 contemporary artists, with works ranging from realistic gardens of florals to Native American images. Hours: Mon–Fri 9–5:30, Thu 9–9, Sat 10–5, Sun 11–2. (Downtown Austin)

WILD ABOUT MUSIC
721 Congress Ave.
Austin
512/708-1700
This is a visual, not a vocal, celebration of sound. Everything—paintings, prints, sculptures, serigraphs by both local and national artists—has a music theme or motif. Hours: Mon–Sat 10–7. (Downtown Austin)

WOMEN AND THEIR WORK
1710 Lavaca
Austin
512/477-1064
Although the gallery mainly focuses on the work—paintings, prints, photographs, and sculpture—of Texas women, it occasionally showcases works by national as well as local women artists. Hours: Mon–Fri 10–5, Sat–Sun 10–4. (North Austin)

© Eleanor S. Morris

7

KIDS' STUFF

Austin is filled with attractions that kids will enjoy. Our Kids, a free monthly newspaper distributed at local stores, is filled with family-oriented articles, a family activities calendar featuring special children's activities across town, family movie reviews, and more.

Austin's beautiful outdoor attractions are a natural draw for families with young children, who will find educational and entertaining diversions, many at little or no cost. Year-round temperate weather conditions have encouraged the construction of many playscapes and parks throughout the city. Stop by the Austin Convention and Visitors Bureau at 201 E. Second Street for a copy of the free 101 Things For Kids to Do in Austin brochure.

ANIMALS AND THE GREAT OUTDOORS

THE ARBORETUM
10000 Research Blvd.
Austin
512/338-4437
This open-air mall may be home to some of Austin's most upscale shopping, but to young visitors it's the location of "the cows." Let the kids climb on top of a life-size cow sculpture on the west side of the mall, then feed the ducks at the lake. (Northwest Austin)

AUSTIN NATURE AND SCIENCE CENTER
301 Nature Center Dr.
Austin
512/327-8180
No need to tell the kids "look but don't touch" at this hands-on educational center. Here exhibits teach ecological lessons about natural history, botany, and more amid 80 acres of canyons and meadows just west of Zilker Park. Kids can even crawl through a "cave" in the "Nature of Austin" exhibit and see over 50 native Texas animals that were orphaned or

Inner Space Cavern

Just up I-35 about 20 minutes beyond Austin's northern limits lies the most accessible cavern in Texas. Discovered during the construction of the interstate highway, this cavern is a cool getaway for summer travelers and was once a hideaway for animals as well. A skull of a peccary (a pig-like hoofed mammal) estimated to be a million years old has been found here, along with bones of a giant sloth and a mammoth. After reaching cave level aboard a small trolley, follow your guide for a tour of cave formations, a small lake, and evidence of those prehistoric visitors. The cavern is located off I-35 west of Austin, exit 259, in Georgetown. It's open 10–5 daily during winter months; 9–6 daily from Memorial Day through Labor Day. For more information, call 512/863-5545.

injured and cannot be returned to the wild. Hours: Mon–Sat 9–5, Sun 12–5. Free. (Southwest Austin)

AUSTIN ZOO
10807 Rawhide Terr.
Austin
512/288-1490 or 800/291-1490
This privately owned zoo located near Oak Hill offers pony rides, train rides, a petting zoo, and plenty of exotic creatures to keep the little ones happy. Animal food is offered for sale, so young visitors can feed some of the inhabitants by hand. Hours: Daily 10–6. $5 adults over 12, $4 kids 2–12, free children under 2, $4 grandparents and seniors. (Southwest Austin)

AUSTIN'S BAT COLONY
Congress Ave. Bridge
at Town Lake
Austin
512/478-0098
Watch 1.5 million Mexican free-tailed bats make their departure from the Congress Avenue Bridge on summer nights. The best viewing is from the hike and bike trail, the bridge, or a free bat-viewing area in the parking lot of the *Austin American-Statesman* (305 S. Congress Ave.). The best viewing months are July and August. For more on the bats, check out the information kiosks at the Four Seasons Hotel (98 San Jacinto Blvd.) and across the river in the parking lot of the *Austin American-Statesman*. (Downtown Austin)

BARTON SPRINGS POOL
2200 Barton Springs Rd.
Austin
512/476-9044
Even little nonswimmers will enjoy splashing around in the shallow waters on the upstream side of Barton Springs Pool. Rest room and changing facilities are available, and a food and drink concession is located just outside the gates. Or bring along a

picnic lunch to enjoy in the shade of the tall oaks. Hours: Daily 5 a.m.–10 p.m. $2.50 adults, 25 cents children. (South Austin)

JOURDAN-BACHMAN PIONEER FARM
11418 Sprinkle Cut-Off Rd.
Austin
512/837-1215
The Jourdan-Bachman Pioneer Farm attraction is well worth the 15-minute drive to introduce youngsters to life in rural central Texas in the 1880s. The living history museum is built on a 2,000-acre cotton farm and populated with docents who carry on the chores of the period. Children can watch a blacksmith shoe a horse or a family cooking its meals over a wood-burning stove. Energetic youngsters can even pitch in and help plant or pick cotton or scrub clothes on a washboard. Hours: Mon–Thu 9:30–3, Sun 1–5. $3 adults, $2 children 3–12, free children under 3. (not shown on map in this chapter) (East Austin)

LADY BIRD JOHNSON WILDFLOWER RESEARCH CENTER
4801 La Crosse Ave.
Austin
512/292-4200
Young botanists can enjoy the children's garden, specially designed to please young visitors. A Children's Little House is especially inviting to young travelers. Don't miss Ralph the Talking Lawnmower! Hours: Tue–Sun 9–5:30. $3.50 adults, $2 students and seniors, $1 children 18 mos.–5 years. (Southwest Austin)

Top Ten Places to Take Preschoolers
by Laurie Kibel, daycare supervisor for over a decade and mother of three daughters

1. **Austin Zoo**, 10807 Rawhide Terr., 512/288-1490.
2. **Log Cabin, Wells Branch Park**, off Wells Branch Pkwy. on Klattenhoff Dr.
3. **Austin Children's Museum**, 1501 W. Fifth St., 512/472-2499.
4. **LBJ Library and Presidential Museum**, 2313 Red River St., 512/482-5136.
5. **Texas Memorial Museum**, 2400 Trinity St., 512/471-1604.
6. **Ice-skating at Northcross Mall**, 512/451-5102.
7. **Zachary Scott Theater**, 1510 Toomey Rd., 512/476-0594.
8. **Kid's Sports**, 8015 Shoal Creek Blvd., 512/452-8775.
9. **Inner Space Cavern**, west off I-35, exit 259, Georgetown, 512/863-5545.
10. **Roller-skating at Skateworld**, 9514 W. Anderson Mill Rd., 512/258-8886.

T I P

If you're looking for an alternative to babysitting, check out the Kids' Night Out at the Hancock Recreation Center. The Saturday night fun runs from 6–11 p.m. for kids 3–12 and includes movie and popcorn. Kids must be registered by 6 p.m. on Thursday; $10 per child. Call 512/453-7765 for information or to register.

LONE STAR RIVERBOAT
Congress Ave. at S. First St.
Austin
512/327-1388
You and your child will feel like Tom Sawyer aboard an old-fashioned paddlewheeler. The 90-minute trip offers a great city view. Hours: Mar–Oct weekends only; hours vary. $9 adults, $6 children under 12, $7 seniors (South Austin)

ZILKER BOTANICAL GARDEN
Zilker Park
Barton Springs Rd.
Austin

512/478-6875
In the Pioneer Settlement in Zilker Park's Zilker Botanical Garden you'll see a collection of historic cabins from Austin's early days. The Esperanza School House was built in the Spicewood Springs area and was in use until about 1873. The Swedish Pioneer Cabin is one of the best-preserved log houses in the country. The blacksmith shop contains equipment used by pioneer blacksmiths to make and shape hand-forged metal implements, and the Mamie Wilson Rowe Summer House is made of cypress wood. If you look closely, you

Austin Nature and Science Center, p. 111

© Permenter and Bigley

Austin Public Library

The Austin Public Library offers a variety of programs including storytimes, films, arts and crafts, and puppet shows. The programs are scheduled at the main library as well as branch libraries scattered throughout the city.

The main library, housed at 800 Guadalupe Street, is named for John Henry Faulk, a well-known Austin humorist and writer. The library system, with an annual budget exceeding $10 million, has over a million holdings.

Youth programs at the Austin Public Library include toddler storytimes for children 18 months to three years with an adult, preschool storytimes for young listeners four to five years old, and additional storytimes for all age groups. A Summer Fun Club is offered every year for children six to 10 years old. Other programs include films, arts and crafts, and puppet shows.

One of the most recognized library programs is the Victory Program. Victory Program Homework Centers offer free tutoring to young Austinites using VISTA volunteers. The program was named one of the top 50 outstanding programs for youth in U.S. schools and public libraries by the American Library Association.

may see some of the original square nails. Hours: 8:30–sunset daily. Free. (South Austin)

ZILKER DINOSAUR TRACKWAYS
Zilker Park
Barton Springs Rd.
Austin
Once restricted to tours only, these invaluable relics of 100 million years ago are now open to the public, but the public is requested to please tread carefully, with soft-soled shoes. The archaeologists who discovered the

tracks in 1991 of what is believed to be an ornithomimus, an ostrich-like dinosaur, say that 30 to 40 percent of the track definitions have been lost due to carelessness. (South Austin)

ZILKER RAILROAD
Zilker Park
Barton Springs Rd.
Austin
Jump aboard this pint-sized train for a three-mile, 20-minute ride through picturesque Zilker Park. The railroad winds past the children's playground

TIP

The Austin Symphony Orchestra regularly schedules kids-oriented concerts and activities such as the Children's Halloween Concert, Children's Day Art Park, and more. For information, call 512/476-6064.

and along the hike and bike trail. Board at the station at Barton Springs Pool, across from the concession stand. Hours: Daily 10–5, weather permitting. $2 adults, $1.25 children and seniors. (South Austin)

MUSEUMS AND LIBRARIES

AUSTIN CHILDREN'S MUSEUM
201 Colorado St.
Austin
512/472-2499
The Children's Museum sets out to make learning fun through hands-on exhibits on all facets of science and technology. Some popular permanent exhibits include the Whole Foods Market, where children learn about nutrition as they "play store"; the Sound Track Studio, where they learn about recording technology with keyboards and microphones; and the Music Room, where they can make music and dance. Hours: Tue–Sat 10–5, Sun 12–5. $2.50 adults, free for children under 2. (Downtown Austin)

CAMP MABRY NATIONAL GUARD
W. 35th St. and Loop 1 (Mo-Pac)
Austin
512/406-6967
Any kids wanting to play soldier can head down to Camp Mabry, headquarters of the Texas Army and Air National

Guard, for a look at the airplanes, helicopters, cannons, and even tanks along the walking trail. If that piques your youngster's interest, stop by the Military Forces Museum for a look at military memorabilia. Hours: Museum Wed–Sun 10–4, closed Mon–Tue. Free. (Northwest Austin)

JOHN HENRY FAULK CENTRAL LIBRARY
800 Guadalupe St.
Austin
512/499-7301
The central library offers excellent youth programs and, for school-age

Blacksmith at Jourdan-Bachman Pioneer Farm, p. 113

© Eleanor S. Morris

children, thorough resources for any school report. Reference assistance is available on the first floor. Hours: Mon–Thu 9–9, Fri–Sat 9–6, Sun 12–6. (Downtown Austin)

LYNDON B. JOHNSON PRESIDENTIAL LIBRARY AND MUSEUM
2313 Red River St.
Austin
512/482-5136

Bring the little ones to stare in awe at the six floors of red, gold-sealed boxes containing the public papers of LBJ's career. Children enjoy a look at the

moon rock, gifts given to the president from people around the world, and especially the top-floor replica of the Oval Office. Buy an inexpensive souvenir in the gift shop, and bring a picnic to enjoy outside by the fountain. Hours: Daily 9–5 except Christmas. Free. (North Austin)

REPUBLIC OF TEXAS MUSEUM
510 E. Anderson Ln.
Austin
512/339-1997

Take the kids to play in "Great Grandma's Backyard" at this historic museum focusing on the years when

---

Branch Libraries

Check with these branch libraries for information about childrens' storytimes:

Carver, *1161 Angelina, 512/472-8954*

Hampton Branch at Oak Hill, *5125 Convict Hill Rd., 512/892-6680*

Howson, *2500 Exposition Blvd., 512/472-3584*

Little Walnut Creek, *835 W. Rundberg Ln., 512/836-8975*

Manchaca Road, *5500 Manchaca Rd., 512/447-6651*

North Loop Area, *2210 Hancock Dr., 512/454-7208*

North Village, *2139 W. Anderson Ln., 512/458-2239*

Oak Springs, *3101 Oak Springs Dr., 512/926-4453*

Old Quarry, *7051 Village Center Dr., 512/345-4435*

Pleasant Hill, *211 E. William Cannon Dr., 512/441-7993*

Riverside Drive, *2410 E. Riverside Dr., 512/448-0776*

Spicewood Springs, *8637 Spicewood Springs Rd., 512/258-9070*

Terrazas, *1105 E. Cesar Chavez St., 512/472-7312*

Twin Oaks, *2301 S. Congress Ave., #7, 512/442-4664*

University Hills, *4721 Loyola Ln., 512/929-0551*

Windsor Village, *5811 Berkman Dr., #140, 512/928-0333*

For the budding novelist in your family, check out the Austin Writer's League Creative Writing Camp, held every summer for middle school students. The AWL also sponsors weekend workshops for young writers. For details, call 512/499-8914.

Texas was an independent republic. Children enjoy the hands-on collection of artifacts that recall Texas' early days in this museum run by the Daughters of the Republic of Texas. Hours: Mon–Fri 10–4. $2 adults, 50 cents children. (North Austin)

STATE CAPITOL
11th St. at Congress Ave.
Austin
512/463-0063
One of the top field trip destinations in Texas, this truly Texas-size building leaves young travelers dwarfed by its massive proportions. Paintings of Texas heroes will also impress youngsters. Starting at the rotunda star, visitors can tour the recently restored structure, and if the legislature's in session, even sit in and watch Texas government at work. Enter the third-floor balconies for a view of the House and Senate chambers. The legislature meets from January through May in odd-numbered years. Guided tours every 15 minutes Mon–Fri 8:30–4:15, Sat 9:30–4:15; open 7 a.m.–10 p.m. weekdays, 9–5 weekends. (Downtown Austin)

TEXAS MEMORIAL MUSEUM
2400 Trinity St.
Austin
512/471-1604
Take your little dinosaur lover to this museum on the University of Texas campus. Youngsters also enjoy a look

at the gem and mineral collection and the wildlife dioramas. Hours: Mon–Fri 9–5, Sat 10–5, Sun 1–5. Free. (North Austin)

PUPPETS AND THEATER

BARNES AND NOBLE
10000 Research Blvd.
Austin
512/418-8985
This two-story bookseller has a separate children's section that encourages young readers to take a place on the floor and curl up with a good book. Regularly scheduled children's events, puppet shows, and readings make this a favorite stop for families. Hours: Daily 9 a.m.–11 p.m. (Northwest Austin)

BOOKPEOPLE
603 N. Lamar Blvd.
Austin
512/472-5050
Austin's largest bookstore has weekly events for children at 10:30 a.m. on Tuesday and Wednesday and 2 p.m. on Saturday, including puppet shows and readings. (Downtown Austin)

BORDERS BOOKS AND MUSIC
10225 Research Blvd.
Austin
512/795-9553
Preschoolers enjoy storytime every Thursday at 10:30 a.m. The Children's

Child-Size Festivals

Austin hosts festivals and special events year-round, and several of these celebrations are designed for younger residents and visitors. Check out these annual events, sure to please kids of all ages:

March: The Austin-Travis County Livestock Show and PRCA Rodeo offers youngsters a chance to feel like a cowboy. Watch professionals compete and schoolchildren show their prize-winning livestock, 512/467-9814.

April: Celebrate spring at Safari, a family festival that recognizes nature and the environment. Sponsored by the Austin Nature Center, 512/327-8180.

June–August: Symphony Square hosts Children's Day Art Park with storytellers and musicians, 512/476-6064.

October: Boo! Ghosts and ghouls make their appearance at two events designed to delight, not terrify, young visitors. The Austin Children's Museum, 512/472-2494, hosts Gruseum, a costumed celebration for young children. The Jourdan-Bachman Pioneer Farm, 512/837-1215, celebrates the season with a Halloween haunt. And finally, bring your costumed youngster to the Austin Symphony's annual Halloween concert for kids, 512/476-6064.

December: Austin becomes the land of Dickens at the Victorian Christmas on Sixth Street, 512/478-8704. Booths sell period costumes and accessories, and carolers share the spirit of the season. Zilker Park lights up with Yulefest and the Trail of Lights, 512/397-1463, a magical wonderland of lights.

Department also schedules special events ranging from tea parties to puppet shows to career awareness seminars. (Northwest Austin)

ZACHARY SCOTT THEATRE
1510 Toomey Rd.
Austin

512/476-0594
Enroll your budding actor or actress in a children's class at the performing arts school for lessons in creative drama, singing, comedy, playwriting, and more. Sessions are divided by age and include children ages 5 to 16. (South Austin)

STORES KIDS LOVE

AMY'S ICE CREAM
1012 W. Sixth St.
Austin
512/480-0673
Boisterous waitpersons serve up frivolity and frozen confection at this Austin institution. Select from dozens of varieties of ice cream—and don't be surprised if the servers toss your order among themselves. Hours vary by store; most open daily at noon and close at midnight. Other locations: 10000 Research Blvd. (Northwest Austin), 512/345-1006; 3300 Bee Caves Rd. (Southwest Austin), 512/328-9859; and 3500 Guadalupe St. (North Austin), 512/458-6895. (Downtown Austin)

ANNA'S TOY DEPOT
2401 S. Lamar Blvd.
Austin
512/447-8697
New and used toys rule at this fun-filled store that has everything from day-care supplies to action figures and games. Hours: Mon–Sat 10–6, Sun 1–5. (South Austin)

CERAMICS BAYOU
3736 Bee Caves Rd.
Austin
512/328-1168
Kids can paint their own pottery at this fun store that sells coffee mugs, bowls, platters, and pots. They'll even glaze and fire the work, making it safe for dining use or display. Hours: Thu–Fri 10–9, Sat 10–6, Sun 12–5. (Southwest Austin)

TERRA TOYS
1708 S. Congress Ave.
Austin
512/445-4489 or 800/247-TOYS
This Austin institution features doll-houses, railroads, science kits, and dolls. You name it, you'll find it in this toy palace. Hours: Mon–Sat 10–7, Sun 12–6. (South Austin)

TOAD HALL CHILDREN'S BOOKSTORE
1206 W. 38th St.
Austin
512/323-2665
This children's bookstore is the kind of place the whole family can enjoy, with regularly scheduled puppet shows and readings for little ones, series books and classics for juveniles, and parenting guides for adults. Hours: Mon–Sat 9–7, Sun 1–5. (North Austin)

TOY JOY
2900 Guadalupe St.
Austin
512/320-0090
This funky shop is a favorite with teens who feel they've outgrown toys but still have room for stickers, figurines, and oddities like boxing nuns. Hours: Sun–Thu 10–10, Fri–Sat 10–12 a.m. (North Austin)

MISCELLANEOUS KIDS' STUFF

CELEBRATION STATION
4525 S. I-35
Austin
512/448-3533
A popular birthday party venue, Celebration Station entertains children any time with Go-karts, batting cages, bumper boats, miniature golf, and more. Rides are priced individually; a play pass gives unlimited access to outdoor attractions. A food court with a pizza restaurant keeps hungry visitors happy. Hours: Memorial Day–Labor Day 10–10; during winter months Sun–Thu 11–10, Fri–Sat 10–12 a.m.

"Pay as You Play" or all-day pass $9.95–$11.95. (South Austin)

DISCOVERY ZONE FUN CENTER
9503 Research Blvd.
Austin
512/346-9666
Another favorite with the birthday party set, this indoor playland has games and playsets for children under 12. Hours: Mon–Thu 10–8, Fri–Sat 10–9, Sun 11–7. Free for adults and children under age 1, $3.99 children 1–3, $5.99 children 3–12. (Northwest Austin)

KIDDIE ACRES AMUSEMENT PARK AND MINI GOLF
4800 W. Howard Ln.
Austin
512/255-4131
Children under 12 can ride ponies and small amusement park rides at this north Austin playland that's been a longtime favorite with Austinites. Its 18-hole miniature golf course is popular, too. Concessions offer hot dogs, ice cream, and snack foods. Wednesday is discount day when tickets are sold at group rates. Hours: Jun–Aug Tue–Sun 10–7; Sep–Oct Tue–Thu 12–7, Fri–Sun 12–9; Nov–Mar Tue–Sun 12–7; Apr–May Tue–Thu 12–7, Fri–Sun 12–9. $1 per ticket or 10 tickets for $8.50; miniature golf rates are $2.50 for adults, $2 for children under 12. (North Austin)

MALIBU GRAND PRIX
7417 N. I-35
Austin
512/454-0283
Older kiddos can take a turn around the track in three-quarter-size Formula 1 race cars and Go-karts or play more than 75 kinds of video games, basketball with a moving hoop, and "Big Bertha," where they can throw balls in Bertha's mouth and watch her get bigger at this high-action fun center. Hours: Sun–Thu 12–10, Fri–Sat 11 a.m.–12 a.m. $2.85–$3.75 for one lap. Need Malibu Grand Prix license, $1.35. (North Austin)

PSEUDO ROCK
200 Trinity St.
Austin
512/474-4375
If restless kids have you climbing the walls, let them have their turn at Pseudo Rock, an indoor climbing facility. The 5,000-square-foot place has 35 different climbing adventures for all skill levels, and youngsters can learn the basics of rock climbing. Hours: Mon–Fri 10–10, Sat–Sun 10–8. $8; equipment rental is $5. (Downtown Austin)

© Eleanor S. Morris

8

PARKS AND GARDENS

Austin has been acclaimed as one of the four best park cities in the nation. Zilker Park is the city's main recreational area, but it's a rare Austin neighborhood that doesn't have its own park, and rarer still to see one empty. No matter how large the city gets, there are spaces aplenty for fun, fitness, and relaxation for everyone. Both visitors and residents take advantage of the typical 300 sunny days a year here by enjoying the outdoors.

PARKS AND RECREATION AREAS

Austin's 191 parks include 89 neighborhood parks, 12 district parks, nine metropolitan parks, 23 greenbelts, and 29 miles of hike and bike trails. Metropolitan parks, which often include a major waterway, offer both the largest and most diversified recreational opportunities. Not only do they serve the city population, in some cases they are tourist attractions. Often more than 200 acres in size, they are also usually located on major roadways. Large parking areas accommodate drivers, public transportation serves these areas, and true to Austin's image as an outdoor

health-conscious community, access by bicycle or foot by way of hike and bike paths is encouraged.

EMMA LONG METROPOLITAN PARK
City Park Rd. 6.2 miles off FM 2222
Austin
512/346-1831
Only about 70 acres of this 1,150-acre park on the shores of Lake Austin are developed. The park has a designated swimming area in the lake, with a large, sandy beach. Rest rooms, dressing rooms, and showers are provided, and lifeguards are on duty noon to six on weekends only, Memorial Day through Labor Day. Boats are not allowed in the swimming area nor

alongside the swimming docks. A city ordinance prohibits swimming beyond 50 feet from the shoreline.

There are two boat ramps, and visitors who have boats but are not staying overnight are restricted to day use of the park. Campers with boats can moor their boats offshore. Park boundaries begin up by Pearce Road, and they include an archery range, a nature trail, and a mountain bike area. The park also has two sand volleyball courts and three sets of volleyball standards.

Contact the Austin Parks and Recreation Department for complete rules and regulations in using the park. Hours: Daily 7–10. Day use: $3 per vehicle Mon–Thu, $5 per vehicle Fri–Sun and holidays; $1 per pedestrian/bicycle per day. Overnight: $6 camping without utilities per night plus first-day entry; $10 utility (RV) area plus first-day entry. (Northwest Austin)

KARST NATURE PRESERVE
3900 Deer Ln.
Austin
512/327-5437
The word "karst" originally referred to a limestone plateau in Germany, but the word now means any area with limestone rocks, deep fractures, and caves that feed rainwater directly into underground lakes and streams. That's

Stairway up Mount Bonnell, p. 127

exactly what characterizes this 10-acre preserve over the Edwards Aquifer Recharge Zone. The preserve features caves, sinkholes, and honeycomb outcroppings along the 1/8-mile trail, a 20-minute, pleasant, winding walk. (South Austin)

MARY MOORE SEARIGHT PARK
907 Slaughter Ln.
Austin
512/440-5150
This 344-acre park creates a large facility for the South Austin area, comparable to Zilker Park in downtown Austin. The park contains a picnic pavilion, volleyball courts, a disc golf

---

T I P

Thousands of people gather along the shores of Town Lake for the Fourth of July fireworks. If the crowd keeps you away, you can catch sight of the skyful of rockets and flares from along Mo-Pac Expressway (Loop 1) along the lake, and even catch glimpses from the Barton Creek Mall parking lots.

---

course, a nature interpretation center, baseball field, basketball and tennis courts, soccer field, 1.5 miles of hiking and bicycle trails, an equestrian center and a two-mile equestrian trail, a model airplane field, and a fully accessible fishing pier on Slaughter Creek. Hours: Daily 5 a.m.–10 p.m. (Southwest Austin)

MAYFIELD PARK
3505 W. 35th St.
Austin
512/327-5437
This 22-acre park next to Laguna Gloria Art Museum, on Barrow Brook Cove at Lake Austin, is also a preserve. Grounds include gardens and lily ponds, peacocks and hens, and trails meander among them through woods and over creek bridges and foot stones. On display is an early 1900s home representative of subur-

ban lake cottage retreats during the turn of the century. Allison Mayfield, chairman of the Railroad Commission and Texas secretary of state, purchased the 23-acre property in 1909 as a summer and weekend retreat for his family. His daughter Mary Frances married University of Texas History Department Chairman Milton Gutsch. The couple designed gardens and received peacocks as gifts from friends. The park was left to the City of Austin in 1972, and descendants of the first peacocks strut through the park today. (Northwest Austin)

McKINNEY FALLS STATE PARK
7102 Scenic Loop
Austin
512/243-1643
This 641-acre state park is located just 13 miles southeast of the Capitol. Activities include a 4.5-mile hike, bike,

Acres and Acres of Developed Parkland

The Operations Division of the Austin Parks and Recreation Department provides maintenance and repair to all parks, recreation facilities, and other city-owned land. More than 3,000 acres of developed parkland are maintained at the present time, and over 14,000 total acres of parkland have been acquired for future development. The Operations Division provides a one-call-does-all number, 512/480-3036, to report a problem with any park or facility, as well as to reserve any of the popular park areas for group activities. The Urban Forestry Program provides many public, tree-related activities such as tree planting, maintenance, and horticulture. The forestry program also provides both education and suppression techniques in Austin's battle against oak wilt, which plagues the beautiful oaks native to the area. Forestry also trims branches causing traffic problems.

T I P

If you want to understand how committed the Austin community is to preserving nature, listen in on a discussion about saving, say, the black-capped vireo, the golden-cheeked warbler, or the endangered Barton Springs salamander. There's often a fierce battle raging between the environmentalists and the developers, and the former often win.

and nature trail (booklet available), fishing, picnicking, camping, and viewing wildlife such as white-tailed deer, raccoons, squirrels, and armadillos. There's bird-watching, too. The mountaintop park is 775 feet above sea level, and there's a shade structure and picnic tables on the bluff overlooking Lake Austin. It's the highest scenic spot (you'll climb 99 steps) for viewing Austin and the surrounding Hill Country. Hours: Daily 8 a.m.–10 p.m. $2 per person. (East Austin)

PEASE PARK
1100 Kingbury St.
Austin

Located on Shoal Creek along Lamar Boulevard, Pease was the first city park, dedicated in 1876 by Governor Pease. One of the city parks with a picnic area for large groups, it has a three-mile hike and bike trail, swimming pool and wading pool, basketball and volleyball courts, picnic facilities, play equipment, children's playground, and rest rooms. It is popular for informal volleyball and softball games. If you need play equipment, you must reserve it in advance by contacting Austin Parks and Recreation, 200 South Lamar Boulevard, 512/499-6700. (North Austin)

SLAUGHTER CREEK
METROPOLITAN PARK
507 W. Slaughter Ln.
Austin

Slaughter Creek Park has 546 acres ideal for soccer, bicycling, and rollerblading. The park is the headquarters for the Southwest Soccer Complex and the Veloway Bicycle Course. There are also facilities for basketball, volleyball, and picnics, as well as an 18-hole disc golf course, a mile of hike

Bluebonnets on Town Lake Greenbelt, p. 129

Austin CVB

Town Lake Metropolitan Park is also the home of Austin's beloved Auditorium Shores, a terraced amphitheater offering a Summer Concert Series and the Austin Symphony Independence Day Concert. The latter draws thousands, creating quite a traffic jam—locals have learned to come early to get a place anywhere close to catch the grand Fourth of July finale of Tchaikovsky's booming 1812 Overture and the magnificent fireworks display that immediately follows.

and bike trails, play equipment, and rest rooms. (Southwest Austin)

TOWN LAKE
METROPOLITAN PARK
Along the Colorado River
Tom Miller Dam
to U.S. 183 Bridge
Austin
This metropolitan park includes 509 acres of parkland along the banks of the Colorado River from the Tom Miller Dam on Red Bud Trail to the Longhorn Dam. The park contains 10 miles of jogging and bicycle trails surrounded by trees and greenery. An athlete's paradise, Town Lake has 17 ballfields for baseball, football, soccer, and rugby, as well as facilities for both team and performance rowing and canoeing. Other facilities include a swimming pool, picnic areas, a

playscape, and a boat ramp. (Downtown and Southwest Austin)

WALNUT CREEK
METROPOLITAN PARK
12138 N. Lamar Blvd.
Austin
512/837-4500
This park is considered an athlete's treat. Home to the Havins Softball Complex, the park features three ballfields, a swimming pool and bathhouse, basketball, volleyball, and multiuse courts, a playscape, and a hike and bike trail along Walnut Creek. The 294-acre park also has concessions. (Northwest Austin)

WILD BASIN
WILDERNESS PRESERVE
805 N. Capital of Texas Hwy.
Austin

T I P

Neighborhood parks are generally close enough to area residents to be accessible by foot or by bicycle. Traditional recreational facilities such as children's playscapes, sports courts, open play areas, swimming pools, and picnicking facilities are usually provided.

Top Ten Park Activities for Children

by Sally Scott, Texas professional home child-care representative

1. Climb the fire escape at **Zilker Park Playscape**, Zilker Park.
2. Hike along **Shoal Creek**.
3. See the owls and walk the nature trail at the **Austin Nature and Science Center**, 301 Nature Center Dr., 512/327-8180.
4. Play "Frisbee Golf" at **Pease Park**, W. 24th St.
5. Try fishing at **Northwest Park**, Shoal Creek at North Park.
6. Climb the rocks by **Lakewood Park** along Bull Creek.
7. Explore the rocks and see the peacocks at **Mayfield Park**, 3505 W. 35th St., 512/327-5437.
8. Enjoy the view from the top of **Mount Bonnell**, 3800 Mount Bonnell Rd.
9. Go to the playscape in **Garrison Park** in South Austin.
10. Picnic, wade, or enjoy the playscape at the **Stacy Park Hike and Bike Trail** in South Austin.

512/327-7622
These 227 acres of beautiful Hill Country were set aside in the mid-1970s to preserve the land through active management, nature education, and research. Operated with the help of trained volunteers, about four miles of trails pass through woodland, grassland, and streamside habitats. Wild Basin is home to some threatened and endangered species of plants, animals, and birds like the golden-cheeked warbler and the black-capped vireo, as well as hundreds of both common and unique species. Hours: Open daily from sunrise to sunset. (Southwest Austin)

WOOLDRIDGE SQUARE
900 Guadalupe St.
Austin
This bright green square with a charming white gazebo is set in the middle of downtown on Guadalupe between 9th and 10th Streets. It's one of four parks deeded in the original city plan when Edwin Waller came to survey the city. It has been the scene of countless weddings and political rallies, and sometimes the city council is sworn in here. (Downtown Austin)

ZILKER PARK
2100 Barton Springs Rd.
Austin
512/476-9044
Downtown on Town Lake, Zilker is one of Austin's most popular parks. Originally the site of temporary Franciscan missions in 1730, the 349-acre park along the shores of the lake was once used by Native Americans as a gathering place. One of its most attractive features is Barton Springs Pool

Walkers, joggers, and mountain bikers all take advantage of the more than 18 miles of well-surfaced scenic trails and 14 miles of natural surface trails in Austin. But there are rules and regulations governing their use. Bicycles may be ridden on the trails, but no motorized vehicles are permitted. Keep to the right unless passing, pass on the left, and use a verbal warning when it seems necessary. The fastest must give way to the slow: Cyclists must yield to joggers, joggers must yield to walkers, and dogs must be controlled. There is a leash law, and it is enforced.

(whose waters were once used by early Austinites as power for several mills). The springs rise from a limestone strata of the Balcones Fault, formed millions of years ago when the Hill Country uplifted to form the Edwards Plateau. The clear springs produce a minimum of 12 million gallons to more than 90 million gallons in any 24-hour period. The swimming pool is more than 300 yards long, and the water varies from 66 to 70 degrees, keeping Austinites pretty cool nowadays as a primary recreational facility for the entire city. Zilker Gardens in the park includes the Oriental Garden, a meditation trail, and the famous Rose Garden, as well as a Swedish log cabin dating from the 1840s; there's also a fine Garden Center. (South Austin)

GREENBELTS

Austin has beautiful greenbelts, parks that follow rivers, creeks, and scenic ravines. These are areas of natural beauty that provide a diversity of recreation, including walking, hiking, jogging, running, bicycling, and even rock climbing. The jewel in the crown is the Barton Creek Greenbelt, an eight-mile-long hiking trail that makes you forget you're in a city. Greenbelt

sizes vary, depending on the location as well as the size and length of the natural feature—river, creek, ravine— they follow. Since almost no maintenance is provided for these natural areas, it's important to pack out what you take in to preserve the beauty of the greenbelts.

BARTON CREEK GREENBELT
Scottish Woods Trail, off Loop 360
Capital of Texas Hwy.
Austin
512/327-5478
Located less than two miles from downtown, this single-track trail is Austin's most accessible, and it offers 7³/4 miles of wooded, beautiful scenery for a quick escape from the daily grind. Access the greenbelt from Scottish Woods Trail, off Loop 360, a mile north of Mo-Pac. The greenbelt also can be accessed from several other locations. The closest to downtown is Zilker Park, west on Barton Springs Road to the park. The trailhead is located by Barton Springs Pool. Another access is south of Mo-Pac at Barton Skyway. Exit and drive to the end of the street. Trail access is across the street from the Stop and Go convenience store. The natural surface is rocky in spots. Be sure to take water as there are no drinking fountains on the trail. Call for trail

conditions in bad weather. (Southwest Austin)

SHOAL CREEK GREENBELT
North side of Town Lake between Guadalupe St. and Lamar Blvd.
Austin
This three-mile trail goes north to 38th Street, passing Duncan Park, Pease Park, and Bailey Park, winding up at Seider's Spring Park. (North Austin)

TOWN LAKE GREENBELT
Loop 1, Mo-Pac Bridge to
S. First St.
Austin
A popular trail where Austinites come to walk, jog, and enjoy the beauty of the city lines the scenic shores on the north and south sides of Town Lake. The best view of the downtown skyline can be seen from the south side of Town Lake. (Downtown and South Austin)

GARDENS

THE COTTAGE GARDENS
AT MAYFIELD PARK
2704 Macken
Austin
512/327-5437
Patterned after the cottage gardens of England, the Cottage Gardens at Mayfield Park are composed of small beds divided by narrow paths. Flowers, vegetables, and herbs are planted in an informal manner and shaded by Mexican plum and peach trees. More than 30 beds of randomly mixed flowers can be seen. Each provide color, texture, and fragrance year-round. Jonquils, pinks, lilies, roses, and honeysuckle, which require less attention than more exotic flora, are among the hearty plants found at Mayfield Park. Rock gardens, too, sport multitiered flower beds of native plants and wildflowers. (Northwest Austin)

LADY BIRD JOHNSON
WILDFLOWER RESEARCH CENTER
4801 La Crosse Ave.
Austin
512/292-4100
Formerly the National Wildflower Research Center, this center is unique in its focus on native plants, resource conservation, and ecologically sensitive design. The center, created by Lady Bird Johnson in 1982 as part of a national beautification project, will give you an eyeful of natural beauty; this is the only institution in the nation dedicated exclusively to conserving and promoting the use of plants native to North America, including 75 species of wildflowers. The 42-acre site includes numerous research display gardens, landscaped areas, theme gardens, preserved woodlands, and natural grasslands. Hours: Tue–Sun 9–5:30. $3.50 adults, $2 students and seniors, $1 children ages 18 mos.–5 years. (Southwest Austin)

ZILKER BOTANICAL GARDEN
2220 Barton Springs Rd.
Austin
512/477-8672
There are seven separate areas to be explored in Zilker Botanical Garden. It all began in October 1954, when seven Austin Garden Clubs petitioned the City of Austin for permission to build a garden center on city property. The City Council allocated space in Zilker Park, and today the center is the site of 45 to 50 garden club meetings each month.

Xeriscape Demonstration Garden: Displaying more than 50 native and low–water-use trees, shrubs, ground covers, and wildflowers, the garden is

Zilker Botanical Garden, p. 129

© Eleanor S. Morris

a showcase of the seven principles of xeriscape design. These are soil improvement, use of mulch, limited lawn areas, native and low–water-use plants, efficient irrigation, and low maintenance.

Cactus and Succulent Garden: In this collection of mostly native West Texas cactus and succulents, the major blooming period is from mid-April to mid-May. These blooming cacti are a wonderful sight.

Isamu Taniguchi Oriental Garden: The unique garden strikes a delicate balance between water and plants, materials that descend in a series of waterfalls, water-lily ponds, and handmade oriental lanterns. Cherry trees bloom mid-March to mid-April, and water lilies bloom mid-June to October, giving soft color to the garden almost all summer. The area was contributed to the Zilker Botanical Garden by Taniguchi, who worked without salary or restrictions as he spent 18 months transforming three acres of rough caliche hillside into this peaceful garden. There is an authentic teahouse in the garden.

Mabel Davis Rose Garden: This is one of the special beauties of the botanical garden. You can wander among beds of roses of every color, ranging from the latest All-America Rose Society award winners to the antique shrub roses of the Republic of Texas collection. There are two special blooming times: April to June and October.

Herb and Fragrance Garden: Dozens of culinary and fragrant plants for visitors to scratch, sniff, and feel are planted in raised beds.

Hamilton Parr Memorial Azalea Garden: Azaleas bloom in Austin in March and April, and no more brilliantly than in these beautifully landscaped azalea beds surrounding a shaded flagstone patio. Nearby, a brook bubbles from a small pond.

Douglas Blachly Butterfly Trail: Local flowers and plants that attract numerous species of Texas butterflies have been placed along this trail. Visitors can view Austin's attractive butterflies and migrating species as well. (South Austin)

© Permenter and Bigley

9

SHOPPING

Vintage clothing to couture, imported coffees to Texas-made crafts, antiques to trendy furniture—no matter what you're seeking, one of Austin's many stores undoubtedly offers it.

Many Austin shops reflect the relaxed lifestyle of the city. Downtown, several shopping districts are filled with funky boutiques, used clothing stores, and unique gift emporiums. Modern malls offer high-end and mass-market shopping for national brands and designer labels on the fringes of the city limits.

SHOPPING DISTRICTS

Shopping West End

As Sixth Street winds beyond the nightlife district and crosses Lamar Boulevard, the atmosphere moves from funky to fine, evolving from hip T-shirt joints to highbrow fashion establishments and gift boutiques.

At the intersection of Sixth and Lamar, some of Austin's largest retail operations have recently sprung to life.

Farther west, the West End offers plenty of excellent shopping in specialty stores sprinkled with a selection of fine restaurants.

COFFEE EXCHANGE
1200 W. Sixth St.
Austin
512/474-5300

It's worth a visit here just to enjoy the heavenly scent of the world's best brews. Coffees, along with teas, wines, champagnes, cheese, and chocolates, are the specialties of this boutique, which also produces gift baskets. Stop in for an espresso, latte, or just a jolt of java. Sandwiches and bagels also available. Hours: Mon–Sat 6:30 a.m.–9 p.m., Sun 6:30 a.m.–4 p.m. (Downtown Austin)

EMERALDS
624 Lamar Blvd.

Top Ten Antique Stores in Austin
by Elizabeth Huber, knowledgeable collector of fine antiques

1. **Whit Hanks Antiques**, 1009 W. Sixth St., 512/478-2101.

2. **Chantal's Antique and Design**, Barton Creek Mall, 2901 Capital of Texas Hwy., 512/328-6376. Also at Northcross Mall, 2525 W. Anderson Ln., 512/451-5705.

3. **1776 House Antiques**, 5530 Burnet Rd., 512/453-6355.

4. **Austin Auction Company**, 8425 Anderson Mill Rd., 512/258-5479.

5. **Attal Galleries**, 3310 Red River St., 512/476-3634.

6. **Antique Marketplace**, 5350 Burnet Rd., 512/452-1000.

7. **L'Elysee Antiques**, 5603 Adams, 512/459-1727.

8. **Austin House Antiques**, 2041 S. Lamar Blvd., 512/445-2599.

9. **Fantastic Finds**, Antique Mall of Texas, 1601 S. I-35, Round Rock (15 miles north of Austin), 512/218-4290.

10. **The Antique Outlet Center**, 4200 I-35, 800/965-8333.

Austin
512/476-4496
This high-priced women's clothing boutique also sells jewelry, house gifts, and stationery. Look for New York fashions, footwear, and furnishings for those with discriminating tastes and discretionary income. Hours: Mon–Sat 10–10, Sun 12–7. (Downtown Austin)

FORTNEY'S ARTFUL HOME FURNISHINGS
1116 W. Sixth St.
Austin
512/495-6505
Check out the one-of-a-kind furnishings in this eclectic shop that combines lodgepole furniture with traditional, Southwest, and contemporary items. Massive couches and bedsteads are accessorized with

imported masks, artist-produced fountains, and sculptures for the home. Hours: Mon–Sat 10–6, Sun 11–4. (Downtown Austin)

NECESSITIES AND TEMPTATIONS
1202-A W. Sixth St.
Austin
512/473-8334
This shop is a good stop for those looking for a Texas souvenir in the form of Texas trinkets, Southwestern jewelry, coffee cups, and more. Texas games test your knowledge of the Lone Star State. Hours: Mon–Sat 10–6, Sun 11–3. (Downtown Austin)

PECAN STREET EMPORIUM
1122 W. Sixth St.
Austin
512/477-4900
Fine European imports, from Swiss

music boxes to German nutcrackers, fill this charming gift shop. Pecan Street claims to have Austin's largest selection of German collectibles. You'll also find Christmas decorations year-round, as well as stationery, stamps, stickers, and more for small gift purchases or just to treat yourself. Hours: Mon–Sat 10–6, Sun 11–4. (Downtown Austin)

WHIT HANKS ANTIQUES AND DECORATIVE ARTS
1009 W. Sixth St.
Austin
512/478-2101
Actually a compendium of 50 shops, this dealership offers American, European, and Oriental antiques including furniture, lamps, china, collectibles, and even architectural features such as paneling, leaded glass windows, doors, lighting, and ironwork. This shop is an excellent place to visit if you're looking for an unusual housewarming gift or just some accessories to make your own abode a little

different. Just down the street, look for a Whit Hanks consignment shop next to TravelFest. Hours: Mon–Sat 10–6, Sun 1–5. (Downtown Austin)

WHOLE FOODS MARKET
Sixth St. and Lamar Blvd.
Austin
512/476-1206
This funky grocery store is a dream for those seeking health foods, organic produce, and anything herbal, from skin treatments to teas to health remedies. You'll also find a large array of wines and cheeses as well as a good inventory of beers from around the globe. And if you get hungry, you'll find a small café ready with healthy sandwiches, soups, snacks, and a juice bar. Hours: Daily 8 a.m.–11 p.m. (Downtown Austin)

Shopping the Drag

For a true Austin shopping experience, consider an afternoon on the Drag, the stretch of Guadalupe Street

Whole Foods Market

© Permenter and Bigley

that runs adjacent to the University of Texas campus. This strip is peppered with shops aimed at the college student, from bookstores to cool clothing outlets.

Unfortunately, the Drag has always had a reputation as a hangout, and runaways from across the nation come to live on its streets. Panhandling is illegal but not unusual.

ANTONE'S RECORD STORE
2928 Guadalupe St.
Austin
512/322-0660
Located directly across the street from Antone's (see Chapter 12 Nightlife), this mega-music store features a little bit of everything, plus some hard-to-find releases. Work by local musicians makes up part of the inventory. Hours: Mon–Sat 11–11, Sun 12–5. (North Austin)

THE CADEAU
2316 Guadalupe St.
Austin
512/477-7276
Look for men's and women's fashions at this trendy store that sells china, crystal, linens, jewelry, home furnishings, and cookware. Often named the top gift store in Austin, this shop has something for everyone. Hours: Mon–Sat 10–6:30. (North Austin)

NOMADIC NOTIONS
2426 Guadalupe St.
Austin
512/478-6200
Beads from around the globe fill this funky store, which is a dream come true for those creative enough to produce their own jewelry. This eclectic shop also sells imported fashions and a few home accessories such as statuettes and wall hangings, many from Indonesia.

Hours: Mon–Sat 11–7, Sun 12–5. (North Austin)

RENAISSANCE MARKET
23rd and Guadalupe Sts.
Austin
Tucked right off the Drag, this open-air market is filled with the work of Austin artisans, who sell handmade jewelry, woodcrafts, tie-dyed shirts, glasswork, toys, pottery, and more one-of-a-kind items. This market claims to be Texas' only continuously operated open-air arts and crafts market. The number of artists varies by season, reaching a crescendo in the weeks before the holidays and a low point during the Christmas break, when most UT students have left town. Hours: Daily 8 a.m.–10 p.m. (North Austin)

TOWER RECORDS
2402 Guadalupe St.
Austin
512/478-5711
This institution is easy to spot: Just look for the two-story mural. New releases, specialty recordings, and local artists are found throughout the store's large inventory. Hours: Daily 9 a.m.–12 a.m. (North Austin)

TOY JOY
2900 Guadalupe St.
Austin
512/320-0090
Funky playthings for the adult child make this a favorite UT shopping spot. Stickers, stamps, figurines, action heroes, and just plain silly items appeal to kids of all ages. It's not everywhere in Austin you can find toy boxing nuns. Hours: Sun–Thu 10–10, Fri–Sat 10–12 a.m. (North Austin)

URBAN OUTFITTERS
2406 Guadalupe St.

Austin
512/472-1621

Clothes with an attitude fill the racks of this trendy two-story shop. Clothing and accessories for fashion-conscious Generation Xers are offered along with home accessories ranging from beaded doors to beanbag chairs. Hours: Mon–Sat 10–9, Sun 12–6. (North Austin)

WHEATSVILLE FOOD CO-OP
3101 Guadalupe St.
Austin
512/478-2667

Owned by consumers, this co-op carries both traditional and natural foods. A deli offers vegetarian items if all this shopping makes you hungry. Membership in the co-op costs $10 a year. Hours: Daily 9 a.m.–11 p.m.; deli closes at 9 p.m. (North Austin)

Shopping Kerbey Lane and Jefferson Square

This charming enclave of boutiques is located just off Austin's medical district on West 35th Street between Kerbey Lane and Jefferson Street. It is lined with homes converted to shops, each filled with unique gift items, collectibles, or fashions. Jefferson Square is a small open-air center with high-priced shops and fine items.

THE GARDEN ROOM
1601 W. 39th St.
Jefferson Square
Austin
512/458-5407

Fashion-conscious Austinites can select from faux reptile bags, silk charmeuse scarves, designer togs,

---

Top Shopping Destinations

Favorite destinations for Austin shoppers are the factory outlets just south of the capital city in the community of San Marcos. Take I-35 south to exit 200 for the **Prime Outlets***, 888/GO-OUTLETS, featuring over 100 shops that sell direct from the factory. Luggage, shoes, leather goods, outdoor gear, china, kitchen goods, and other specialties are offered for sale. Stores are open daily.*

Just across the road, the **Tanger Factory Outlet Center***, 512/396-7444, tempts shoppers with over 30 shops that feature name-brand designers and manufacturers. Housewares, footwear, home furnishings, leather goods, perfumes, and books are offered in Reebok, American Eagle, Levi's, and other outlet shops. Stores are open Monday through Saturday from 9 to 9 and Sunday from 11 to 6.*

and home accessories in this upscale boutique. Hours: Mon–Sat 10–5:30. (North Austin)

KERBEY LANE DOLL SHOPPE
3706 Kerbey Ln.
Austin
512/452-7086
Whether you're looking for a doll as a children's gift or as a collector's investment, you'll find plenty to select from in this home with room after room of dolls. Antique and modern dolls fill shelves and display cases, along with doll-related accessories and stuffed toys. This shop also buys and repairs dolls. Hours: Mon–Sat 10–5. (North Austin)

KERBEY LANE DOLLHOUSES AND MINIATURES
3503 Kerbey Ln.
Austin
512/454-HAUS
You'll feel like Gulliver in this Lilliputian world of tiny furnishings and accessories designed to help collectors design and furnish miniature versions of their dream homes. Hours: Mon–Sat 10–5. (North Austin)

POSSESSIONS GIFT GALLERY
1600 W. 35th St.
Austin
512/302-1132
Unique gift items, from glass picture frames to Indonesian ornaments to funky jewelry, fill this shop. Hours: Mon–Fri 10–6, Sat 10–5. (North Austin)

SECOND TIME AROUND
3704 Crawford
Austin
512/451-6845
Recently named the best resale boutique in Austin, this consignment store offers fine fashion and everyday wear at affordable prices just steps

from Kerbey Lane. Four rooms filled with seasonal wear make this shop a favorite stop for budget shoppers with an eye for fashion. Hours: Tue–Fri 10–6, Sat 10–5. (North Austin)

TRENDS AND TRADITIONS JEWELERS
3707 Kerbey Ln.
Austin
512/450-1121
Owners Cathy and Monte Franzetti create custom jewelry using fine diamonds and gemstones. You'll also find jewelry that's easy on any budget, with silver imports, amber, and more. Hours: Mon–Sat 10–5. (North Austin)

Shopping South Congress Avenue

Funky collectibles, Mexican imports, out-of-this-world costumes, and a truly flippant Austin atmosphere make this an eclectic district for those looking for something a little different. Park and walk from shop to shop.

ALLEN BOOTS
1525 S. Congress Ave.
Austin
512/447-1413
If you want to dress like a cowboy or even an urban version of one, here's your chance. Along with boots, this shop will have you moseying out in a cowboy hat, Western shirt, jeans, and, of course, the obligatory Western rodeo belt buckle. Hours: Mon–Sat 9–8, Sun 12–6. (South Austin)

ANTIGUA
1508 S. Congress Ave.
Austin
512/912-1475
Shop for imported items such as wood carvings, handcarved furniture, primitives, silver, colonial art,

Top Ten Places for Teens to Shop
by Lauren Bigley, Age 17

1. **Electric Ladyland**, 1506 S. Congress Ave., 512/444-2002.
2. **Limbo**, 5015 Duval St., 512/302-4446.
3. **Half-Price Books**, 2110 Guadalupe St., 512/451-4463.
4. **Bookpeople**, 603 N. Lamar Blvd., 512/472-5050.
5. **Urban Outfitters**, 2406 Guadalupe St., 512/472-1621.
6. **Tower Records**, 2402 Guadalupe St., 512/478-5711.
7. **Old Navy Clothing Co.**, 9607 Research Blvd., 512/346-1991.
8. **Barnes and Noble**, 10000 Research Blvd., 512/418-8985.
9. **Nomadic Notions**, 2426 Guadalupe St., 512/478-6200.
10. **Renaissance Market**, 23rd and Guadalupe Sts., 512/397-1456.

santos, tin mirrors, and Mexican antiques at this delightful store. Hours: Tue–Sat 10–6:30, Sun 12–6. (South Austin)

ARMADILLO ANTIQUES AND JEWELRY
1712 S. Congress Ave.
Austin
512/443-7552
Whatever you're looking for is probably here: The question is will you ever find it? Display cases overflow with antique and imported silver jewelry, walls sag with innumerable displays, and tables creak with figurines and collectibles. Hours: Daily 10–5. (South Austin)

LUCY IN DISGUISE WITH DIAMONDS/ELECTRIC LADYLAND
1506 S. Congress Ave.
Austin
512/444-2002
This store defines funky with an inventory of vintage clothing and costumes. Dress—for parties or just to portray your personality—in everything from

mariachi outfits to French maid uniforms to '70s disco polyester. Along with rentals, the shop also sells clothing, shoes, hats, unique jewelry, and costume accessories. Hours: Mon–Fri 11–7, Sat 10–7, Sun 12–5. (South Austin)

OFF THE WALL
1704 S. Congress Ave.
Austin
512/445-4701
If you're looking for a collectible portraying any animal—from armadillo to zebra—look here first. Ceramics, wooden boxes, wall plaques, and more, all featuring animals, make up much of the shop, along with some antiques, handmade wooden clocks, and home accessories. Hours: Mon–Sat 10–6:30, Sun 12–6. (South Austin)

RUE'S ANTIQUES, INC.
1500 S. Congress Ave.
Austin
512/442-1775
Whether you are shopping for an antique movie poster or an oak

wardrobe, make a stop at this antiques shop with a varied and changing inventory. Hours: Mon–Sat 10–6, Sun 12–6. (South Austin)

TERRA TOYS
1708 S. Congress Ave.
Austin
512/445-4489
This toy shop's motto is "If you can't play with it, why bother?" The multiple rooms of this fun store invite play from shoppers of all ages. Imported dolls, toddlers' indestructible toys, stamps, stickers, gift wrap, books, and more fill the shelves. Hours: Mon–Sat 10–7, Sun 12–6. (South Austin)

TINHORN TRADERS
1608 S. Congress Ave.
Austin
512/444-3644
This small store specializes in architectural details and imported housewares. Look at its collection of oversized planters and other purchases to make your home unique. Hours: Tue–Sat 10:30–6. (South Austin)

UNCOMMON OBJECTS
1512 S. Congress Ave.
Austin
512/442-4000
Yes, you will find truly uncommon objects in this shop where you can easily spend an hour or two checking out the architectural details such as old doors and gate lamps, the clothing that harks back to the '40s and '50s, and antique imports from south of the border. Hours: Mon–Fri 10:30–6, Sat 12–5. (South Austin)

Shopping West Lynn

The quiet mood of the residential neighborhood of West Lynn, west of

the Capitol, is reflected in the laid-back shops of this district. Enjoy some shopping, then a snack at a genuine drug-store fountain.

GARNER AND SMITH ANTIQUES, ETC.
1013 West Lynn St.
Austin
512/474-1518
Fine home furnishings, china, books, and antiques fill this elegant shop. A home behind the main store houses more casual furniture including tables, wardrobes, dressers, and bookcases. Hours: Tue–Sat 11–5:30, Sun 2–4. (Downtown Austin)

NAU ENFIELD DRUG
1115 West Lynn St.
Austin
512/476-1221
This old-fashioned drug store is a favorite with Austinites, whether they're looking for a birthday card or cosmetics. The real draw, though, is the soda fountain, which serves up breakfast and lunch as well as tasty malts and sundaes. Hours: Mon–Fri 7:30 a.m.–9 p.m., Sat 8 a.m.–9 p.m., Sun 10 a.m.–6 p.m. (Downtown Austin)

BOOKSTORES AND NEWSSTANDS

BOOKPEOPLE
603 N. Lamar Blvd.
Austin
512/472-5050
This mega-store calls itself the largest bookstore in the U.S., spanning four floors with over 300,000 titles, 2,000 magazines and newspapers, and plenty of space just to hang out and browse. New Age books, music, and gifts are a specialty. An espresso bar fills the first floor with the scent of

fresh brew. Hours: Daily 9 a.m.–11 p.m. (Downtown Austin)

HALF PRICE BOOKS RECORDS MAGAZINES
2110 Guadalupe St.
Austin
512/451-4463
Half Price Books is one of Austin's most tempting places to stop and browse. An Austin institution, this sprawling bookstore carries all types of reading and listening materials. Shop for some new or used books or sell some of your old ones. Hours: Mon–Sat 10–10, Sun 12–9. (North Austin)

TRAVELFEST
1214 W. Sixth St.
Austin
512/469-7906
The creator of Bookstop founded this store, which combines travel books, travel gadgets, and a travel agency under one roof. Separate rooms are dedicated to different parts of the globe with videos, guides, and maps to plan any trip. Travel magazines and gadgets designed to do everything from purify water to hide money are located in the front of the store, alongside a full-service travel agency. Hours: Daily 9–9. (Downtown Austin)

UNIVERSITY CO-OP
2244 Guadalupe St.
Austin
512/476-7211

For over 90 years, this bookstore has supplied UT students with all the essentials. Over 70,000 titles, Texas souvenirs and clothing, and more can be found here; there's a complete camera department on the second floor. The main floor offers UT and Texas souvenirs, or head upstairs for the popular book collection. Textbooks are located in the basement. Hours: Mon– Fri 8:30–7:30, Sat 9:30–6, Sun 11–5. (North Austin)

OTHER NOTABLE STORES

AUSTIN COUNTRY FLEA MARKET
9500 U.S. 290 East
Austin
512/928-2795
If you're into flea markets, here's a mega-market with over 500 booths. You'll find jewelry, clothing, furniture, records, tools, and more at this combination shopping extravaganza and festival. Hours: Sat–Sun 10 a.m.–6 p.m. (East Austin)

CALLAHAN'S GENERAL STORE
501 U.S. 183
Austin
512/385-3452
Like a true general store, this sprawling store has just about everything a person could want. Western wear, saddles, boots, household items, and, yes, even chicks and ducks make up the extensive inventory. Hours: Mon–Sat 8–6. (East Austin)

TRIVIA

Austin has the highest per capita bookstore sales of the U.S.'s 50 largest cities.

Central Market

CENTRAL MARKET
4001 N. Lamar Blvd.
Austin
512/206-1000
More than a mere grocery store, Central Market is an international smorgasbord of produce, wines, meats, fish, and seasonings from around the globe.

Regularly scheduled cooking classes offer visitors the chance to learn techniques from pros. Hours: Daily 7 a.m.–10 p.m. (North Austin)

CLARKSVILLE POTTERY AND GALLERIES
4001 N. Lamar Blvd.
Austin
512/454-9079
Shop for handmade stoneware, from bowls to goblets to decorative ware, at this fine crafts gallery.

Another location can be found in The Arboretum market. It is convenient for shoppers in northwest Austin. Hours: Mon–Wed, Fri–Sat 10–6, Thu 10–8, Sun 12–6. (North Austin)

MITCHIE'S FINE BLACK ART GALLERY AND BOOKSTORE
5312 Airport Blvd.
Austin
512/323-6901
African American, Caribbean, and African arts and collectibles fill this eclectic shop, which also sells books and all types of materials related to black art and history. Framing is available. Hours: Mon–Sat 10–7, Sun 1–6. (North Austin)

TRAVIS COUNTY FARMERS' MARKET
6701 Burnet Rd.
Austin
512/454-1002
Look for homegrown produce and homemade products at this 3½-acre market. Start with a walk through the 5,000-square-foot barn for a look at Texas antiques and primitive furnishings, then shop for homegrown fruits and vegetables. Barbecue, tamales, soups, sandwiches, and fresh-baked goods are also available. Hours: Daily 7 a.m.–6 p.m. (North Austin)

MAJOR DEPARTMENT STORES

DILLARD'S DEPARTMENT STORE
Barton Creek Square Mall
2901 Capital of Texas Hwy.
Austin
512/327-6100
This extensive department store sells clothing, jewelry, perfumes, housewares, gift items, and more. Other locations are found at Highland Mall in far north Austin and Lakeline Mall in northwest Austin. Hours: Mon–Sat 10–9, Sun 12–6. (Southwest Austin)

FOLEY'S DEPARTMENT STORE
Highland Mall
6001 Airport Blvd.
Austin
512/329-2238
Shop for fine housewares, women's and men's fashions, fine and costume jewelry, cosmetics, and more at this Texas-based department store. Hours:

The Arboretum shopping center

© Permenter and Bigley

Mon–Thu 10–9:30, Fri 10–10, Sat 9 a.m.–10 p.m., Sun 11–7. (North Austin)

MERVYN'S DEPARTMENT STORE
Lakeline Mall
Austin
512/219-0088
Moderately priced clothing for the entire family as well as limited housewares, jewelry, and accessories draw shoppers to this two-story department store. Other locations include Brodie Oaks Shopping Center, 4040 S. Lamar Blvd., in south Austin and 8000 Research Boulevard in far north Austin. Hours: Mon–Sat 9:30–9:30, Sun 10–8. (Northwest Austin)

MAJOR SHOPPING MALLS

THE ARBORETUM
10000 Research Blvd.
Austin
512/338-4437
Austin's largest collection of exclusive shops is fun for window shopping when you can't afford the lofty price tags. The open-air mall is Austin's most scenic, dotted with oaks and including a sculpture-filled garden that's home to Blues on the Green, a series of free blues concerts every summer. Hours: Mon–Sat 10–8, Sun 12–5. (Northwest Austin)

BARTON CREEK SQUARE
2901 Capital of Texas Hwy.
Austin
512/327-7040
Austin's largest shopping mall is home to Foley's, JC Penney, Dillard's, Montgomery Ward, Sears, and many specialty shops. Hours: Mon–Sat 10–9, Sun 12–6. (Southwest Austin)

BRODIE OAKS SHOPPING CENTER
4115 S. Loop 360

Capital of Texas Hwy.
Austin
512/474-9900
This open-air shopping center is filled with medium-priced stores such as Mervyn's. Hours: Mon–Sat 10–9, Sun 12–6. (South Austin)

CAPITAL PLAZA SHOPPING CENTER
5400 N. I-35
Austin
One of Austin's original shopping centers, built in 1961, Capital Plaza includes Bealls, Office Max, Montgomery Ward, Toys R Us, Weiner's, and several discount shops. Hours vary by store. (North Austin)

GATEWAY
U.S. 183 North at Loop 360
Capital of Texas Hwy.
Austin
A new addition to the Austin scene, this open-air mall includes Whole Foods, Linen's N Things, Old Navy Clothing Company, TravelFest, CompUSA, and Marie Callender's restaurant. Hours vary by store. (Northwest Austin)

HIGHLAND MALL
6001 Airport Blvd.
Austin
512/451-2920
Over 180 shops in this two-story mall include Foley's, Dillard's, and JC Penney as well as specialty shops selling books, housewares, jewelry, music, and sporting goods. A large food court on the second floor offers fast food, salads, and baked goods. Hours: Mon–Sat 10–9, Sun 12–6. (North Austin)

LAKELINE MALL
11200 Lakeline Mall Dr.
Austin

512/257-SHOP
Austin's newest enclosed mall, this two-story compendium of shops includes Foley's, JC Penney, Sears, Montgomery Ward, Dillard's, a food court, movie theaters, and Austin's first interactive video arcade. Hours: Mon–Sat 10–9, Sun 12–6. (Northwest Austin)

NORTHCROSS MALL
2525 W. Anderson Ln.
Austin
512/451-7466
Perhaps best known as home of Austin's first ice-skating rink, this enclosed mall includes Bealls and Oshman's Super Sports, a food court, and several movie theaters. Hours: Mon–Sat 10–9, Sun 12–5:30. (North Austin)

FACTORY OUTLET CENTERS

DELL FACTORY OUTLET
8801 Research Blvd.
Austin
512/728-5656
Austin's own homegrown computers, designed by Austinite Michael Dell, are sold at substantial discounts. Hours: Mon–Sat 10–6. (North Austin)

HAROLD'S OUTLET BARN
8611 N. Mo-Pac Expwy.
Austin
512/794-9036
Harold's, a San Antonio women's fashion store, offers upscale items at outlet prices. Harold's barn-shaped building is located on the east side of Mo-Pac just south of U.S. 183 or Research Boulevard. Hours: Mon–Fri 10–7, Sat 10–6, Sun 12–6. (North Austin)

NEIMAN MARCUS LAST CALL
Brodie Oaks Shopping Center
4115 S. Capital of Texas Hwy.
Austin
512/447-0701
Yes, you can have haute couture on a budget, thanks to this outlet store for the world-famous, Dallas-based Neiman Marcus store. Clothing discounted 40 to 70 percent. Hours: Mon–Tue 10–6, Wed–Sat 10–7:30, Sun 12–6. (South Austin)

© Permenter and Bigley

10

SPORTS AND RECREATION

Austin has plenty for sports lovers to enjoy, both as participants and observers. Fun comes in many forms, from bicycling to bowling, from disc golfing to day hikes. Many of the outdoor activities revolve around the water, with windsurfing, boating, fishing, and other watersports among the most popular.

In the summer months, Austin really lives up to its nickname of "The River City." Austinites beat the heat on Lake Austin and Lake Travis, happily taking to the water to enjoy swimming, boating, scuba diving, and waterskiing. Weekends on the lake are a central Texas ritual; the activity level of these outings ranges from siesta to fiesta. Note: The map in this chapter shows locations of major sports venues only.

PROFESSIONAL SPORTS

HOCKEY
Austin Ice Bats
Travis County Exposition Center
512/927-PUCK
Austin's first professional sports team is the newly formed Ice Bats, part of the Western Professional Hockey League. The team plays 64 games from mid-October through mid-March and has quickly drawn loyal fans throughout the city eager to learn more about a game new to Austin spectators. (East Austin)

HORSE RACING
Manor Downs
512/272-5581
Quarter horses race from early March through mid-June at this pari-mutuel track located in the community of Manor, just east of Austin. You can try your luck at the simulcast races year-round. Call for post times. (East of map)

Soccer

AUSTIN LONE STARS
12th St. and Lamar Blvd.

Austin
512/335-0427
This semi-pro team plays at House
Park Field, at 12th Street and Lamar
Boulevard. An average of 1,000 fans
frequent every home game. (Downtown Austin)

AMATEUR SPORTS

*The University of Texas is the clos-
est Austin gets to professional
league sports in most fields, and
their play is followed closely by fans
of the Burnt Orange throughout the
city. The Longhorns football team
draws huge crowds to Austin with
every home game at Darrell K.
Royal-Texas Memorial Stadium, formerly Memorial Stadium. During the
winter months, both the Lady Longhorns women's and the Runnin'
Horns men's basketball teams play
at the Frank Erwin Center; the round
venue located just off I-35 is also
used for Austin's largest indoor concerts. The women's UT volleyball
team also serves up a rousing game
during the winter months, usually at
the UT Recreation Sports Center,
followed in the spring by UT baseball at Disch-Falk Field, just east
of I-35.*

UT BASEBALL
512/471-3333
This baseball team plays just east of
I-35 in a newly improved stadium.
Over the years the popular team has
produced many professional players
including pitcher Roger Clements.

UT BASKETBALL, MEN'S
512/471-3333
The Runnin' Horns, participants in the
Big 12 Conference, play a rousing
game at the Frank Erwin Center.

UT BASKETBALL, WOMEN'S
512/471-3333
Lady Longhorns coach Jody Conradt
has brought widespread attention to
this popular team.

UT FOOTBALL
512/471-3333
The Longhorns, part of the Big 12
Conference, have been in the na-
tional spotlight thanks to Heisman
Trophy winner Ricky Williams.

UT VOLLEYBALL, WOMEN'S
512/471-3333
This energetic team has a devoted
following in the city of Austin.

RECREATION

Biking

*Austin offers a network of more than
30 miles of bike trails. Eighteen of
them are on well-surfaced scenic*

TRIVIA

You don't need to listen to
the nightly news to find out
how the Longhorns fared—
just have a look at the
University of Texas Tower.
With every win, the top of
the tower is illuminated with
orange lights. Conference
titles earn orange lights all
over the building, and when
there's a national cham-
pionship, a number "1"
appears in lights down the
side of the building.

Capital Metro buses are equipped with bike racks, so your bike can ride the bus along with you, making it convenient to get to your favorite riding trail. For more information, call 512/474-1200.

paths following natural greenbelts into all areas of the city, making excellent trails available to all. Also, there are an additional 14 miles of natural surface trails to follow, with varied terrain for any level of biker. The hills to the west of Austin are a popular training ground for competitive-level cyclists. All trails have a curfew in effect from 10 p.m. to 5 a.m. No motor vehicles are allowed at any time. Dogs must be controlled; Austin has a leash law enforced by the Austin Park Police (Rangers). For maps of the seven hike and bike trails of Austin, contact the Parks and Recreation Department at 512/499-6700 weekdays from 8 a.m. to 5 p.m.

BARTON CREEK GREENBELT
Some bikers prefer paths that follow picturesque creeks. Here you'll find 7.5 miles of natural surface both east and west of Mo-Pac (Loop 1).

DUNCAN PARK
Eighth–10th Sts. along
Shoal Creek
Austin
The south side of the neighborhood park is outfitted with dirt features to allow motocross riders to jump and perform tricks. (Downtown Austin)

EMMA LONG MOTORCROSS PARK
City Park Rd.
Austin
Located just outside the Emma Long Metropolitan Park, this five-mile motocross park offers intermediate and difficult trails for mountain bikers. (Southwest Austin)

TOWN LAKE GREENBELT
A host of bikers enjoy Town Lake Trail

Bike Rentals

Bike rentals are available at these cycling shops:
A-1 Bikesmith, *4034 Guadalupe St., 512/467-2453*
Bicycle Sport Shop, *13376 Research Blvd., 512/258-7278 and 1426 Toomey Rd., 512/477-3472*
University Schwinn, *2901 N. Lamar Blvd., 512/474-6696*

The Texas Longhorn football team will always hold the last Southwest Conference title.

because of the visual beauty of its 10 miles of granite, gravel, and concrete. Loop A, from Mo-Pac Bridge to Lamar Boulevard, is 2.9 miles; Loop B, Mo-Pac Bridge to South 1st Street, is 4.1 miles.

VELOWAY
Off Slaughter Ln.
Austin
512/480-3032
The Veloway is a 3.1-mile paved asphalt loop used by bicyclists to wind through scenic parkland. Catch the Veloway from behind Bowie High School or from south Loop 1 (Mo-Pac). Open from dawn until dusk. (Southwest Austin)

WALLER CREEK WALKWAY
East of Downtown
Austin
Just east of the main downtown area, Waller Creek Walkway follows the creek from 15th Street to where it flows into Town Lake, ¾ mile of gravel, concrete, and brick surface. The Waterloo Park area, 15th Street south to 10th Street, is a quarter-mile. Lower Waller Creek Development, 10th Street south to Town Lake, is half a mile.

Boating

Motorboats are prohibited on Town Lake, a haven for canoeists and rowers, but watercraft action picks up on Lake Austin. The 22-mile-long lake has four public boat launch sites: Emma Long Metropolitan Park, a 1,150-acre facility on the north side of the lake; Quinlan County Park; Fritz Hughes Park; and the Walsh Boat Landing, next to Tom Miller Dam. Lake Travis is 65 miles long, and more than 3 miles across in some spots, with literally hundreds of coves and inlets along its snakelike boundaries. Much of the land on Travis' shores is controlled by the Lower Colorado River Authority and remains undeveloped, but there are several excellent public parks. On narrow Lake Austin, boaters are required to stay to the right as they proceed on the lake, unless they're picking up a downed waterskier. You must have a Coast Guard–approved personal flotation device for each person on board. Class A and Class 1 motorboat passengers under 13 years of age are required to wear lifejackets.

EMMA LONG METROPOLITAN PARK
City Park Rd.
Austin
512/346-1831
Boat ramps offer easy access into beautiful Lake Austin at this park located 6.2 miles off FM 2222. The park includes a boat dumping station. A 10 p.m. curfew is strictly enforced and gates are locked. Hours: 7 a.m.–10 p.m. daily. $3 per vehicle Mon–Thu, $5 per vehicle Fri–Sun and holidays. (Northwest Austin)

Enjoying Austin's Lakes

Austin is often called the River City, a moniker that aptly describes its longtime connection with the Colorado River. From the river, Austin enjoys two lakes, located back to back and completely within city limits. Lake Austin, 22 miles long, begins at the foot of Lake Travis and flows through the hills surrounding the western part of the city. There's high-priced residential development along the shores, but much of the countryside is still preserved in public parks.

Lake Austin flows into Town Lake, a narrow stretch of water that meanders for five miles through the very heart of downtown Austin. The shoreline is composed of beautifully planted greenbelts, with 15 miles of hike and bike trails, popular with local residents on cool summer evenings. Swimming and motor boating are prohibited, except for canoe and sailboat rentals.

By contrast, Lake Austin is a boater's haven with four public boat launch sites. The most popular of these is located in City Park on the north side of the lake. Besides the ramp, the park contains RV hookups, picnic and camp sites, restrooms, swimming areas, and a bath house.

Several other areas on Lake Austin also provide boaters with public launch facilities. Quinlan County Park, with picnic areas and restrooms, and Fritz Hughes Park, with a picnic area, are both launch sites. The Walsh Boat Landing, next to Tom Miller Dam, has a launch site but no picnic sites or restrooms.

Lake Austin's warm waters and the city's sunny climate attract water sports of every description—from cruisers to windsurfers to waterskiers. Even during busy summer weekends, there's room to get away for a quiet cruise beside the rocky bluffs that line much of the lake. Early morning and evening boaters may be lucky enough to spot a white-tailed deer. There's plenty of color along the banks, too, from the deep blue of the spring bluebonnets to the surprisingly brilliant blossoms of the prickly pear cactus, which clings precariously to the cliffs, seeming to grow out of sheer rock.

Anglers casting their lines in Lake Austin won't be disappointed by the black bass, catfish, perch, white bass, and crappie found in these clear waters. The lake is stocked throughout the year. A Texas fishing license, available through most bait and convenience stores, is required.

T I P

Test your jogging abilities at the annual Capitol 10,000. One of the nation's largest road races, this event draws about 20,000 participants. The race starts at 15th Street and Congress Avenue and winds along the 10K route to Auditorium Shores. The event is generally scheduled for late March; call 512/445-3598 for information.

JUST FOR FUN
6410 Hudson Bend Rd.
Austin
512/266-9710

Ski boats, Jet skis, and pontoon and party boats for groups of up to 150 people are available for rent at this operation at Lake Travis Marina. (West of map)

LAKE AUSTIN YACHT CLUB
2215 Westlake Dr.
Austin
512/327-2110

This harbor offers ski boats, sailboats, pontoon, fishing, and paddle boats by the hour, half day, or full day. Wave runners are also available for rent. (Southwest Austin)

SKIP'S BOAT AND RV RENTALS
4702 Hudson Bend Rd.
Austin
512/266-1446

Ski boats and pontoon boats are available for hourly, daily, and weekly rental, with discounts available for weekday rentals. (West of map)

Bowling Alleys

AMS SHOWPLACE LANES
9514 N. I-35
Austin
512/834-7733

Austin's premier lanes frequently host bowling competitions and tours. Open 24 hours daily. $2.10 before 5:30 p.m., $3.25 after 5:30 p.m; shoe rental $2. (North Austin)

DART BOWL
5700 Grover
Austin
512/452-2518

This is one of Austin's larger family bowling alleys. It offers 32 lanes, 20 of which have bumpers (they help to eliminate gutter balls for small children). The Dart Bowl cafe's enchiladas have been rated the best in Austin by a local paper. The vinyl ceiling and walls give a backdrop effect of a lower ceiling, making the large alley quite cozy feeling. Right at the front door is a little gallery, with a collection of bowling souvenirs such as trophies, clocks, and little bowling figurines. Hours: Sun–Thu 9 a.m.–11 p.m., Fri–Sat 9 a.m.–2 p.m. $2.45 before 6 p.m., $2.95 after 6 p.m.; shoe rental $1.75. (North Austin)

HIGHLAND LANES
8909 Burnet Rd.
Austin
512/458-1215

Hours: Fri–Sat 9:30 a.m.–1 p.m., Sun–Thu 9:30–11. $2.45 before 6 p.m., $2.95 after 6 p.m.; shoe rental $1.60. (North Austin)

Waterskiing on Lake Austin, p. 147

Canoeing

ZILKER PARK BOAT RENTALS
2000 Barton Springs Rd.
Austin
512/478-3852
Enjoy the quiet beauty of Town Lake as you glide through the water in a canoe. Bring an ID to rent canoes. Hours: 11–dusk; weekends only during winter months. $7.75 per hour, $28.50 per day. (Southwest Austin)

Day Hikes

You'll find over 25 miles of hiking trails along the major creeks in town. For a free hiking and biking guide, contact Austin Parks and Recreation, 200 S. Lamar Blvd., 512/499-6700. Austin has several hiking groups that offer regularly scheduled hikes and classes. For classes in hiking, contact the University of Texas Recreational Sports department at 512/471-1093.

BARTON CREEK GREENBELT
3755-B Capital of Texas Hwy.
Austin
Stretching 7¾ miles, this greenbelt is a favorite with hikers as well as mountain bikers. The single-lane dirt walkway can be accessed from the Barton Springs Pool parking lot, Mo-Pac at Barton Skyway, or off Loop 360. (Southwest Austin)

TRIVIA

Austin has a grand total of 11,800 acres of greenbelt—uncultivated land preserved for recreational activities: picnics, jogging, hiking and biking, bird-watching, and kite-flying for the entire community.

Top Ten Places to Hike

by Sheryl Smith-Rodgers, author of *Weekends Away!
Camping and Cooking in Texas State Parks*
(Eakin Press, 1998)

1. **McKinney Falls State Park**, 7102 Scenic Loop, 512/243-1643.
2. **Mount Bonnell**, 3800 Mount Bonnell Rd.
3. **Town Lake hike and bike trail**, Mo-Pac Bridge to S. First St.
4. **Zilker Park** (also Zilker Botanical Gardens and Zilker Nature Preserve), Barton Springs Rd.
5. **Mayfield Park and Preserve**, 3505 W. 35th St., 512/327-5437.
6. **Wild Basin Wilderness Preserve**, 805 N. Capital of Texas Hwy., 512/327-7622.
7. **Barton Creek Greenbelt**, Mo-Pac at Barton Creek.
8. **Waller Creek Walkway**, 15th St. to Town Lake on Waller Creek.
9. **Hamilton Pool Wilderness Preserve**, Hwy. 71, 30 miles from Austin, 512/264-2740.
10. **Westcave Preserve**, FM 3238, 210/825-3442.

BUTTERMILK BRANCH GREENBELT
7500 Meador Ave.
Austin
Here you'll find a ballfield and basketball court with play equipment, as well as picnic and barbecue facilities and a half-mile hike and bike trail. ♿ (East Austin)

JOHNSON CREEK GREENBELT
2100 Enfield
Austin
Austin is blessed with many creeks, which all flow into the Colorado River. The river is dammed into a series of lakes, making Austin a delightful outdoor recreational area. There is a 1.11-mile hike and bike trail off Enfield Road, which follows Johnson Creek. The route is lined with trees and bushes

and lots of greenery. The greenbelt is popular with bird-watchers and often, while you walk this trail, you can hear songbirds. (North Austin)

MARY MOORE SEARIGHT TRAIL
907 Slaughter Ln.
Austin
This greenbelt, with four miles of hike and bike trails, is in a metropolitan park with a ballfield; an 18-hole disc golf course; two tennis and two volleyball courts; playground, picnic, and barbecue facilities; rest rooms; a pavilion; and shelters. (South Austin)

SHOAL CREEK GREENBELT
Town Lake to 38th St.
Austin
There are 2.5 miles of hiking and biking

trails here, as well as a shelter and picnic facilities. (North Austin)

TOWN LAKE GREENBELT
Mo-Pac Bridge to S. First St.
Austin
The 10.1-mile hike and bike trail is one of the most popular attractions in Austin. Every day, year-round, you'll find locals and visitors jogging, walking, and biking around Town Lake. The north shore is the least secluded, just a few paces from the road, but when the trail turns south the atmosphere gets quieter. (Downtown and South Austin)

WALLER CREEK WALKWAY
15th St. to Town Lake
Austin
This lovely walkway along Waller Creek is located on the eastern edge of downtown Austin. It runs from 15th Street on the north edge of downtown all the way to Town Lake, the body of water that divides Austin between north and south. There are some picnic facilities along the three-mile walk, and the natural scenic beauties along the way attract a variety of recreational activities. (Downtown Austin)

WILD BASIN WILDERNESS PRESERVE
805 N. Capital of Texas Hwy.
Loop 360
Austin
512/327-7622
Several trails over varying degrees of

difficulty offer everyone a chance to enjoy the natural side of Austin in this 227-acre park along Bee Creek. Trails range from an easy-access trail for the mobility impaired with benches every 300 feet, to Triknee Trail (the name says it all), which winds through a rocky incline. No pets, bikes, or motorized vehicles. Open from light until dark daily. (Southwest Austin)

Disc Golf

Disc golf, commonly known as "Frisbee golf," is popular with Austin's younger set, who are often seen tossing the disc at courses across the city. Disc golf is played similarly to golf but instead of holes there are metal poles with a chain basket to catch the discs.

BARTHOLOMEW PARK
E. 51st St.
Austin
Located just north of Robert Mueller International Airport, this park includes an 18-hole disc golf course. Other Batholomew Park features include the brown and green play equipment that keeps little tots and kids ages five and above busy for hours. A system of raised walkways, ramps, ladders, and bridges connects each piece of equipment. The swings are also a big hit here. (East Austin)

PEASE PARK
W. 24th St. off Lamar Blvd.
Austin

TRIVIA

Producers found the soccer fields at Zilker Park to be the ideal setting for *The Big Green*, a movie about soccer-playing youths.

Top Spots for Outdoor Sports Enthusiasts

by Warren E. Johnson, avid and experienced fly fisherman, downhill skier, golfer, waterfowl hunter, and boundary water canoe guide

1. *Archery: Archery Country*, 8910 Research Blvd., 512/452-1222.

2. *Fly Fishing Tackle, Equipment, Guide Service: Austin Angler*, 312 ½ Congress Ave., 512/472-4553.

3. *Fishing Rod Building and Instruction: Rodmakers*, 7739 Northern Dr., 512/452-7637.

4. *Golf Equipment, Club Components, Instruction, Apparel: Golfsmiths*, 11000 N. I-35, 512/837-4810.

5. *Hunting Gear and Equipment: McBride Guns*, 2915 San Gabriel, 512/472-3532.

6. *McKinney Falls State Park*, 5808 McKinney Falls Pkwy, 512/243-1643.

7. *Trap, Skeet, Sporting Clays: Capitol City Trap & Skeet Club*, 8707 Lindell Ln., 512/272-4707.

8. *Trout Unlimited*, Guadalupe River Chapter, 207 Finn St., 512/261-4409.

9. *Sportswear and Equipment: Oshman's Super Sport*, 2525 W. Anderson Ln., 512/459-6541.

This area is yet another example of why Austin has such a wonderful reputation for the great outdoors. Bordering Shoal Creek along Lamar Avenue, the area can be easily accessed. The park contains picnic facilities, a three-mile hike and bike trail, play equipment, rest rooms, tennis courts, a 14-hole disc golf course, and a very popular volleyball court. The disc golf course is a favorite of students attending the nearby University of Texas. (North Austin)

ZILKER PARK
Barton Springs Rd.
Austin
You can savor nature here as well as enjoy a nine-hole disc golf course. Other Zilker Park features include a swimming pool, a 60-acre preserve featuring a meadow along a creek, a

high cliff with shallow caves and a rock-walled ramada overlooking both the preserve and downtown Austin. Foot trails begin under the Loop 1 Bridge, with interpretive signs along the well-marked trail. (South Austin)

Fishing

Fishermen casting their lines in Lake Austin won't be disappointed by the black bass, catfish, perch, white bass, and crappie found in these clear waters. The lake is stocked throughout the year.

Licensing

Fishing licenses, required for everyone over the age of 17, are available in most bait and convenience stores. Issued by the Texas Parks and Wildlife Department, the licenses are valid from September 1 to the end of August each year.

A year-round fishing license for a resident of Texas costs $13 and is required of anyone who fishes in the public waters. A temporary (14-day) Resident Sportfishing License is available to residents for $10 and is valid for 14 days in a row. A special $6 license is available for any Texas resident who is 65 years of age or who is legally blind.

Out-of-state visitors must obtain a Non-Resident Fishing License ($30) or the Temporary Five-Day Non-Resident Fishing License ($20). If you are under 17, or 65 years of age or older from Kansas or Louisiana, or 64 years of age or older from Oklahoma, this license is not required. The temporary license is valid for five days in a row for nonresidents.

Real fishing lovers can obtain a Lifetime Resident Fishing License for $400, valid for the lifetime of a Texas

resident. Applications may be obtained from the Texas Parks and Wildlife Department offices or by calling the department at 800/792-1112 (Mon–Fri 8–5).

TOM MILLER DAM
Red Bud Trail at Lake Austin
Austin
800/776-5272

Tom Miller Dam is just south of the Walsh Boat Landing, with four acres for day use only, providing picnicking, boat ramps, and access to Lake Austin. It's illegal to climb on the dam, but you can fish in the lake below the dam. Fishermen park along Red Bud Trail and walk down to the lake shore to cast their lines, hoping to catch catfish and bass. (Southwest Austin)

Fitness Clubs

These clubs offer day passes for visitors.

BIG STEVE'S GYM AND AEROBICS CENTER
1126 S. Lamar Blvd.

Scuba divers in Lake Travis, p. 158

© Permenter and Bigley

Austin Municipal Golf Courses

Austin has five municipal golf courses, each with a pro shop, food and beverage concession, and equipment rental. For general information on Austin's municipal golf courses, stop by the office at 901 West Riverside Drive or call 512/480-3020. The 18-hole courses include driving ranges.

Austin
512/445-2348
Since 1982 this gym has served Austinites who are serious about fitness. Lynn Helton (Mrs. Big Steve) is a certified American College of Sports Medicine fitness instructor and has been teaching aerobics since 1986. Big Steve has trained professional athletes and even a former governor. Day passes for visitors cost $6. (South Austin)

THE HILLS FITNESS CENTER
4615 Bee Caves Rd.
Austin
512/327-4881
This fitness facility covers 12 wooded acres and includes indoor and outdoor pools, racquetball, squash, basketball, an outdoor track, spa services, massage, and a café. Day passes cost $14 and are good on a come-and-go basis. (Southwest Austin)

Golf

Austin boasts some of the top names in golfing, including the late Harvey Penick and his protégés Ben Crenshaw and Tom Kite.

HANCOCK GOLF COURSE
811 E. 41st St.
Austin
512/453-0276
This shady course is the oldest golf course in Texas. It's for walkers: $7.50 for 9 holes and $13 for all 18. Senior discounts are available. Tee times are taken one day in advance and walk-ons are welcome. Weekend reservations are taken on Friday. (North Austin)

JIMMY CLAY-ROY KYZER
GOLF COURSE
5400 Jimmy Clay Dr.
Austin
512/444-0999
The Roy Kyzer 18-hole course is a link-style course. Greens fees on Roy Kyzer Mon–Thu $17, Fri–Sun $23. Tee times are taken three days in advance; weekend reservations are taken on Tuesday. (Southwest Austin)

LIONS GOLF COURSE
2910 Enfield
Austin
512/477-6963
This 18-hole course is located in northwest Austin. Greens fees are $12 on weekdays, $13.50 on weekends and holidays. Senior discounts are available. Tee times are taken one day in advance. (Northwest Austin)

MORRIS WILLIAMS GOLF COURSE
4305 Manor Rd.
Austin
512/926-1298
Greens fees at this hilly course are $12 on weekdays, $13.50 on weekends and holidays. Senior discounts are available. Tee times are taken one day in advance. (East Austin)

Horse Stables

BLUE STAR RIDING CENTER
9513 S. U.S. 183
Austin
512/243-2583
Over 50 acres in Travis County, the riding center boasts indoor and outdoor arenas for lessons in Western, English, hunter-jumper, dressage, and cross-county. Open Tue– Sun. (East Austin)

CAMERON EQUESTRIAN ENTER
13404 Cameron Rd.
Austin
512/272-4301
The center offers hour-long rides on a 70-acre ranch. The price is $30 for one person, $25 for two people, and $20 for three or more. (East Austin)

MEDWAY RANCH
13500 Pecan Dr.
Austin
512/263-5151
This 500-acre ranch is considered one of Texas' most beautiful. An hour ride for one person costs $30; two for $25 each; and three or more $20 each. Children 6 and older are permitted to ride the trail; there are pony rides for children under 6. (Northwest Austin)

OL' CACTUS JACK
13433 W. Hwy. 71,
Bee Caves Rd.

Austin
512/263-2388
Enjoy a trail ride at this ranch, which spans over 300 acres of the Hill Country. An hour's ride costs $20 for one person, $16 for two or more. Children must be 8 years or older to ride. (Southwest Austin)

VALLEY CREEK STABLES
8601 Bluff Springs Rd.
Austin
512/282-6248
There is a regular trail ride here every Wednesday evening at 5:30; other hourly trail rides are by appointment. For three or more persons, the charge is $25 per person, $35 per couple or individual. Children as young as 6 are permitted to ride alone. (South Austin)

Ice-Skating

Ice-skating was once a pretty foreign concept in Texas, but the increased number of northern transplants has increased the popularity of this sport.

Town Lake Greenbelt, p. 158

© Permenter and Bigley

TIP

When you go to rent a horse, look for a copy of the certificate required by the State of Texas at stables that rent horses. It must be on public display and should be an assurance that the animals are being treated humanely. Violations can be reported to the Texas Health Department, 512/458-7255.

The establishment of the Ice Bats will undoubtedly make ice-skating and hockey a fun diversion for the younger set as well.

AUSTINICE
2525 W. Anderson Ln.
Austin
512/451-5102
Located in Northcross Mall, this ice rink offers public skating and lessons. Hours: Daily 12–5, Tue–Thu 7:30 p.m.–9:30 p.m., Fri–Sat 7:45 p.m.–10:15 p.m. $5 plus $2 skate rental. (North Austin)

CHAPARRAL ICE
14200 N. I-35
Austin
512/252-8500
Public skating, lessons, and birthday parties are available at this new rink. Hours: Open Sun–Mon, hours vary. $5 plus $2.50 skate rental. (North Austin)

In-line/Roller Skating

PLAYLAND SKATING CENTER
8822 McCann
Austin
512/452-1901
One of the largest indoor skating centers in Texas, this facility offers family nights and adult nights. Birthday parties are especially popular here. In-line skates are permitted. Hours: Tue 4–6, 7 p.m.–10 p.m.; Thu 4–6, 7 p.m.–9 p.m.; Sat–Sun 2–5. $4 including skates. (North Austin)

SKATEWORLD
9514 Anderson Mill Rd.
Austin
512/258-8886
A popular birthday party site, this rink is also used by adults looking for a fun way to get in shape. Hours: Thu 3:30–5:30; Fri 7:30 p.m.–11 p.m.; Sat 10–5, 7:30 p.m.–10 p.m.; Sun 2–5. $3–$5; $2 rental for rollerblades. (Northwest Austin)

VELOWAY
Off Slaughter Ln.
Austin
512/480-3032
The Veloway is a 3.1-mile paved asphalt loop used by bicyclists as well as in-line skaters to wind through scenic parkland. Located behind Bowie High School. Catch the Veloway from behind Bowie High School or from south Loop 1 (Mo-Pac). Open dawn until dusk. (Southwest Austin)

Jogging

CAMP MABRY
W. 35th St. and Loop 1 (Mo-Pac)
Austin

512/465-5059
Located on the grounds of historic Camp Mabry, this mile-long jogging trail is a favorite with families on the city's west side. No wheeled vehicles except for strollers are permitted. Leave the pets at home. (Northwest Austin)

TOWN LAKE GREENBELT
Mo-Pac Bridge to S. First St.
Austin
Austin's top jogging spot is filled with downtown office workers after 5 p.m. and during the lunch hour. Workout posts offer a chance to do a few chin-ups and stretches as you go; or just enjoy the jog with the best view of the city's skyline. During the spring months, you'll see blooming flowers and shrubs. (Downtown and South Austin)

Rock Climbing

PSEUDO ROCK
200 Trinity St.
Austin
512/474-4376
Whether you're a beginner or an advanced rock climber, you'll find plenty of challenge at this indoor climbing center. Over 5,000 square feet of sculpted climbing surface offer sporting opportunities regardless of the weather. Hours: Mon–Fri 10–10, Sat–Sun 10–8. $8 plus $5 equipment rental. (Downtown Austin)

YMCA SOUTHWEST
Oak Hill
Austin
512/891-9622
This YMCA includes an indoor climbing facility and offers instruction in climbing techniques. Hours: Mon–Fri 6 a.m.–10 p.m., Sat 8 a.m.–7 p.m., Sun 1 p.m.–7 p.m. YMCA members

© Permenter and Bigley

Sailboat on Lake Travis

only; $99 to join, $40 per month for individual membership. (Southwest Austin)

Sailing

You'll find licensed sailing instruction at several places in the Austin area. The Sail and Ski Center offers sailing instruction; call 512/258-0733. Texas Sailing Academy, 512/261-6193, offers instruction and rents vessels. Dutchman's Landing, on the north shore of Lake Travis near Volente, offers sailing instruction as well; call 512/267-4289. Commander's Point Yacht Basin rents vessels and offers instruction for all levels of sailors; call 512/266-2333.

Scuba Diving

Scuba divers find good conditions for year-round diving in Lake Travis, a top Texas dive spot because of good visibility. A popular deep dive is at Mansfield Dam Park. Windy

Austin Recreation Centers

Austin recreation centers offer everything from organized fun to classes. Call the individual centers for a rundown of their facilities and services.

Alamo Recreation Center, *2100 Alamo St., 512/474-2806*

Austin Recreation Center, *1301 Shoal Creek Blvd., 512/476-5662*

Dittmar Recreation Center, *1009 Dittmar, 512/441-4777*

Doris Miller Auditorium, *2300 Rosewood Ave., 512/476-4118*

Dottie Jordan Recreation Center, *2803 Loyola Ln., 512/926-3491*

Dove Springs Recreation Center, *5405 S. Pleasant Valley Rd., 512/447-5875*

Givens Recreation Center, *3811 E. 12th St., 512/928-1982*

Hancock Recreation Center, *811 E. 41st St., 512/453-7765*

Martin Recreation Center, *1601 Haskell, 512/478-8716*

McBeth Recreation Center, *2401-A Columbus Dr., Zilker Park, 512/327-6498; TDD service line, 512/327-6662*

Metz Recreation Center, *2407 Canterbury, 512/478-8716*

Montopolis Recreation Center, *1200 Montopolis, 512/385-5931*

Northwest Recreation Center, *2913 Northland, 512/458-4107*

Pan Am Recreation Center, *2100 E. Third St., 512/476-9193*

Parque Zaragoza Recreation Center, *741 Pedernales, 512/472-7142*

Rosewood Recreation Center, *2300 Rosewood Ave., 512/472-6838*

South Austin Recreation Center, *1100 Cumberland Ave., 512/444-6601*

Point is a good access point; other divers enter from the shoreline of Hippie Hollow/MacGregor Park.

AQUATIC ADVENTURES
12129 RR 620 North
Austin

512/219-1220
This operation includes an on-site heated pool for instruction. Scuba lessons, air fills, scuba gear sales, and dive travel are available. Serious divers will find Nitrox facilities here. (Northwest Austin)

DEEP BLUE SCUBA
4006 S. Lamar Blvd.
Austin
512/326-4344
Lake Travis boat charters are available from this PADI operation. Open-water instruction, basic and advanced Nitrox instruction, rebreather courses, and more are offered. (South Austin)

GREAT OUTDOORS AQUA SPORTS
4403 Guadalupe St.
Austin
512/453-1852
This center includes an on-site heated pool, swimming, and snorkeling. Scuba equipment is available for a fee. (North Austin)

OCEAN'S WINDOW
13376 Research Blvd.
Austin
512/258-8000
This PADI five-star facility offers private and group classes, all-inclusive course fees, and all ranges of training. Underwater photography and video facilities are offered as well. The in-house travel agency specializes in dive travel. (North Austin)

PISCES SCUBA
11401 RR 2222
Austin
512/258-6646
Lake Travis boat dives are offered by Pisces. Other services include an on-site heated pool, air fills, sales, and dive travel. (Northwest Austin)

TOM'S DIVE AND SKI
5909 Burnet Rd.
Austin
512/451-3425
www.tomsscuba.com
Since 1983 this SSI training facility has offered professional scuba instruction as well as sales and rentals.

An on-site heated pool is available. (North Austin)

Skiing/Jet Skiing

Waterskiing is a popular summer activity on Lake Austin and Lake Travis. Use of Jet skis, wet bikes, or similar devices on Lake Austin is prohibited during the holiday weekends of Memorial Day, Labor Day, and July 4. The holiday weekend ban runs from 5 p.m. Friday to 6 a.m. Tuesday. Heavy water traffic during those peak times makes this safety law important.

Swimming Pools

With Austin's active population and soaring summer temperatures, it's easy to see why swimming would be a popular pastime. Pools fill with children and adults alike during the summer months, and many locals enjoy a swim in the area lakes. However, swimming is prohibited in Town Lake.

BARTON SPRINGS POOL
2200 Barton Springs Rd.
Austin
512/476-9044
You'll find dedicated swimmers braving the constant 68-degree spring water that makes this one of Texas' most beautiful (and chilliest) year-round swimming holes. Located in Zilker Park, the pool includes a diving board and a shallow end for children to enjoy but maintains the look of a natural swimming hole. Rest room and changing facilities available. Hours: Daily 9 a.m.–10 p.m. $2.50 adults, 25 cents children. (Southwest Austin)

DEEP EDDY POOL
401 Deep Eddy
Austin

512/472-8546

Swim laps or just hang out at this spring-fed pool. Its cool waters are a favorite with dedicated swimmers and young kids. (Northwest Austin)

STACY POOL
800 E. Live Oak
Austin
512/476-4521

This spring-fed pool is another beautiful spot to cool off during Austin's long, hot summers. During the cooler months, the warm water of this artesian hole draws dedicated swimmers. Hours: Mon–Fri 6 a.m.–9 a.m. and 11 a.m.–7 p.m., Sun 12–7 p.m., closed Sat. $2 adults, 50 cents juniors, 25 cents children. (South Austin)

Tennis

Austin has over 15 tennis facilities for a total of over 200 courts—so many, in fact, that Tennis *magazine has named the city the "10th Best U.S. Tennis City in the Nation." Public tennis facilities have a time limit of 1½ hours for sin-gles and two hours for doubles. Cost is $3 for singles and $2.50 per person for doubles. For information on public courts, call 512/480-3020.*

AUSTIN HIGH SCHOOL
TENNIS CENTER
2001 Cesar Chavez St.
Austin
512/477-7802

After school hours, tennis buffs will find eight courts for play at this high school located just off Town Lake. Hours: Mon–Thu 5 p.m.–10 p.m., Fri 5 p.m.–8 p.m., Sat 8:30 a.m.–6 p.m., Sun 9 a.m.–6 p.m. (Downtown Austin)

AUSTIN RECREATION CENTER
1301 Shoal Creek Blvd.
Austin
512/476-5662

There is no cost for use of the courts, which are available on a first-come first-served basis (although classes have priority). Four lighted tennis courts are available at this central facility 7:15 a.m.–10:15 p.m. (North Austin)

Austin City Pools

Call individual pools for their schedules. For general information on neighborhood pools, call 512/476-4521 or the Swimming Pool Administration, 512/476-4521.

Bartholomew Pool, *1800 E. 51st St., 512/928-0011*
Barton Springs Pool in Zilker Park, *512/867-3080*
Deep Eddy Pool, *401 Deep Eddy, 512/472-8546*
Garrison Pool, *6001 Manchaca Rd., 512/442-4048*
Mabel Davis Park *(lake access), 3427 Parker Ln., 512/441-5247*
Northwest Pool, *7000 Ardath, 512/453-0194*
Walnut Creek Pool, *12138 N. Lamar Blvd., 512/834-0824*

CASWELL TENNIS CENTER
24th St. and Lamar Blvd.
Austin
512/478-6268
Nine lighted courts are available for public play at this center, which also offers lessons and does restringing of rackets. Hours: Mon–Thu 8:30 a.m.–10 p.m., Fri–Sun 8:30 a.m.–9 p.m. (North Austin)

PHARR TENNIS CENTER
4201 Brookview Dr.
Austin
512/477-7773

This tennis center offers eight lighted courts. Operated by the City of Austin, the courts are especially busy on weekends. Hours: Mon–Thu 8 a.m.–10 p.m., Fri–Sun 8 a.m.–9 p.m. (East Austin)

SOUTH AUSTIN TENNIS CENTER
1000 Cumberland Dr.
Austin
512/442-1466
Ten lighted courts are available for daily play at this center. Hours: Mon–Fri 8:30 a.m.–10 p.m., Sat–Sun 8:30 a.m.–6:30 p.m. (South Austin)

© Permenter and Bigley

11

THE PERFORMING ARTS

Like so much else in Austin, the arts are thriving. Austin is committed to excellence, supporting the growth of artistic centers that are enriching life in the city by placing a premium on creativity and professionalism. The University of Texas Performing Arts Center hosts music, dance, Broadway, and comedy performances regularly, presenting major stars, great diversity, artistic integrity, and just plain fun. Itzhak Perlman, Pinchas Zukerman, Leontyne Price, Merce Cunningham, Willie Nelson, Marcel Marceau, and Asleep at the Wheel are some of the nationally and internationally known artists who grace the boards at Bass Concert Hall and Bates Recital Hall and the Paramount Theater. Music runs the gamut from choral to concert, from light opera to classics presenting guest artists.

Austin is so music-happy there are even noonday concerts at four venues. In dance, Ballet Austin and the Sharir Dance Company are joined by other local companies, such as Austin Contemporary Ballet, presenting everything from ballet to jazz to postmodern and innovative dance. Note: The map in this chapter shows locations of major performing arts venues only.

THEATER

AUSTIN CIRCLE OF THEATERS
823 Congress Ave.
Austin
512/499-8388
This theater alliance is a nonprofit corporation and umbrella organization for theater in Austin, funded in part by the City of Austin and the Austin Arts Commission and by a joint grant from the Texas Commission on the Arts and the National Endowment for the Arts. Call them to find out what's going on about town theatrically. (Downtown Austin)

MUSICAL THEATER

CAPITOL CITY COMEDY CLUB
8120 Research Blvd.
Austin
512/467-2333
Here you'll find live, professional stand-up comedians, like Ellen Degeneres and Bobcat Goldthwait, who have performed on shows like *David Letterman*, *The Tonight Show*, HBO, and Showtime. An evening here can keep you in stitches. (North Austin)

DOUGHERTY ARTS CENTER
1110 Barton Springs Rd.
Austin
512/397-1468
This public visual and performing arts center offers theater performances, gallery exhibitions, and affordable arts education to all residents of Austin. The 150-seat proscenium theater, 3,700 square feet, is complete with lighting and sound systems, box office and concession areas, dressing rooms with showers, gallery entrance, and outdoor marquee. There is ample lighted parking for drama, dance, or music events. (South Austin)

ESTHER'S FOLLIES
525 E. Sixth St.
Austin
512/320-0553
Esther's Follies is one of Texas' premier musical and comedy troupes, performing hilarious original and topical satire and musical parody. Both revered and feared for its biting wit, the Follies are a centerpiece of Sixth Street with such buffoonery as Boris Yeltsin tap dancing his way back to health, Madonna making Argentina cry, and Chi Chi LaBomba picking her man of the year. Not to mention Esther's classics like "Ode to Football Joy" and "The Jalapeño Chorus." Tickets $10 to $14. (Downtown Austin)

FRONTERA @ HYDE PARK THEATER
511 W. 43rd St.
Austin
512/452-6688
Known for interesting and provocative works, the group Frontera is the resident company of the Hyde Park Theater in the historic Hyde Park neighborhood. The company puts on performances such as one called "the fringe theater event of the Southwest," with playwrights, dancers, and actors mixing media. (North Austin)

HYDE PARK THEATER
511 W. 43rd St.
Austin
512/452-6688
Productions range from comedy to tragedy and everything in between in this theater in the Hyde Park Historical District. (Downtown Austin)

All University of Texas student recitals are free; they take place at four locations: Bates Recital Hall, Jessen Auditorium, McCullough Theater, or the Recital Studios. Call the Music Department's hotline: 512/471-5401.

T|I|P

There are free movie screenings at the Texas Union Theater on Tuesday nights, hosted by the Austin Film Society. Foreign, classic, and independent films are shown. For more information, call 512/322-0145.

LIVE OAK THEATER
200 Colorado St.
Austin
512/472-5143

The only local professional theater performing on a regular basis and featuring local talent. The company, with more than 15 years of experience, has performed the *Dead Presidents' Club*, *Cabaret*, and *Sweeney Todd*. (Downtown Austin)

LOUISE T. PETER THEATER
Concordia Lutheran College
3400 N. I-35
Austin
512/452-7661

Concordia University shows, either premiere or popular, are on the program here in the auditorium of the Peter Building. A recent offering was *A Midsummer-Night's Dream;* interesting speakers are featured as well. (North Austin)

MARY MOODY NORTHERN THEATRE
St. Edward's University
3001 S. Congress Ave.
Austin
512/448-8484

St. Edward's University has a fine drama department. This campus theater is the venue for the drama department's

Austin Symphony Orchestra outdoor concert, p. 170

Austin CVB

plays, often enhanced by well-known guest directors and stars. (South Austin)

MCCULLOUGH THEATRE
2400 East Campus Dr.
University of Texas
Austin
512/471-1444
Small operas and dance are mounted at the McCullough Theatre. Call the number above for tickets and information about student performances at the College of Fine Arts and for performances at Bass Concert Hall at the Performing Arts Center. (North Austin)

MEXIC-ARTE MUSEUM
419 Congress Ave.
Austin
512/480-9373
Director Francisco Jacobi presents three plays a year of cross-cultural performances in the main gallery of this museum. The group within the museum, Teatro Communitario en Español, performs works in Spanish by contemporary Mexican playwrights. Tickets are $5. (Downtown Austin)

PARAMOUNT THEATRE
713 Congress Ave.
Austin

512/499-8388
Like many others in the past, this new theater company is making its debut as a project sponsored by the Austin Circle of Theaters. The directors of the company, both professional performers, decided that Austin was ripe for a sophisticated production company of classic musicals. The musicals combine Broadway-caliber leads with Austin's best actors, dancers, and singers. (Downtown Austin)

THEATRE ROOM
23rd St. at San Jacinto Blvd.
Austin
512/471-1444
Call the number above for tickets and information about student performances at the College of Fine Arts and the Performing Arts Center. You'll enjoy small University of Texas shows in this cozy room, and you might spot a rising star. (North Austin)

VELVEETA ROOM
521 E. Sixth St.
Austin
512/469-9116
Down on Sixth Street where much of Austin's entertainment happens, the Velveeta Room offers stand-up comedy and cabaret-style selections.

TRIVIA

The Arts in Public Places ordinance sets aside one percent of the total construction budget for all new or remodeled public buildings, parks, parking facilities, and decorative commemorative structures for the commission, purchase, and installation of art. The Award of Cultural Contracts is another way the city promotes the arts, and these contracts allow local nonprofit, tax-exempt cultural arts organizations to apply for funding from the city. Contract categories include dance, literature, theater, visual arts, mixed art, and music.

T I P

Get half-price tickets for some venues on the same day as the theatrical performance. Call ahead, because the selection varies. Dougherty Arts Center, 1110 Barton Springs Rd., Wed–Fri 11:30–1:30 and 4:30–6:30, Sat 11–2. Also at the Visitors Center, 201 E. Second St., Mon–Fri 8:30–5, Sat 9–5, Sun 12–5. To find out what's available, call 512/320-7168 or 512/397-1450.

Get into the act on open-mike nights. (Downtown Austin)

VICTORY GRILL/KOVAC THEATRE
1104 E. 11th St.
Austin
512/474-4494

This east side cabaret-style venue for small musical and theatrical productions aims to provide cultural and community revival through music. Wednesdays are usually devoted to Harold McMillan's Voodoo Jazz Jam, featuring different performers weekly. On any given night the club will be open and there will be something interesting going on, whether it's older, established musicians or younger, unknown players. You might see dance, a Shakespeare play, or a group of teenage playwrights from the Outreach Program collaborating on a performance. (East Austin)

VORTEX THEATER AT THE PLANET THEATRE
2307 Manor Rd.
Austin
512/472-8644

This repertory company presents a variety of bold, alternative theater. A cutting-edge production of Shakespeare's *Julius Caesar*, for example, alternates with a cybernetic opera

such as *Panoptikon*, a trilogy by Ethos. Tickets range from $9 to $12. (East Austin)

ZACHARY SCOTT THEATRE
1510 Toomey Rd.
Austin
512/476-0541

This professional theater is named for an Austin native turned movie star. There are two theaters in one: the main stage in the larger building and the Arena, a theater in the round around the corner. The long season runs from September to August, so interested visitors ought to be able to catch something. Productions in this regional theater (using both local and national talent) include musicals, contemporary comedy, and hard-hitting drama. (South Austin)

ZILKER SUMMER MUSICALS
Zilker Hillside Theatre
Austin
512/479-9491

The Zilker Summer Musical was created in 1959 as a project of the City of Austin Parks and Recreation Department and is funded both by the city and private patrons. Amateur and professional talent combine to provide memorable evenings with full orchestra and innovative sets, costumes, and

Zilker Hillside Theatre

The Zilker Hillside Theatre is Austin's oldest performance space, a popular "people place" that has been a showcase for a wide variety of local performing arts groups. The natural grassy hillside can accommodate more than 2,500 people, who bring blankets to enjoy an open-air picnic supper while watching free quality entertainment. The theater is available to both arts groups and individual artists for performance events. Rental fees are reasonable; contact the Special Events office at 512/397-1463.

choreography. The free performances at the Zilker Hillside Theatre have run the gamut of successful musicals, from *Seventeen* in 1959 to *Once Upon A Mattress* in 1996. (South Austin)

CLASSICAL MUSIC AND OPERA

AUSTIN CHAMBER MUSIC ENSEMBLE
512/345-3399
The ensemble meets in private residences of their most devoted fans during their Intimate Concert Series; you'll feel right at home.

AUSTIN CHORAL UNION
512/472-9600
This community group meets in various locations and is open to any Austinite over 16 who has experience as well as musical skills. Typically Austin, it's a very democratic organization. It serves as a backup chorus for the University of Texas Opera and presents its own season October to June.

AUSTIN CIVIC CHORUS
Scottish Rite Temple
18th St. and Lavaca
Austin
512/451-8863
It's tempting to join in after one of these popular choral concerts, presented in various venues around town. The group consists of three entities. The first is composed of an oratorio group of 130 community volunteers,

TRIVIA

When the English National Opera's production of *War and Peace* came to the United States, it played in only two venues in the entire country: New York's Metropolitan Opera and Bass Concert Hall at the University of Texas Performing Arts Center, where the facilities, amenities, and audiences are first class.

Austin Lyric Opera

chosen by audition. A major orchestral chorus, they present a season of four concerts by subscription. (Tickets are $36 for the four performances.)

The second group, the New Austin Singers, presents shorter and more diverse choral works of the sixteenth through the twentieth centuries. (Tickets range from $5 to $10.)

The third group is the Summer Musicals for Children, with eight performances during weekends in early August. Past productions include *Snow White*, *Cinderella*, and the *Golden Goose*. (Admission is free, with donations welcome at the door.) (North Austin)

AUSTIN GILBERT AND SULLIVAN SOCIETY
2026 Guadalupe St.
Austin
512/472-4772

Since 1976 Austin audiences have been proud to have their own Gilbert and Sullivan Society, delighting in the lilting lyrics and scores of such light comic operas as *The Pirates of Penzance*, the *Mikado*, and *HMS Pinafore*. Informal monthly musicals are free and open to the public, held at various homes of society members; more formal productions have been held at the auditorium of St. Stephen's School. There is a grand annual production at a local theater. The society also takes the performances into the public schools so that youngsters can be exposed to music they might not otherwise have the opportunity to hear. (Northwest Austin)

AUSTIN LYRIC OPERA
1111 W. Sixth St.
Austin
512/472-5927

For more than 10 years this professional company has been performing such works as their signature opera, *The Magic Flute*, as well as other operatic favorites like *La Bohéme*. Local artists fill the choir and orchestra, with guest artists from major opera companies all over the world performing. They offer three annual productions, four performances of each, in the University of Texas' Bass Concert Hall. Tickets range from $10 to $80. (North Austin)

AUSTIN SYMPHONY ORCHESTRA
1101 Red River St.
Austin
512/476-6064
The oldest symphony orchestra in Texas is under the leadership of Maestro Sung Kwak, former assistant conductor of the Cleveland Orchestra. With its high level of performance, the orchestra delights Austin music lovers. The orchestra performs at the University Performing Arts Center, Bass Concert Hall, monthly, September through May. (North Austin)

AUSTIN VOCAL ARTS ENSEMBLE
603 N. Lamar Blvd.
Austin
512/442-1685
The ensemble, formerly the Handel-Haydn Society, has become one of Austin's favorite chamber choirs. Some of the area's most talented singers consistently present quality choral music, both a cappella and with an orchestra. (Downtown Austin)

NOONDAY CONCERT SERIES
512/472-2445
For a pleasant lunchtime break, try some noon tunes at one of Austin's noonday concert series chamber music performances. There are several to choose from: Central Presbyterian Church, 512/472-2445; Regents' Plaza, 512/469-1766; the Texas Medical Association, 512/370-1300; and right downtown at 311 Congress Avenue, 512/320-7001. (Downtown Austin)

RIVER CITY POPS
McCallum High School
U.S. 290 and Cameron Rd.
Austin
512/345-7420
At these delightful choral concerts, the River City Pops pulls out all the stops, in costume and dance, presenting fully staged Broadway and show tunes in two major productions, winter and spring, each year. The chorus of 40 community members performs at McCallum High School, which operates a fine arts academy and provides a handsome auditorium. Tickets are $10 to $13. (East Austin)

UNIVERSITY OF TEXAS OPERA THEATRE
512/471-1444
Call the above number for tickets and information about student performances at the College of Fine Arts and for performances at Bass Concert Hall at the Performing Arts Center. (North Austin)

Austin's Annual Festival of Dance, which takes place every March, features local, national, and international dance companies. A sampling of what might await you: the San Francisco Ballet and the Dallas Black Dance Company, among others. Call 512/406-6401 for festival information.

DANCE

AUSTIN CONTEMPORARY BALLET
4601 S. Lamar Blvd.
Austin
512/892-1298
Formed in 1986, this is Austin's second-largest ballet company. The ballet maintains a professional academy with workshops taught by professionals from such companies as Alvin Ailey American Dance Theater, Atlanta Ballet, Lar Lubouvitch Dance Company, and the Royal Winnepeg Ballet. The company usually performs at the Paramount Theater. (Downtown Austin)

Ballet Austin

BALLET AUSTIN
3002 Guadalupe St.
Austin
512/476-2163
Austin's first professional ballet company, formed under the direction of Eugene Slavin and Alexandra Nadal (like the Austin Civic Ballet), presents both classical and contemporary works during its fall-to-spring season. The company keeps getting better and better, testing itself constantly with new material and blending other forms of dance, such as tap dancing and tango, with more classical pliés and battements. But the annual offering, the classic reliable *Nutcracker*, is still performed every December to the delight of Austin and area children of all ages. (North Austin)

LOZANO'S ROY BALLET FOLKLORICA
1928 Gaston Place Dr.
Austin
512/928-1111
This folklorica dance company has a fine reputation for authentic dances from south of the border, from the states of Jalisco, Nayarit, Nuevo

León, and others. Formed in 1982, they perform professionally at the Paramount Theater (adults $12, children and seniors $7) as well as at the Zilker Hillside Theatre and perform free open-air concerts in local hotels and in the Austin Convention Center. They also perform in the Capitol Rotunda, and not too long ago their audience contained no less than the Queen of England.

SHARIR DANCE COMPANY
College of Fine Arts
University of Texas
Austin
512/458-8158
The Sharir Dance Company was organized in 1982 as the professional dance company in residence at the University of Texas College of Fine Arts. Led by award-winning choreographers Yacov Sharir and Jose Luis Bustamante, it has become the leading innovative postmodern dance company in Texas. The company produces three to four home season productions in addition to touring nationally and internationally. (North Austin)

Dial up Danceline, 512/474-1766, for a full listing of upcoming dance performances.

TAPESTRY DANCE COMPANY
2521 Rutland Dr.
Austin
512/837-8909
All forms of rhythm and motion are combined in the diverse style of this company. This local touring company, directed by Deirdre Strand and Acia Gray, weave modern dance, jazz, ballet, tap, and rhythm into performances by the 12 members, 3 full-time dancers, and 4 apprentices. The company performs in Austin three times a year at the Paramount Theater. Tickets range from $15 to $18. (North Austin)

UNIVERSITY OF TEXAS DANCE REPERTORY THEATRE
512/471-1444
Call the number above for tickets and information about student performances at the College of Fine Arts and for performances at Bass Concert Hall at the Performing Arts Center. (North Austin)

CONCERT VENUES

AUSTIN MUSIC HALL
208 Nueces St.
Austin
512/495-9962
The roomy music hall hosts concerts running the gamut from rock to country, gospel to reggae. (North Austin)

FRANK ERWIN CENTER
University of Texas
Off Red River and 15th Sts.
Austin
512/477-6060
The Frank Erwin Center is one of the largest live music venues in Austin. The 17,871-seat arena hosts a myriad of musical events and professional performances, often hosting concerts by touring mega-stars. (North Austin)

PARAMOUNT THEATRE
713 Congress Ave.
Austin
512/472-5411
Built in 1915, the Paramount is one of those ornate beauties left over from vaudeville days. Now beautifully restored, it's considered one of the country's most beautifully detailed historic theaters, and it shines for both classic movies on a big screen and local and national touring artists. (Downtown Austin)

SOUTHPARK MEADOWS
9600 S. I-35
Austin
512/280-8771
National touring acts love to play at Austin's largest outdoor concert venue. During spring and summer the sounds are mostly alternative music to heavy rock and country-western, with such groups as the Steve Miller Band, Hootie and the Blowfish, Def Leopard, Jimmy Buffett, Sting, and

the Horde Festival performing. Bring a blanket and sit on the lawn, or pay some more and have a reserved seat up front. (South Austin)

UNIVERSITY OF TEXAS PERFORMING ARTS CENTER
23rd St. at East Campus Dr.
Austin
512/471-1444 or 800/687-6010

Constructed in 1981, with no expense spared in building and equipping the center with state-of-the-art facilities, the Performing Arts Center is actually a complex consisting of five buildings. The acoustics are ideal at all of them. Bass Concert Hall is a 3,000-seat venue large enough to host the world's most renowned performers in touring Broadway shows or symphony orchestras. The lighting is controlled by computer and the orchestra pit can be raised and lowered. The smaller Bates Recital Hall is designed for smaller ensembles and for soloists. It contains one of the world's largest organs. The Opera Lab Theater is reserved for chamber operas, dance programs, and productions of the university's drama department. The Center has hosted everyone from schoolchildren to princes and presidents; thousands visit the theater each year, which accomplishes the university's main aim: to bring people together to witness the marvels of the arts, to view exhibits, and to share ideas. (North Austin)

ZILKER HILLSIDE THEATRE
Zilker Park
Barton Springs Rd.
Austin
512/479-9491

This is a free entertainment venue out under the stars in Austin's favorite downtown park. Pack a picnic to savor while you enjoy live music, a lively musical, or some very fine dance. For music under the stars, summer musicals feature local Austin performers mid-July to mid-August.

Texas Young Playwrights Festival

To encourage young playwrights-to-be, Austin's annual Texas Young Playwrights Festival, sponsored by the Dougherty Arts Center, the Capitol City Playhouse, and the University of Texas Department of Theater and Dance, invites all Texas writers under the age of 19 to submit plays to be considered for the festival. The submission deadline is in February, and selected works are given public readings and professional performances in the ensuing summer, giving young playwrights the opportunity to work with theater professionals. The program is made possible by a grant from the Texas Commission on the Arts and funds from Austin's City Opportunity for Youth Programs.

The Bard Under the Stars brings Shakespeare to the park September through October; call 512/454-2273. (South Austin)

BUYING TICKETS

AUSTIX
512/397-1450
A ticket service giving information on both half-price "day of performance" tickets and full-service theater tickets for theater, dance, and performing arts events, depending upon availability. AusTix is located at both BookPeople (603 N. Lamar Blvd.) and the Austin Visitors Center (2nd St. and San Jacinto Blvd.). (Downtown Austin)

THE BOX OFFICE
603 N. Lamar Blvd.
(Inside Book People)
512/499-8497
The Box Office is a full-price ticket service for smaller companies, offering sales over the phone via Master-Card/Visa as well as information. (Downtown Austin)

PAC (PERFORMING ARTS CENTER, UNIVERSITY OF TEXAS)
512/471-1444
For events at the UT Performing Arts Center (Bass Hall, Bates Recital Hall, McCullough Theatre). For many but not all PAC events, tickets are sold through UTTM, 512/477-6060 (see below). (North Austin)

STAR TICKETS
512/469-7469 or 800/966-7469
Handles touring acts and local concerts by phone and through a dozen locations in the central Texas area.

TICKET SERVICES
Austin Circle of Theaters
Performance Hotline
Austin
512/320-7168
This is a service provided by Austin's theaters, updated every Monday and Thursday morning, giving theater listings, ticket availability, and information on box offices and where half-price tickets are available.

UTTM
in Texas Union Building
Austin
512/477-6060
University of Texas TicketMaster handles sales for the Frank Erwin Center and other UT facilities as well as some Paramount Theatre events and sports events. There are UTTM outlets at all central Texas H.E.B. grocery stores. (North Austin)

© Permenter and Bigley

12

Austin is known for its music scene. Over 100 clubs have helped Austin earn the title "The Live Music Capital of the World," and any type of music can be heard nightly from local and internationally known talents.

Much of the music takes place on Sixth Street. This historic seven-block area, which is sometimes compared to New Orleans' Bourbon Street, is home to many nightclubs and restaurants. Here the music starts late and the fun lasts until the early hours of the morning. All types of music are represented along this bustling street, where Austinites and visitors can enjoy an evening of club-hopping any night of the week.

Outside of Sixth Street, the beat continues in clubs near the UT campus, at special events in venues ranging from the shores of Town Lake to high-tech concert halls, and at restaurants and bars throughout the city. The Austin Chronicle, *a free alternative weekly that's distributed at bookstores and grocery stores throughout town, gives an excellent rundown of who's playing where so that you can plan your night on the town. The Thursday "XLent" section of the* Austin American-Statesman *also offers a good look at the happenings in town.*

Many nightclubs enforce a "21 and over" age restriction. Those permitting youth admission are noted in the text.

DANCE CLUBS

CALLE OCHO CAFE Y CLUB
706 Congress Ave.
Austin
512/474-6605

The Calle Ocho Cafe y Club is like the real thing. The Latin rhythm of salsa or merengue at this pulsating dance club make you feel like you are really in Latin America. Stop by early for a lesson, then head out onto the dance floor. (Downtown Austin)

DANCE ACROSS TEXAS
2201 E. Ben White Blvd.
Austin
512/441-9101
Dance to live or DJ music with a country beat. Wednesday is ladies' night with no cover for ladies, a $2 buffet from 5 to 8, and $1 drinks from 8 to 11. This club claims to have the largest dance floor in Austin. (East Austin)

RUMORS
13233 Pond Springs Rd.
Austin
512/258-9717
Shuffle to country-western tunes in this neighborhood bar and dance hall. Live bands are scheduled on Friday and Saturday night, with karaoke on Tuesday. Pool, shuffleboard, darts, and a large-screen TV keep things lively. (Northwest Austin)

TANGERINE'S
9721 Arboretum Blvd.
Austin
512/343-2626

Part of the Renaissance Hotel but with a separate entrance, this dance club plays current faves. (Northwest Austin)

MUSIC CLUBS

Jazz

CEDAR STREET
208 W. Fourth St.
Austin
512/708-8811
Shaken, not stirred could well be the motto of this popular nightspot that's known for its martinis. Over 30 vodkas and 20 gins stock the bar with enough spirits to keep even the choosiest drinker happy. The bar is also home to Gigantè, a cedar-lined humidor with some of the world's finest cigars. (Downtown Austin)

DRISKILL LOBBY BAR
604 Brazos St.
Austin
512/474-5911
The quiet ambience of the elegant Driskill Hotel makes this lobby bar the

SXSW

The South by Southwest Music and Media Conference, better known as SXSW, attracts over 15,000 music buffs—including professional critics, musicians, and fans—to the capital city for music seminars and nighttime entertainment. Held in mid-March, the four-day festival brings over 600 acts to perform at 42 clubs throughout town. Wristbands permit music lovers to take in show after show, from rock to blues to Cajun music. The activities begin with the Austin Music Awards. For information, call 512/467-7979.

T I P

You'll find free blues concerts every week during summer months at Blues on the Green, a concert series held at the Arboretum in far north Austin at the intersection of U.S. 183 and U.S. 360.

perfect place for a quiet drink and a chat. (Downtown Austin)

ELEPHANT ROOM
315 E. Congress Ave.
Austin
512/473-2279
Jazz lovers are well acquainted with this basement club. Very popular with the cool cats, the club is at the top of the list for true jazz buffs. (Downtown Austin)

PETE'S PEANUT BAR AND PIANO EMPORIUM
421 E. Sixth St.
Austin
512/472-PETE
Jazz and piano tunes keep the crowds happy at this centrally located bar. (Downtown Austin)

TOP OF THE MARC
618 W. Sixth St.
Austin
512/472-9849
Located on the second floor above Katz's Deli and Bar (see Chapter 4, Where to Eat), this rooftop club hosts names like the Guy Forsythe Band. Jazz happy hour shows start the evening off right. (Downtown Austin)

VICTORY GRILL/KOVAC THEATER
1104 E. 11th St.
Austin
512/474-4494

Musical and theatrical acts are the usual fare, but on Wednesday check out Harold McMillan's Voodoo Jazz Jam, featuring different performers weekly. (East Austin)

Blues

311 CLUB
311 E. Sixth St.
Austin
512/477-1630
You don't have to worry about remembering the address for this club, located at 311 E. Sixth Street. The smoke-filled club is small and nothing

Saxophone player at an Austin music club

Austin CVB

*Guitar player at one of Austin's
many music clubs*

Austin CVB

fancy but offers some of the best blues licks in the city. (Downtown Austin)

ANTONE'S
213 W. Fifth St.
Austin
512/320-8424
Known as "Austin's Home of the Blues," this legendary nightspot on the north end of the Drag has entertained audiences for over two decades. Since 1975, Clifford Antone has been drawing music lovers with some of the best blues names in the country. All ages welcomed. (Downtown Austin)

CATFISH STATION
408 E. Sixth St.
Austin
512/477-8875
Look for musicians like Blues Boy Hubbard and the Jets at this soulful bar and restaurant. Chase away the blues with a plate of catfish and all the fixins. (Downtown Austin)

STUBB'S BAR-B-Q
801 Red River St.
Austin
512/480-8341
Barbecue, beer, and blues—Stubbs has it all. The late Charles "Stubb" Stubblefield of Lubbock opened this popular joint that smokes with meat and music. A Sunday gospel brunch is scheduled weekly at 11:30 and 1:30. (Downtown Austin)

Rock

BABE'S
208 E. Sixth St.
Austin
512/473-2262
Rock as well as blues and country music keep Babe's hoppin'. Check out the schedule for both the restaurant (which serves up burgers along with the blues) and the stage next door. (Downtown Austin)

BACK ROOM
2015 E. Riverside Dr.
Austin
512/444-ROCK
This venue calls itself "The Home of Rock 'n' Roll." Games and music keep the action moving. (East Austin)

CONTINENTAL CLUB
1315 S. Congress Ave.
Austin
512/441-2444
Enter through doors that look like they belong on a '50s diner, then enjoy a happy hour show from 6:30 to 8:30 or a headliner act during late evening. Advance tickets are available for some performers. (South Austin)

EMO'S
603 Red River St.
Austin
512/477-3667

Emo's is well known as the place to go in Austin to hear music when the funds run low. Enjoy national acts as well as local names at this alternative lounging club that has some of the lowest cover prices in town. All ages welcomed for all shows. (Downtown Austin)

FLAMINGO CANTINA
515 E. Sixth St.
Austin
512/474-9336
Enjoy rock, reggae, and ska at this downtown club. Names like the Killer Bees headline here. (Downtown Austin)

HOLE IN THE WALL
2538 Guadalupe St.
Austin
512/472-5599
Located on the north end of the Drag, this joint truly does look like a "hole in the wall." For over two decades, fans have come here to enjoy local alternative bands. Don't come here for comfort, but for some of Austin's best sounds. (North Austin)

LA ZONA ROSA
Fourth St. and Rio Grande
Austin
512/472-9075
Dine on Tex-Mex either indoors or outdoors, then enjoy the show. Early dinner shows feature Austin singer-songwriters. A Sunday gospel brunch and all-you-can-eat buffet is sched-uled from 11 a.m. to 3 p.m. (Downtown Austin)

LIBERTY LUNCH
405 W. Second St.
Austin
512/477-0461
One of Austin's best-known clubs, this place is especially popular with touring bands. The large venue holds over 1,000 music lovers. (Downtown Austin)

MAGGIE MAE'S
512 Trinity St.
Austin
512/478-8541
Located at the corner of Sixth and Trinity Streets, this club is always popular. Along with the bar, a party deck on the roof overlooking Sixth Street makes this a popular stop for live music. (Downtown Austin)

STEAMBOAT 1874
403 E. Sixth St.
Austin
512/478-2912
Steamboat has rocked with names like the Will Sexton Band, Ian Moore, Chris Duarte, and the Red Hot Chili Peppers. Today it's a favorite for those enjoying original live music. Beatles fans will find an entire wall of Beatles artwork, and on October 9 the club celebrates the birthday of John Lennon with a special show when Austin musicians perform the late singer's tunes. (Downtown Austin)

TRIVIA

Some top names on the Austin scene past and present include Rick Trevino, Ian Moore, Nanci Griffith, Tish Hinojosa, Butch Hancock, Joe Ely, Marcia Ball, the late Stevie Ray Vaughan, Willie Nelson, and Jerry Jeff Walker.

Austin City Limits

Many television viewers around the world get their first glimpse of the capital city through Austin City Limits, *a public television program produced in a television studio on the University of Texas campus. Over 300 markets carry the popular show, which spotlights Texas music, especially Austin performers. Past productions have included Willie Nelson, Guy Clark, Gary P. Nunn, Jerry Lee Lewis, Bonnie Raitt, and Austin's own guitarist, the late Stevie Ray Vaughan.*

Tickets to the taping of the show are free but difficult to obtain. Call the KLRU hotline at 512/475-9077 and listen for the artist, taping date, time, and the radio stations that will be handling ticket distribution. Radio stations will announce the time the tickets will be given away. Once the radio announcement is made, go to the KLRU offices in Communications Building "B" at the corner of 26th and Guadalupe Streets on the UT campus. Two tickets per person are given away, but be warned—they often disappear within five minutes of the radio announcement. And once you have a ticket, you don't have a guaranteed seat at the taping. To ensure a full house, the staff distributes more tickets than there are available seats. Get there early the night of the show.

Even if you don't get to see the taping of the show, you can schedule a look at the Austin City Limits *studio. Call 512/471-4811 to arrange a visit.*

Country-Western

BROKEN SPOKE
3201 S. Lamar Blvd.
Austin
512/442-6189
The Broken Spoke is a real country dance hall—and also a restaurant, with chicken-fried steak a big item on the menu. The Broken Spoke is famous for being the spot where Willie Nelson came to fame, and you're likely to find a cross-section of Austinites here two-steppin' around the dance floor to the music of Don Walser, Dale Watson, or the Geezinslaws. The dance hall is closed Sunday and Monday. (South Austin)

DALLAS NIGHTCLUB
7113 Burnet Rd.
Austin

512/452-2801

They say they're "a two-step above the rest." For almost two decades this nightclub has featured country and contemporary tunes. (North Austin)

DONN'S DEPOT
1600 Fifth St.
Austin
512/478-0336

Styled like an old railroad depot, Donn's is a favorite with Austinites looking for the Sixth Street atmosphere without the parking hassles. The saloon includes a live band and dancing nightly featuring '50s tunes, country, and easy listening. (Downtown Austin)

HANG 'EM HIGH SALOON
201 E. Sixth St.
Austin
512/322-0382

Located right in the heart of Sixth Street, this dance club looks like an old-fashioned, Wild West saloon. (Downtown Austin)

TEXAS BAR AND GRILL
14611 Burnet Rd.
Austin
512/255-1300

This casual bar sports an open mike weekly as well as scheduled performers several times a week. (North Austin)

OTHER GREAT MUSIC SPOTS

CACTUS CAFE
24th and Guadalupe Sts.
Austin
512/475-6515

Located in the Texas Union, the student union building on the University of Texas campus, this café features folk and acoustic performances in a smoke-free environment. Hours and cover vary with performer. (North Austin)

SAXON PUB
1320 S. Lamar Blvd.
Austin
512/448-2552

Singer-songwriter performances by artists like James McMurtry and W.C. Clark make this pub a popular stop. (South Austin)

SHADY GROVE
1624 Barton Springs Rd.
Austin
512/474-9991

Acoustic and singer-songwriter sets, along with an excellent menu, bring Austinites to this funky eatery near Zilker Park. Tucked beneath tall pecan trees, enjoy music on Thursday nights with local talent like Asleep At the Wheel, Bad Livers, and such. (South Austin)

TEJANO RANCH
7601 N. Lamar Blvd.
Austin
512/453-6616

Dance to sounds of Tejano and *conjunto*, a pop twist with a Tex-Mex beat. Live bands on Sunday, Tuesday, and Thursday. (North Austin)

PUBS AND BARS

THE BITTER END BISTRO AND BREWERY
311 Colorado St.
Austin
512/478-2337

Enjoy fine dining at this brew pub (see Chapter 4, Where to Eat) or just come in for a taste of some of Austin's best brews. (Downtown Austin)

CopperTank Brewing Co.

512/322-9168
This bar boasts that it has the longest happy hour in town, extending from 2 p.m. to 7 p.m. The fun here includes pool tables and darts. (North Austin)

DRAUGHT HORSE PUB AND BREWERY
4112 Medical Pkwy.
Austin
512/452-6258
This German-style pub lies tucked in a quiet residential neighborhood near Austin's medical center. Sample brews from around the globe, and on warm evenings enjoy a brew and a bratwurst at outdoor picnic tables. Live entertainment scheduled regularly. (North Austin)

BOAR'S HEAD PUB AND TAVERN
700 W. Sixth St.
Austin
512/472-2739
Select from 38 different varieties of beer at this charming pub, located on the west end of Sixth Street. Pub grub, from grilled turkey sandwiches to seven-layer taco salads to chicken-fried steak, is offered. (Downtown Austin)

COPPERTANK BREWING CO.
504 Trinity St.
Austin
512/478-8444
Brick walls and wood floors give this brewpub the warm atmosphere of a restored warehouse. Favorite brews here include Big Dog Brown Ale, River City Raspberry Ale, Fire House Stout, and White Tail Pale Ale. (Downtown Austin)

CROWN AND ANCHOR
2911 San Jacinto Blvd.
Austin

GINGERMAN PUB
304 W. Fourth St.
Austin
512/473-8801
Located directly next door to Waterloo Brewing Company, choose from a wide variety of brews at this pub. (Downtown Austin)

WATERLOO BREWING COMPANY AND AMERICAN GRILL
401 Guadalupe St.
Austin
512/477-1836
Come to this brewpub with a thirst. Some specialties of the house include Ed's Best Bitter; Clara's Clara, a golden ale named for Clara Driskill; O. Henry's Porter; and Guytown I.P.A, an India Pale Ale. The pub is a popular lunchtime eatery as well, with plenty of pub grub, including burgers and sandwiches as well as pasta, tacos, salads, and daily specials that include everything from pecan-crusted trout to veal parmigiana to pork empañadas. (Downtown Austin)

COMEDY CLUBS

CAPITOL CITY COMEDY LUB
8120 Research Blvd.
Austin
512/467-2333

Get ready to laugh at this club tucked in a strip center along busy U.S. 183. Top names like Ellen Degeneres and Bobcat Goldthwait have entertained audiences here, as have up-and-coming comedians. (North Austin)

Austin's Best Brews

Brewpubs quickly sprouted up in downtown Austin when the state law regarding breweries was changed. Here Luis Ayala, a brew aficionado and home brewmaster, selects the best Austin-made brews and pubs.

Says Ayala, "Whether you are a beer connoisseur or just a beer lover, Austin is sure to have a brew just for you! Following is a list of selected local breweries and a few of the beers they make. Please note that not all breweries sell beer on their premises, and that not all of these beers are sold bottled outside the breweries."

1. *The Bitter End Bistro and Brewery*, 311 Colorado St., 512/478-2337. A very good selection of house beers and a complete food menu.

2. *Celis Brewery*, 2431 Forbes Dr., 512/835-0884. Tours available, no food, sold in stores. Try Celis White or Celis Grand Cru.

3. *Copper Tank Brewing Company*, 504 Trinity St., 512/478-8444. Full food menu most of the day. Try Cliffhanger Alt or Altbiers Big Dog Brown Ale.

4. *Draught Horse Pub And Brewery*, 4112 Medical Pkwy., 512/452-6258. Limited food menu. Seasonal house beers and a good selection of imported beers.

5. *Hill Country Brewing Company*, 730 Shady Ln., 512/385-9111. Available in stores only. Try Red Granite Pale Malt.

6. *Waterloo Brewing Company and American Grill*, 401 Guadalupe St., 512/477-1836. Texas' oldest brewpub offers a full food menu, some beers bottled to go. Try Sam Houston Austin Lager or Vienna Lager's O. Henry's Porter.

Velveeta Room

ESTHER'S FOLLIES
525 E. Sixth St.
Austin
512/320-0553
Since 1977, Esther's Follies has been satirizing Texas politics, parodying musical styles, and just tickling the funny bones of those lucky enough to take in a show. All ages welcomed. Seating is on a first-come, first-seated basis, so it's recommended that you arrive at least a half-hour ahead of showtime. (Downtown Austin)

VELVEETA ROOM
521 E. Sixth St.
Austin
512/469-9116
Down on Sixth Street where much of Austin's entertainment happens, visit the Velveeta Room for stand-up comedy and cabaret-style selections, and perhaps get into the act on open-mike nights. (Downtown Austin)

CONCERT VENUES

AUSTIN MUSIC HALL
208 Nueces St.

Austin
512/495-9962
This large venue has hosted performers such as Eric Clapton, Bonnie Raitt, Robert Earl Keen, and Sheryl Crow. (Downtown Austin)

THE BACKYARD
13101 W. Hwy. 71
Austin
512/263-4146
On the west side of town, relax beneath shady oaks and enjoy an open-air concert at The Backyard. With rock walls, some picnic tables, and a casual atmosphere, the venue lives up to its name. National acts including Joni Mitchell and The Band have played here. (Southwest Austin)

FRANK ERWIN CENTER
University of Texas
Off Red River and 15th Sts.
Austin
512/477-6060
Also the home of Longhorn basketball, this 17,871-seat circular auditorium hosts nationally recognized touring acts. Concertgoers enjoy concessions

TRIVIA

Austin has more movie screens per capita than any other American city.

and reserved theater-style seats in this venue. (North Austin)

SOUTHPARK MEADOWS
9600 S. I-35
Austin
512/280-8771
Bring along a blanket and stretch out to enjoy a top act at this outdoor venue. Some of Austin's largest concerts are held at this south Austin meadow located just off I-35. Sting, Hootie and the Blowfish, and R.E.M. have drawn crowds to this open-air venue. (South Austin)

MOVIE HOUSES OF NOTE

Austin is sprinkled with movie houses. With its young, moviegoing population, the city is often selected as a test market for flicks, so check for "sneak preview" listings in the movie ads.

ARBOR 7
10000 Research Blvd.
Austin
512/346-6937
Located in the Arboretum, this cinema features seven screens, serves bottled water at the concession stand, and even has a high-tech lightning and thunder show every few minutes that flickers across the lobby ceiling. $3.50 before 6 p.m.; $6.50 adults, $3.50 seniors and children after 6 p.m. (Northwest Austin)

VILLAGE CINEMA ART
2700 W. Anderson Ln.
Austin
512/451-8352
In this day of multiscreen movieplexes, the Village has one screen that's dedicated to the artsy films that rarely make it to the mall theaters. $3.50 before 6 p.m., $5.50 after 6 p.m. (North Austin)

© Eleanor S. Morris

13

DAY TRIP: Fredericksburg and Enchanted Rock State Natural Area

Distance from Austin: 1 hour, 15 minutes/78 miles
This Hill Country town of just over 7,000 residents located southwest of Austin bulges with visitors every weekend as travelers seek its small-town hospitality and distinct German atmosphere. Whether your idea of a weekend getaway is curling up in front of a fireplace in a secluded log cabin, shopping for antiques, or touring historic sites, Fredericksburg's the spot for you.

Fredericksburg has plenty of historic attractions, including the **Admiral Nimitz State Historical Park**, 340 E. Main Street, where the contributions of Fredericksburg native Admiral Chester Nimitz, World War II Commander-in-Chief of the Pacific, are recalled through museum displays. Behind the museum lies the **Garden of Peace**, a gift from the people of Japan. Follow the signs from the Garden of Peace for one block to the **Pacific History Walk**, filled with a collection of military artifacts.

For a look at early Fredericksburg, visit the **Pioneer Museum Complex** at 309 W. Main Street. The **Fort Martin Scott Historic Site**, two miles east of town on U.S. 290, was the first frontier military fort in Texas. Today the original stockade, a guardhouse, and a visitors center are open to tour, and historic reenactments keep the history lesson lively.

Fredericksburg is the capital city of Texas bed-and-breakfast inns. Give **Gastehaus Schmidt** a call at 830/997-5612 to learn about more than 100 properties, including cottages, log cabins, and a 125-year-old rock barn.

AUSTIN REGION

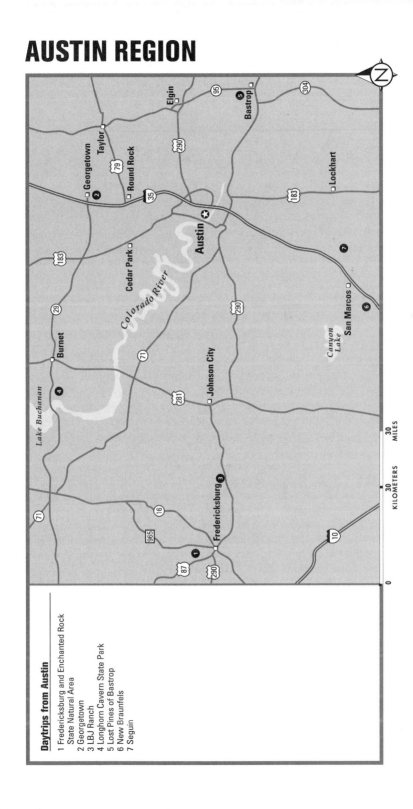

Daytrips from Austin

1 Fredericksburg and Enchanted Rock
  State Natural Area
2 Georgetown
3 LBJ Ranch
4 Longhorn Cavern State Park
5 Lost Pines of Bastrop
6 New Braunfels
7 Seguin

A few miles north of Fredericksburg, **Enchanted Rock**'s enormous dome of pink granite rises 325 feet above the small stream flowing at its base like a massive bald mountain. Covering over a square mile, the formation is second in size only to Georgia's Stone Mountain.

See the granite for yourself with a walk up the dome. Take your best walking shoes for the trek. Except when wet or icy, it is a fairly easy climb, though, and the view is worth the effort. Experienced rock climbers can scale the smaller formations located next to the main dome. These bare rocks are steep and dotted with boulders and crevices, and their ascent requires special equipment.

Enchanted Rock

© Permenter and Bigley

If you'd like to extend your stay at the park, tent camping and backpack camping is available.

For more information on Fredericksburg, call the Convention and Visitors Bureau at 830/997-6523. For more information on Enchanted Rock State Natural Area, call 915/247-3903.

Getting there from Austin: *Take U.S. 290 for 48 miles to the town of Johnson City; continue west for 30 miles to Fredericksburg. Enchanted Rock is located 18 miles north of Fredericksburg on RR 965.*

DAY TRIP: Georgetown

Distance from Austin: 30 minutes/25 miles

Start with a small Texas county seat. Add a sprinkling of cultural attractions, a pinch of recreational sites, a dash of locally owned businesses and a heaping helping of restored historic buildings and what do you have? The perfect recipe for one charming small town.

Georgetown has refined its recipe for community charisma as the city has grown and prospered. With 18,000 residents and serving as seat for Williamson County, the second-fastest-growing county in the nation, Georgetown continues to hang onto its cozy charm. The town comfortably incorporates **Southwestern University**, the oldest college in Texas; rich Victorian architecture from the late 1800s; and newer arrivals, such as retirement community **Del Webb's Sun City Georgetown** and businesses that have benefited the Georgetown economy without altering its environment. The result? A town where residents and visitors can shop for produce from local growers in the daytime, and then enjoy a world-class piano concert or theater performance at night. While some communities have tried and failed in their attempts at enjoying the best of both worlds, Georgetown may have just found the secret ingredient: preservation.

"Georgetown's ability to recognize and preserve its treasured assets is the reason, I believe, that we have been able to maintain our small-town charm in the midst of tremendous growth and change," explains longtime Georgetown Mayor Leo Wood. "The continuing revitalization of the historic downtown square, protecting and enhancing the San Gabriel river corridors, and the creation and enhancement of our local parks system all contribute to this community's identity and sense of place."

Preserving that appeal has been a communitywide effort. From 1982 to 1986, Georgetown participated in the Main Street project, renovating and rejuvenating historic structures to bring back the look of the 1890s. With the help of the National Trust for Historic Preservation, over $8 million was invested in this project.

Recognition of Georgetown's success in integrating its past and present has come from several national sources. Georgetown was selected in 1997 as one of five national winners of the National Trust's Great American Main Street Award. Today visitors walking along that award-winning downtown square get a feel for the small-town atmosphere that makes Georgetown so special. The courthouse square still thrives as the heart of the Georgetown business community.

For visitors, the square holds special appeal because of its many specialty shops. The square really comes alive during seasonal special events. Just as it did a century ago, when it was used for First Monday horse-trading days or events like the firemen's picnic, this site hosts many of Georgetown's get-togethers. MayFair on the Square and the Christmas Stroll unite residents and visitors in a spirit of celebration and pageantry on the historic square.

Georgetown's recognition has also come from many national publications, thanks in part to Southwestern University. The university offers residents and visitors big-city recreational and cultural opportunities, from a public golf course to music and theater productions. North of the courthouse square, **San Gabriel Park** has served for centuries as a gathering place. Native Americans camped on the verdant grounds, pioneers met here, and early Georgetown residents congregated on the river banks for parades and meetings, including one event that featured speaker Sam Houston.

Today park lovers enjoy shady picnics on the oak- and pecan-dotted grounds. Children romp on the playscape while fishermen try their luck from the grassy river banks. West of the park at **Blue Hole**, where river waters reflect limestone cliffs, a revitalization has made this beautiful spot again a place to be appreciated by residents and visitors. Upstream, the **North San Gabriel River** has been controlled to create Lake Georgetown, a 1,310-acre lake popular with fishermen, boaters, waterskiers, and swimmers. Four shoreline parks draw campers, hikers, and day visitors.

South on I-35, **Inner Space Cavern**, discovered during the construction of the highway, draws family travelers. It remains one of the most accessible caverns in the state due to its roadside location. Guests enter the cavern on a cog railroad car, descending from the visitors center to the well-lighted, easy-to-follow trail.

Over 80,000 years of dripping water carved the Inner Space Cavern from the easily eroded limestone. Today visitors view discoveries such as the remains of Ice Age mastodons, wolves, sabre-toothed tigers, and glyptodon (a kind of prehistoric armadillo) as well as delicate cave formations on their walk through the cool cave.

Just across the highway lies another popular visitor attraction: the **Georgetown Candle Factory**, owned by Paul and Ellen Nuckolls. This operation really "lights up" for visitors, and on most days travelers can watch workers producing the candles. "This is one of the few places you can still find hand-dipped tapers made like they were 100 years ago," says Paul Nuckolls.

The Georgetown Candle Factory typifies the kind of business Georgetown attracts: clean industry that integrates into the community. The large operation makes hundreds of styles of candles in an assortment of colors, scents, and sizes, from tiny votives to hand-painted candles, arrangements, and ceramic candleholders.

For more information on Georgetown, contact the Georgetown Convention and Visitors Bureau, 800/GEO-TOWN.

Getting there from Austin: Follow I-35 north for 25 miles.

DAY TRIP: LBJ Ranch

Distance from Austin: 1 hour/63 miles
If you're looking for a day of history and heritage, head to Johnson City. This is the land that President Lyndon Baines Johnson (LBJ) called home, just as his ancestors had years before when Texas was first being settled.

Start your visit in downtown Johnson City at the **LBJ National Historic Park** (U.S. 290 and Ninth Street). Stop by the visitors center for brochures and a look at some exhibits on the late president's family, then walk to the president's **Boyhood Home and the Johnson Settlement**, a restoration of the cabin and buildings that belonged to Sam Ealy Johnson, Sr., LBJ's grandfather. It's just a short drive to the **LBJ State Historical Park**, the home of the late president. Leave Johnson City on U.S. 290 to Stonewall, then turn on Ranch Road 1 to the park entrance. When LBJ was alive, much of this area comprised his private ranch. Security was very tight, and Secret Service men guarded the grounds.

Today, however, the National Park Service conducts tours of the LBJ Ranch. Your visit to the park begins at the visitors center, a building of native rock constructed in a typical Texas style. Displays of LBJ's family, the ranch, and the Hill Country can show you what life was like during the pioneer times, as well as the hectic days when LBJ was president. A short walk away from the building are pens of huge buffalo, native white-tailed deer, and wild turkeys.

While you're in the visitors center, sign up for a guided tour of the ranch. An air-conditioned bus, with a guide, will take you on a drive around the ranch and the back pastures. Along with featuring landmarks such as the Texas White House, the tour includes a look at this working ranch and offers visitors a peek at central Texas ranch life. Cattle graze lazily over the many pastures; ranch hands cut hay; workers clean the stockbarn used for cattle sales. For information on Johnson City, call 830/868-7684.

Getting there from Austin: Follow U.S. 290 west for 42 miles to the intersection of U.S. 281. Turn north and continue for six miles to Johnson City. The LBJ Ranch is located about 15 miles west of Johnson City on U.S. 290.

DAY TRIP: Longhorn Cavern State Park

Distance from Austin: 1¹/₂ hours/60 miles

The area west of Austin is riddled with caverns, but the granddaddy of all Hill Country caves is **Longhorn State Cavern**, near Burnet. Longhorn boasts an extensive history from prehistoric day through the early years of this century.

The earliest use of the cavern was by prehistoric man, but the most interesting events have occurred since the 1800s. Comanches once kidnapped a young woman named Mariel King and took her back to the cavern. The Indians did not realize they were being followed by three Texas Rangers. When the Indians prepared a campfire, the Rangers opened fire on them, grabbed Mariel King, and raced for the entrance. Meanwhile, the surviving Comanches regrouped and began their counterattack, falling upon the Rangers before they reached the cavern entrance. A desperate hand-to-hand battle took place, with the Rangers finally escaping with Mariel King. Ending the story with a fairy-tale flourish, Miss King later married one of her rescuers, Logan Van Deveer, and the couple made their home in Burnet.

Years later, Confederate soldiers used the cave's main room as a munitions factory. Bat guano from the cave was an ingredient in the manufacture of gunpowder. Additional small rooms in the back reaches of the cavern were used as storerooms for the gunpowder.

The cave went unused for several decades until the Roaring Twenties. A local businessman opened a dance hall in the largest room of the cave, building a wooden dance floor several feet above the limestone. When it proved successful, he then opened a restaurant in the next room, lowering food through a hole in the cavern ceiling. Next, an area minister decided to take advantage of the cool temperature and built bleachers to accommodate crowds for Sunday services. When the Depression struck, business declined. The private owners were forced to sell the cave. It was purchased by the state and opened as **Longhorn Cavern State Park** in 1932.

Burnet is also home to several other natural attractions. The **Vanishing Texas River Cruise** tours Lake Buchanan, then heads up the cliff-lined passages of the Colorado River. During the winter months, this cruise is popular with bird-watchers, who come to sight the American bald eagles that nest along the shores. Campers enjoy **Inks Lake State Park** on TX 29, a 2,000-acre park with camping, lakeside picnicking, swimming, and a golf course.

For more information on Burnet-area attractions, call the Chamber of Commerce at 512/756-4297.

Getting there from Austin: *Take U.S. 183 north to the intersection of TX 29. Drive west on TX 29 for 22 miles to Burnet. Longhorn Cavern State Park is located on Park Road 4 off TX 29.*

DAY TRIP: Lost Pines of Bastrop

Distance from Austin: 25 minutes/25 miles

According to legend, the Lost Pines of Bastrop were a gift from an Indian brave to his new bride, who was homesick for East Texas. Scientists provide a less romantic explanation: the coniferous trees were left in central Texas when a shallow sea receded 80 million years ago. A prehistoric forest thrived across much of the state, but when conditions changed, only an island of loblolly pines remained.

Regardless of the explanation, one thing's for certain: the Lost Pines are far from lost. This forest enclave southeast of Austin is found by over 600,000 guests annually. Today Bastrop State Park is one of the most visited parks in the Lone Star State.

Some of the most popular features of the park are the cabins, built by the Civilian Conservation Corps in the late 1930s. (Cabins fill up quickly; reserve them far in advance.) Two work companies came to the newly created park to plant pine seedlings and to construct buildings using native red sandstone. Paid about one dollar a day, these skilled craftsmen left a legacy of rustic-style cabins furnished with handcrafted tables and carved fireplace mantels. Bastrop State Park also boasts a 365,000-gallon swimming pool, and a nine-hole golf course that's consistently cited as one of the top two public courses in the state.

But the popularity of this park has not infringed on the small town atmosphere of Bastrop. With a population of just 4,000 within the city limits and 20,000 in the community, this historic town holds onto its small-town roots.

Bastrop dates back to 1829, the first in Stephen F. Austin's "little colony," located where the Camino Real, or King's Highway, crossed the Colorado River. Bastrop holds the honor as one of the oldest settlements in the state. Settlers came by the wagonload from around the country to claim a share of this fertile land and to establish a home in this dangerous

Admiral Nimitz Museum at the Admiral Nimitz State Historical Park, p. 186

territory. Even as homes were being erected, Indian raids continued in this area for many years.

Stop by the Bastrop Chamber of Commerce (927 Main Street) for a copy of *A Walking Tour of Historic Bastrop*. The tour takes you past the 1883 courthouse, the Old Colorado River Bridge, and many downtown businesses and homes.

Contact the Bastrop Chamber of Commerce at 512/321-2419 for brochures on lodging, shopping, and historic attractions. For reservations at Bastrop State Park, call 512/389-8900. For general information on Bastrop State Park, call 512/321-2101 or write Park Superintendent, Bastrop State Park, Box 518, Bastrop, TX 78602.

Getting there from Austin: *Bastrop is located about 25 minutes southeast of Austin on TX 71.*

DAY TRIP: New Braunfels

Distance from Austin: 45 minutes/50 miles

Grab your lederhosen and run, don't walk, to New Braunfels. No matter what time of year you visit, you'll find that this community, known as the antique capital of Texas, greets visitors with a warm *Wilkommen*.

Founded by a group of immigrant farmers from the Solms-Braunfels region of Germany, this city of 25,000 has never forgotten its ties to the old country. German is the main language in many local homes, and every fall the town hosts **Wurstfest**, one of the largest German festivals in the country.

Warm weather means outdoor activities in this community, many along the banks of the **Comal River**, at only two miles long holding the title as the world's shortest river. The river flows through **Landa Park**, a 300-acre center for family picnics and gatherings. New Braunfels' other river is the **Guadalupe**, where you can drift downriver in an inner tube beneath the tall cypress trees for hours. Outfitters will meet you at a predetermined point and pick you up at the end of your journey. White-water rafting and canoeing enthusiasts will also find plenty of activity on the Guadalupe.

Water lovers can't miss **Schlitterbahn**, the state's largest water park. With a German theme, the park offers stomach-churning thrill rides with names like Der Bahn. For those looking for a slower pace, there's a huge hot tub and paddleboats. You're welcome to bring a picnic lunch to enjoy along the riverbanks.

The rivers are just part of New Braunfels natural attractions. Drive out to Texas' largest cave, **Natural Bridge Caverns**, for a look at what lies beneath the Hill Country. Natural Bridge is a spectacular limestone cave formed by underground waters. It's a showcase of glittery stalactites and stalagmites, with huge flowstones and rooms larger than football fields.

Just next door, animals are the star attractions at **Natural Bridge Wildlife Park**. This drive-through park is filled with both native and exotic species, ranging from some very pushy ostriches to excited zebras. You'll receive a bucket of food when you arrive, and the animals come right up to the car (and inside the vehicle if you leave your window down!).

It's easy to see why this town earned the title of antique capital of Texas. There are antique malls with dozens of vendors, small one-room stores, and warehouses of antiques for sale all over town. Another top attraction is the **Hummel Museum**, which chronicles the life of German nun Sister Maria Innocentia Hummel through her sketches, paintings, and personal diaries. It's filled with 350 original paintings and early sketches that spawned the popular Hummel figurines, plates, and other collectibles.

For more information on New Braunfels attractions, call the New Braunfels Chamber of Commerce at 800/572-2626.

Getting there from Austin: *New Braunfels is located south of Austin on I-35.*

DAY TRIP: Seguin

Distance from Austin: 1 hour/50 miles

Just as readers of *Gone with the Wind* might go looking for Scarlett's home, fans of *True Women* come to Seguin looking for a peek into the past. In this community located southeast of Austin, book buffs enjoy both docent-led and self-guided tours to sites mentioned in this Texas bestseller that has been made into a television miniseries.

The book chronicles the story of author Janice Woods Windle's ancestors in the Seguin. Travelers interested in learning more about the sites mentioned in *True Women* and more about the community in general can take part in guided tours, scheduled through the Seguin Chamber of Commerce. Led by local docents, the tours take a look at sites that play an important role in the historical novel: the live oak-shaded **King Cemetery**, the old **First Methodist Church** where two *True Women* characters were married, and the river bottom where horses were daringly rescued in the tale.

One of the most memorable stops is the **Bettie Moss King Home**, near the King Cemetery. With its wraparound porch and shady lawn, the home saw generations of the King family and was also the childhood home of author Janice Woods Windle. Today the home is inhabited by Windle's mother, Virginia Woods, who often opens her home to tour groups. Woods points out her ancestors' belongings, including the dining room table that played a part in *True Women*, both in the story and in the writing of the family saga. "Janice came home about once a month, and each time I had something from the records, and we would sit here and see how it fit," Virginia Woods recalls.

You can also enjoy a self-guided tour to these sites, which are identified with red, white, and blue markers. Stop by the Seguin Area Chamber of Commerce office at 427 N. Austin St. to pick up a free brochure that traces the path of this novel.

Several of the stops along the tour route feature concrete buildings, a reminder of Seguin's first claim to fame. Once called "The Concrete City" and later the "Athens of Texas," Seguin was the home of a nineteenth-century chemist who held several of the first patents on the production of concrete. His invention was used to construct over 90 area buildings. Seguin's history also boasts a link to the days of the Texas Revolution. The town is named for Lieutenant Colonel Juan Seguin, a hero of the revolution.

For another look at the history of this region, make a stop at **Los Nogales Museum** at 415 S. River St., open Sunday afternoons from May through September. This small museum is housed in an adobe building constructed in 1849 by some of the area's earliest settlers. Next door, peek in the windows of the **Doll House**, a child-size Victorian gingerbread home built by local cabinetmaker Louis Dietz in 1909. Today the home is filled with children's toys and dolls.

This shady community combines its historic attractions with the natural beauty of its surroundings. Don't miss **Starcke Park**, the perfect spot for a picnic beneath towering pecan, oak, and cypress trees. Those pecan trees cover not just the park but the yards of most downtown residences, and several local pecan houses sell the nut by the pound. The town is home to what it claims is the "World's Largest Pecan," a statue located on the courthouse lawn at Court Street.

Even if you don't make it to Seguin for a special event, you'll find plenty of reasons to make a day trip to this city of 22,000 residents. History and architecture buffs should plan a visit to **Sebastopol State Historical Park**, one of the best examples of the early use of concrete in the Southwest. Sebastopol, once a private home, was constructed of concrete with a plaster overlay. Today it is open for tours and contains exhibits illustrating the construction of this historic building and its restoration in 1988.

For other visitors, it's not the historic but the new attractions that make a day trip to Seguin special. Youngsters love **Buffalo Roam**, a drive-through animal park located on I-10 at exit 617. Here over 40 species, including buffalo, camels, zebras, antelopes, gazelles, and many exotic species, roam the ranch, eager for a handout from travelers. Unlike many drive-through wildlife parks, Buffalo Roam has chosen to leave the natural vegetation—the mesquite trees, cactus, and oak. Although removal might have aided spotting of the animals, the unaltered setting gives visitors the chance to see the animals in a more natural habitat with behaviors closer to what might be witnessed in the wild.

Another popular summer spot is the **Wave Pool**, located in Starcke Park East. In this Texas-sized pool, youngsters can cool off under the Mushroom Shower or splash in the simulated waves. Nearby, the sprawling Kids Kingdom Playscape makes an excellent stop for energetic young travelers as well. For more information on Seguin, call 800/580-7322.

Getting there from Austin: *Follow U.S. 183 south to Luling. In Luling, turn west on U.S. 90A and continue to Seguin.*

RECORDED INFORMATION

Time
512/416-5700 or 512/973-3555

Road Conditions
512/832-7084

HOSPITALS AND EMERGENCY MEDICAL CENTERS

Austin Diagnostic Medical Center
12221 N. Mo-Pac Expwy.
512/901-1000

Brackenridge Hospital
601 E. 15th St.
512/476-6461

Children's Hospital of Austin at Brackenridge
601 E. 15th St.
512/480-1818

Pro Medical Emergency Center
North: 2000 W. Anderson Ln.
512/459-4367
South: 3801 S. Lamar Blvd.
512/447-9661

Round Rock Hospital
2400 Round Rock Ave.
512/255-6066

St. David's Hospital
1005 E. 32nd St.
512/476-7111

Seton Medical Center
1201 W. 38th St.
512/323-1000

South Austin Medical Clinic
2555 Western Trail Blvd.
512/892-6600

POST OFFICE

U.S. Post Office
8225 Cross Park Dr.
512/342-1253

VISITOR INFORMATION

American Automobile Association
512/335-5222

Austin Convention & Visitors Bureau
800/926-2282
Events Line, 800/888-8287

Austin Visitors Center
512/478-0098 or 800/926-2282

Better Business Bureau
512/445-2911

Citizen Information/Help Center
512/480-0370 or 512/499-CITY

Greater Austin Chamber of Commerce
512/478-9383

CITY TOURS

Around Austin
512/328-6690

Austin Adventure Company
512/451-3719 or 800/326-2264

Central Texas Tours
512/376-5000

Clark Travel & Tours
512/272-5568

Gray Line Austin
512/345-6789 or 800/950-8285

Heart of Texas Tours
512/345-2043

Sjo-Pro Tours
512/467-2345 or 800/776-4126

Unique Tour and Travel
512/882-3791

CAR RENTAL

Advantage Rent-A-Car
800/777-5500

Alamo Rent-A-Car
800/327-9633

Avis Rent-A-Car
800/831-2847

Budget Rent-A-Car
800/527-0700

Enterprise Rent-A-Car
800/325-8007

Hertz Rent-A-Car
800/654-3131

National Car Rental
800/227-7368

Payless Car Rental
800/729-5377

Thrifty Car Rental
800/367-2277

DISABLED ACCESS INFORMATION

ADAPT of Texas
(Services for the Disabled)
512/442-0252

SERVICES FOR THE DEAF

Relay Texas
800/735-2989 TDD
800/735-2988 Voice

MULTICULTURAL RESOURCES

Asian Chamber of Commerce
512/472-7262

Capital City Chamber of Commerce
(African American Chamber)
512/459-1181

Hispanic Chamber of Commerce
512/476-7502

OTHER COMMUNITY ORGANIZATIONS

Austin Latino/a Gay & Lesbian
Organization
512/472-2001

Austin Stonewall Chamber of
Commerce for Professional Gays
and Lesbians
512/707-3794

Metropolitan Community Church of
Austin (church group supportive of
gay and lesbian relationships)
512/708-8002

Out Youth Austin (education and support group for gays, lesbians, and bisexuals age 22 and younger) 512/708-1234

Parents, Families and Friends of Lesbians and Gays (P-FLAG) 512/302-FLAG

Youth Help Line 512/477-HELP

Women's Chamber of Commerce of Texas 512/346-2676

BABYSITTING/CHILDCARE

Austin Families 512/834-0342 or 512/834-0748

Kid Care Locators 512/892-3135

Texas Department of Protective and Regulatory Services 512/834-0162

NEWSPAPERS

The Austin American-Statesman 512/445-3500

The Austin Chronicle 512/454-5766

The Daily Texan 512/471-5422

MAGAZINES

The Austin Business Journal 512/328-0180

BOOKSTORES

B. Dalton Booksellers 1202 Highland Mall, 512/452-5739 Northcross Mall, Burnet Rd. and Anderson Ln., 512/454-5125

Barnes and Noble Booksellers 1000 Research Blvd., 512/418-8985 701 Capitol of Texas Hwy. S., West Lake Hills, 512/328-3155 2246 Guadalupe St., 512/457-0581

BookPeople 603 N. Lamar Blvd., 512/472-5050

Book Source 13729 Research Blvd., 512/472-1313 4543 S. Lamar Blvd., 512/891-9588

Bookstop Crossroads Shopping Center, 9070 Research Blvd., 512/451-5798 Lincoln Village Shopping Center, 6406 N. Interregional Hwy., 512/453-7297 Sunset Valley Market Fair, 5400 Brodie Ln., 512/892-1580, or 4001 N. Lamar Blvd., 512/452-9541

Borders Books and Music 10225 Research Blvd., 512/795-9553

Congress Avenue Booksellers 716 Congress Ave., 512/478-1157

Waldenbooks Barton Creek Square, 2901 Capitol of Texas Hwy., 512/327-1668

RADIO STATIONS

KASE 101 (country)
KEYI 103.5 (current favorites and classic rock)
KFON AM 1490 (talk radio)
KLNC-FM 93.3 (smooth jazz)
KQQQ FM 92.1 La Nueva (Spanish)
KVET AM 1800 FM 98.1 (news, classical music, etc.)
MAJIC 95.5 (current favorites and classic rock)

TELEVISION STATIONS

KLRU 18 (PBS)
KNVA 54 (Warner Brothers)
KTBC 7 (FOX)
KVUE 24 (ABC)
KXAN 36 (NBC)

INDEX

You'll Feel like a Local When You Travel with Guides from John Muir Publications

CiTY·SMART™ GUIDEBOOKS

Pick one for your favorite city: *Albuquerque, Anchorage, Austin, Calgary, Charlotte, Chicago, Cincinnati, Cleveland, Denver, Indianapolis, Kansas City, Memphis, Milwaukee, Minneapolis/St. Paul, Nashville, Pittsburgh, Portland, Richmond, Salt Lake City, San Antonio, St. Louis, Tampa/St. Petersburg, Tucson*

Guides for kids 6 to 10 years old about what to do, where to go, and how to have fun in: *Atlanta, Austin, Boston, Chicago, Cleveland, Denver, Indianapolis, Kansas City, Miami, Milwaukee, Minneapolis/St. Paul, Nashville, Portland, San Francisco, Seattle, Washington D.C.*

TRAVEL✦SMART®

Trip planners with select recommendations to: *Alaska, American Southwest, Carolinas, Colorado, Deep South, Eastern Canada, Florida Gulf Coast, Hawaii, Illinois/Indiana, Kentucky/Tennessee, Maryland/Delaware, Michigan, Minnesota/Wisconsin, Montana/Wyoming/Idaho, New England, New Mexico, New York State, Northern California, Ohio, Pacific Northwest, Pennsylvania/New Jersey, South Florida and the Keys, Southern California, Texas, Utah, Virginias, Western Canada*

Rick Steves' GUIDES

See *Europe Through the Back Door* and take along guides to: *France, Belgium & the Netherlands; Germany, Austria & Switzerland; Great Britain & Ireland; Italy; Russia & the Baltics; Scandinavia; Spain & Portugal; London; Paris;* or the *Best of Europe*

ADVENTURES IN NATURE

Plan your next adventure in: *Alaska, Belize, Caribbean, Costa Rica, Guatemala, Honduras, Mexico*

JMP travel guides are available at your favorite bookstores. For a FREE catalog or to place a mail order, call: 800-888-7504.

John Muir Publications P.O. Box 613 ✦ Santa Fe, NM 87504

Cater to Your Interests on Your Next Vacation

**The 100 Best Small Art Towns in America
3rd edition**
Discover Creative Communities, Fresh Air, and
Affordable Living
U.S. $16.95, Canada $24.95

**The Big Book of Adventure Travel
2nd edition**
Profiles more than 400 great escapes to all corners
of the world
U.S. $17.95, Canada $25.50

Cross-Country Ski Vacations
A Guide to the Best Resorts, Lodges, and Groomed
Trails in North America
U.S. $15.95, Canada $22.50

Gene Kilgore's Ranch Vacations, 5th edition
The Complete Guide to Guest Resorts, Fly-Fishing,
and Cross-Country Skiing Ranches
U.S. $22.95, Canada $35.50

Indian America, 4th edition
A traveler's companion to more than 300 Indian
tribes in the United States
U.S. $18.95, Canada $26.75

Saddle Up!
A Guide to Planning the Perfect Horseback
Vacation
U.S. $14.95, Canada $20.95

Watch It Made in the U.S.A., 2nd edition
A Visitor's Guide to the Companies That Make Your
Favorite Products
U.S. $17.95, Canada $25.50

The World Awaits
A Comprehensive Guide to Extended Backpack
Travel
U.S. $16.95, Canada $23.95

**JMP travel guides are available
at your favorite bookstores.
For a FREE catalog or to place a
mail order, call: 800-888-7504.**

John Muir Publications ◆ P.O. Box 613 ◆ Santa Fe, NM 87504

ABOUT THE AUTHORS

Eleanor S. Morris is a freelance travel journalist and photographer based in Austin. She has been widely published in national newspapers and magazines and is the author of *Recommended Country Inns of the Southwest* (Globe Pequot), *Country Roads of Texas, Country Towns of Texas*, and *Texas Fairs and Festivals* (Country Roads Press), and the SATW award-winning *Great Destinations: The Texas Hill Country* (Berkshire House Press) among others. She is a member of ASJA (American Society of Journalists and Authors) and SATW (Society of American Travel Writers).

Paris Permenter and John Bigley are a husband-wife team of freelance travel writers and photographers based in Austin. Widely published in magazines and newspapers, the pair have authored 18 guidebooks to Texas and the Caribbean including *Cayman Islands Alive!* (Hunter), *Adventure Guide to the Cayman Islands* (Hunter), *Caribbean with Kids* (Open Road), *Day Trips from San Antonio* (Globe Pequot), *Day Trips from Austin* (Globe Pequot), *Gourmet Getaways* (Callawind), and *Texas Barbecue* (Two Lane), named Best Regional Book by the Mid-America Publishers Association. Both Paris and John are members of ASJA (American Society of Journalists and Authors) and SATW (Society of American Travel Writers). More about their travels can be found on their Web site: www.parisandjohn.com.

JOHN MUIR PUBLICATIONS and its City•Smart Guidebook authors are dedicated to building community awareness within City•Smart cities. We are proud to work with Literacy Austin as we publish this guide to Austin.

Literacy Austin's mission is to provide basic literacy and English as a Second Language instruction for adults who read below the fifth-grade level.

In Austin/Travis County, it is estimated that one in six adults lacks the ability to understand even the most basic written information. They can't read job announcements, medicine bottles or even warning signs. As a result, they lead marginal—even dangerous—lives.

Literacy Austin occupies a crucial position at the starting point of the educational path for adults. It does not charge for services, and has no minimum educational or language proficiency prerequisites for becoming a student.

To fulfill its mission, Literacy Austin recruits and trains tutors from the community who volunteer three hours per week, for a minimum of six months, to work with students one-to-one or in small groups. Volunteer tutors receive 12 hours of training before being matched with students. Presently our volunteers donate more than 45,000 hours of service each year.

For more information, please contact:
Literacy Austin
2002 A Manor Road
Austin, Texas 78722
512/478-7323

LITERACY AUSTIN